A
MYSTERIOUS
COUNTRY

Also by Norman Mailer

A MYSTERIOUS COUNTRY

THE GRACE AND FRAGILITY OF AMERICAN DEMOCRACY

NORMAN MAILER

EDITED BY
J. MICHAEL LENNON
AND JOHN BUFFALO MAILER

Arcade Publishing • New York

First Edition

Arcade Publishing books may be purchased in bulk at special discounts for sales promotion, corporate gifts, fund-raising, or educational purposes. Special editions can also be created to specifications. For details, contact the Special Sales Department, Arcade Publishing, 307 West 36th Street, 11th Floor, New York, NY 10018 or arcade@skyhorsepublishing.com.

Arcade Publishing® is a registered trademark of Skyhorse Publishing, Inc.®, a Delaware corporation.

Visit our website at www.arcadepub.com.
Visit the author's site at jmichaellennon.com.

10 9 8 7 6 5 4 3 2 1

Library of Congress Cataloging-in-Publication Data is available on file.
Library of Congress Control Number: 2022949744

Cover design by Erin Seaward-Hiatt
Cover photo: Fred W. McDarrah/Getty Images

ISBN: 978-1-956763-37-9
Ebook ISBN: 978-1-956763-59-1

Printed in the United States of America

We dedicate this book to our wives,
Donna Pedro Lennon and Claudia Maree Mailer.

Without their generous help, this book would not exist.

Re-reading the bulk of my work in the course of a spring and summer, one theme came to predominate—it was apparent that most of my writing was about America. How much I loved my country—that was evident—and how much didn't I love it at all! Our noble idea of democracy was forever being traduced, sullied, exploited, and downgraded, through a nonstop reflexive patriotism. And every decade our great land lay open more and more to all the ravages of greed.

What a curiosity is our Democracy, what a mystery. No novelist unwinds a narrative so well.

The Time of Our Time (1998)

Contents

Editors' Note

Mailer, like most writers of his time, used the word "Negro" when referring to someone from the Black community. It was meant as a term of respect, much the way "African American" is intended as a term of respect today. Mailer also uses the masculine pronoun when referring to humankind, which was the standard for writers of his generation but can seem off-putting when read through the lens of today's filters.

Given the sensitivities of the current climate, we considered updating some of the verbiage Mailer employed from the earlier decades covered in this book in order to accurately reflect his intentions to the younger audience of today, but thought better of it. To change words in Mailer's sentences would be the equivalent of plucking notes out of a symphony from another day. So, we ask the reader to read Mailer's words within the context of the time in which he was writing and to savor the cornucopia of prescient insights he offers us on how we, Americans all, have arrived at the troubled waters we now navigate, and how we can reach safe haven.

Square brackets are used throughout for editorial additions to the excerpts from Mailer's work. Source notes at the end of the book provide detailed bibliographical information on the contents. Mailer's original titles are in quotation marks; those of the editors are not.

Introduction

At the midpoint of *The Big Empty*, a 2006 collection of speeches, interviews, and conversations between Mailer and his son John Buffalo about the state of the nation after the 9/11 attacks and the Iraq War they precipitated, Mailer made a prophetic statement:

> You know, under all my remarks rests a very unhappy premise. Fascism may be more to the tastes of the ruling powers in America than democracy. That doesn't mean we'll be a fascist country tomorrow. There are any number of extensive forces in America that would resist it. On the other hand there are also huge forces in America that are promoting fascism in one way or another.

Mailer had spoken and written of his fears many times prior to this, all the way back to 1948 when, during a campaign speech for Henry A. Wallace, the Progressive Party presidential candidate, he called Wallace "the only national figure who is an obstacle to fascism in America." But his 2006 comment to his son is perhaps the clearest statement about the predilections in the American character for a homegrown variety of fascism. Mailer's commentary over the decades notes that, like twentieth-century European varieties, the American brand would be rooted in racism, xenophobia, cronyism, flag-waving, and fraudulent elections. But he also foresaw that creeping fascism would incorporate idiosyncratic native traits—rugged individualism (guns aplenty), corporate freebooting, religious fundamentalism, and an indifferent if not rapine attitude toward the environment. He rejected the idea that such a serious and divisive ultranationalistic movement could be imported. After the fall of the Soviet Union in 1991, his warnings increased and became more vehement as he watched the loss of a common enemy turn our anger and fear upon ourselves.

Now, after the assault on the Capitol and the ever-increasing divide between those who feel enthusiasm for Donald Trump and those who view him as an unprecedented threat to our democracy; after a global pandemic and a growing divide between rich and poor; after peaceful demonstrations have led to chaotic violence in the streets fueled in part by social media—the worldwide experiment started with no understanding about the effects it would have on our collective psyche and our freedom—now, as Americans find themselves navigating the overlapping effects of these profound events and changes, it is clear that Mailer was correct: fascism, not yet dominant, is festering within the American body politic.

His premonitions can be traced back to his mother, who came to the United States in 1894 as a three-year-old refugee from Lithuania. As Mailer recalled a year before the end of his life, Fan Mailer was deeply affected by the European wars and dislocations during the first decades of the twentieth century. The horrendous events in Germany in the 1930s "caused my mother pain," he said, adding that it seemed she knew in advance what would happen.

His understanding of how fascism came to Europe became more sophisticated during an eighteen-month period in 1949–50 when he was tutored by Jean Malaquais, a Polish Jew whom he met in France. A leftist intellectual whose parents died in the Holocaust, Malaquais immersed Mailer in the history of Russia and Europe from the later czars to the 1917 revolution to the purges of Stalin in the late 1930s, Hitler's astounding rise, the Spanish Civil War—Malaquais was a veteran—and the Cold War that began shortly after World War II ended. He gave Mailer a vivid sense of the forces and counterforces of war, peace, genocide, economic disaster, and revolution and—the central point—that both the Russian and American political and economic systems, although profoundly different, were geared for war and vulnerable to populist authoritarianism. They also discussed Hitler's rise to power as a reaction against the harsh economic penalties imposed on Germany after World War I.

Mailer's early novels abound with fears of reactionary encroachments in the US. In *The Naked and the Dead* (1948), the crypto-fascist General Cummings tells his Lieutenant Hearn, his aide, that fascism is "far sounder than communism if you consider it, for it is grounded in men's actual natures." In his next novel, *Barbary Shore* (1951), Cummings's predictions of the rightward turn in postwar America are dramatized in the conflict between an FBI agent, Hollingsworth, and McCleod, a former high official of the Communist Party, who played a role in the murder of Stalin's rival Leon Trotsky but left the party in disgust at Stalin's brutality. The Red Scare and the blacklist of leftist writers and artists, stoked by the demagoguery of another American reactionary, Senator Joseph McCarthy, is the backdrop to Mailer's 1955 Hollywood novel, *The Deer Park*. Mailer's portrait of Herman Teppis, the right-wing studio head, and the insidious corruptions of Hollywood Babylon is based on his eighteen months spent working as a scriptwriter, along with Malaquais, at Warner Brothers.

In the 1950s, Mailer described himself as a "libertarian socialist," a phrase that captures his desire to join the emerging polarities of his thinking, to build a radical bridge between the Left and the Right, to create an alliance that would stand as a bulwark against reactionary nativism. Because the encroachments of totalitarianism knew no boundaries and were present in the programs of both the Left and the Right from the start, the effort to keep democracy alive had to take place in every venue of American life. Consequently, as he stated in a 1955 interview, "politics as politics interests me less today, than politics as part of everything else in life." Mailer was a proponent of sexual freedom, minority and worker civil rights, and an end to literary censorship; he was also opposed to corporate greed, environmental destruction, jingoistic patriotism, and the growing and powerful seductions of advertising, all of which he saw as the hydra heads of totalitarianism. Dismayed by these trends and forces, he stepped away from party politics and did not vote again until 1960.

He was enticed back to the political arena by the candidacy of John F. Kennedy, whose "New Frontier" platform gave promise of a rejuvenation of civic life as the dull fog of conformity during the 1950s began to recede. Kennedy, he believed, could perform the essential duties of governing while also satisfying the nation's psychological yearnings for greatness, which he called "the dream life of the nation." Mailer's deepest aspiration was to create a dialectical relationship not only between the political Left and Right but also between traditional politics and psychology—more Jungian than Freudian—linking the world of practical affairs with the world of movies, myths, and dreams. His deepest fear was that a polarized nation would devolve into a failed nation. He described the gulf between these oppositions in the nation's psyche in "Superman Comes to the Supermarket," one of his most brilliant and influential essays, which is also a portrait of candidate Kennedy at the 1960 Democratic convention in Los Angeles.

Another reactionary spasm, a powerful one, followed the massive protests against the Vietnam War and led to the election of the anti-communist Republican Richard M. Nixon as president. Mailer chronicled these protests in his Pulitzer Prize–winning account, *The Armies of the Night,* and *Miami and the Siege of Chicago,* both published in 1968. The same pattern of a major national or international upheaval leading to a confusing period of discontent, rage, and scapegoating occurred after the fall of the Soviet Union in 1992 and again following the destruction of the Twin Towers and the attack on the Pentagon in 2001. In 1995, in a commencement speech at Wilkes University, Mailer proposed a metaphor for this pattern of upheaval, one that unleashed rage and anger and moved the country closer each time to political polarization.

> Looking back on it, we were like magnetic filings in the power of a huge electromagnet, the Cold War, and almost all of us pointed in the same direction. When the Cold War ended, it was as if the great switch on this huge electromagnet was released and now all the fragments went in all directions. Filings were scattered, and being so scattered we discovered that the anger and the rage that we have been able to channel toward the Soviet Union was now being directed toward ourselves in every way.

To the end of his life, Mailer continued to warn about the alarming manifestations of fascism in the United States in interviews, letters, speeches, political reportage, essays, and fiction. For this collection, which spans six decades, from 1945 to 2007, we have drawn from the vast trove of Mailer's work (published, unpublished, and/or uncollected), presenting his contemporaneous observations and analyses in rough chronological order but departing from this whenever he cast back to consider events and phenomena from an earlier time.

Most if not all of Mailer's statements and insights on the grace and fragility of democracy employ one or more of the four rhetorical methods employed by the Old Testament prophets: revilements of excesses and abominations; lack of awareness, care, and understanding of those with whom we disagree; warnings of impending ruination and suffering; and visionary promises of a stronger, more equitable society. More specifically, he recommended six ways that democracy could be strengthened, all of which are emphasized and reemphasized in the excerpts from his work in this collection:

1. Exercise free speech and encourage civic involvement.
2. Build left-right bridges and dialogue.
3. Be wary of corporate power and create equity between worker rewards and corporate profits.
4. Mend the wounds of slavery and eliminate all forms of discrimination.
5. Distrust flag-waving patriotism.
6. Never forget the past.

The role of the artist in society, Mailer wrote, "is to be as disturbing, as adventurous, as penetrating as his energy and courage make possible." He had hoped to become an adviser to President Kennedy, a member of the Camelot roundtable, but this never came to pass. His voice, however, especially after Kennedy's assassination, proved to be far more potent as an unfrocked seer speaking with the same foreboding passion as the Old Testament prophets Isaiah, Daniel, Jeremiah, and Ezekiel. His death on November 10, 2007, was a huge loss for the advocates of free speech and honest debate, racial harmony, civil comity, social justice, and a vigorous and secure democracy.

A
MYSTERIOUS
COUNTRY

OPENING REMARKS

BY NORMAN MAILER

The following "Opening Remarks" set the tone and direction for this collection by establishing Norman Mailer's deep and abiding fears about the many threats to American democracy, as well as some thoughts on how they may be successfully met. Throughout these excerpts (taken from two books published four decades apart, The Big Empty, *2006, and* The Presidential Papers, *1963), Mailer's profound anxiety about the nation's careless, if not feckless, attention to these threats resounds like a tolling bell. There is also a short piece from the transcript of a French television documentary,* Dreams and Nightmares: Mailer's America, *from 2000.*

Democracy Is a Grace

We, so great a democracy, have demonstrated already that we have little real comprehension of democracy itself. We don't seem to understand that it has to be built from the ground up, from the inner midnight will of the people who live in that country. No external power can offer you democracy as a gift. If you are not willing to die for your own idea of democracy, then you are not going to have one.... But democracy, however, is not an antibiotic to be injected into a polluted foreign body. It is not a magical serum. Rather, democracy is a grace. In its ideal state, it is noble. In practice, in countries that have lived through decades and centuries of strife and revolution and the slow elaboration of safeguards and traditions, democracy becomes a political condition which can often withstand the corruptions and excessive power-seeking of enough humans to remain viable as a good society. It is never routine, never automatic. Like each human being, democracy is always growing into more or less. Each generation must be alert to the dangers that threaten democracy as directly as each human being who wishes to be good must learn how to survive in the labyrinths of envy, greed, and the confusions of moral judgment. Democracy, by the nature of its moral assumptions, has to grow in moral depth, or commence to deteriorate. So, the constant danger that besets it is the downward pull of fascism. In all of us there is not only a love of freedom, but a wretchedness of spirit that can look for its opposite—as identified with the notion of order and control from above.

Power and Metaphor

The fight now in America as I see it—the primal fight, if you will, the one that underlies all the others—is the level of American intelligence. A democracy depends on the intelligence of its people. By that I don't mean literary intelligence. . . . Rather, it is the willingness to look into difficult questions and not search for quick answers. You can measure real intelligence by that ability to live with a difficult question. And patriotism gobbled up, sentimentalized, and thereby abased is one of the most powerful single forces to proliferate stupidity. . . .

A nation's greatness depends, to a real extent, on how well-spoken its citizens are. Good things develop out of a populace that really knows how to use the language and use it well. Would Great Britain have been able to manage the empire in the nineteenth century without their three hundred and more years of reading Shakespeare? Where would Ireland be today without Joyce? Not as prosperous, I suspect. As language deteriorates, becomes less eloquent, less metaphorical, less salient, less poignant, a curious deadening of the human spirit comes seeping in.

By now, America has shifted from being a country with a great love of freedom and creativity (in constant altercation with those other Americans who want rule and order) into a country that's now much more interested in power. And power, I can promise you, is not interested in metaphor. Metaphor is antagonistic to power because it pushes you to think in more poetic and contradictory ways. Power demands a unilinear approach. Power does not welcome poetic concepts.

The Masks of Fascism

We're not necessarily headed for disaster, but we may be. I don't know much about the Greeks, but the little I have learned about them in recent years does inspire some respect on this matter. Because they saw life as a dynamic mixture of hope and despair. In other words, you never live without the possibility that disaster may be near. That's part of the human condition. Any attempt to wipe out one's fear of the possibility of disaster is totalitarian, and this is a spectrum that extends all the way from political correctness over to the worst of Hitler. We are not living with a guarantee of a happy ending. Anyone who purveys such a notion is not working for humanity, but against it. I would go as far as to say that.

Under all my remarks rests a very unhappy premise. Fascism may be more to the tastes of the ruling powers in America than democracy. That doesn't mean we will become a fascist country tomorrow. There are any number of extensive forces in America that would resist it. There are also huge forces in America that are promoting fascism one way or another. . . .

I sneer at people who say we are comparable to Germany in the thirties. The difference is immense. Germany was suffering through absolute demoralization. The profound insult of the Versailles Treaty hung over them. Both sides had been equally guilty in starting that war [World War I], but they were made the sole criminals. Germans saw that as an outrage. The reparations they had to pay were extreme. And then there was their inflation. At one point in the early twenties, the German mark became a joke. People used their currency as wallpaper—literally—it wasn't worth the paper it was printed on. The mark had once been as substantial to them as the dollar. So, yes, everything had gone wrong in Germany, and to top it off you had a weak liberal government that wasn't even liberal. . . . If fascism does come here, it will come slowly. The one thing we can count on is it won't be called fascism, and there won't be party men in uniform. If it is a hundred miles from here to Hitler, we've gone one mile so far. Every time someone opens their mouth and says, "This is like Hitler," they are just encouraging their own people to grow more stupid. The one thing the Left has got to do, if it is not to become more intellectually anemic (a.k.a. politically correct) is to keep some balance in its critical spirit.

Capitalism and Technology

An immensely powerful global capitalism is shaping up. That capitalism does not need or look for inquiry into delicate matters. Its need, rather, is to keep the bullshit train running at top speed. It has to enforce the self-serving notion that big business is the only way to do it. The last thing those gentlemen need are novels.

Part of the genius of corporate capitalism is that they've found ways to control people that are so much subtler than the old Stalinist procedures. Those methods were brutal, dull, cold, stupid, and openly oppressive. The modern form of oppression is nuanced; it gets into your psyche—it makes you think there's something wrong with you if you're not on the big capitalism team. So they don't want writers exploring their morality. They want one morality, theirs. Unlike Stalinism at its worst, it's more of a benign regime, superficially open and ready for the development of technology that will make all our lives extraordinary—sure, technology will end up keeping us alive for 150 or 200 years, even if three-quarters of each of us will be replacement parts. I'm not sure that's either God's intention or the real human intention. It may be an ultimate destruction of the human spirit to stay alive after a certain point. Maybe death is as important to life as life itself.

Corporations and Technology

As they make plastic stronger, more analogous to steel—which they will—so, in turn, cars are going to be made entirely of plastic because economically speaking, the plastic substitute offers more profit. No surprise then if the mediocrities have taken over the world under the banner of technology, corporate vision, and the unholy urge to purvey democracy to all countries of the world, whether they're ready for it, or capable of it. But we tell them, in effect, "You're going to end up a democracy whether you want it or not." This turns democracy into a farce because democracy is a grace. Any true democracy is sensitive enough to be perishable, and we're in danger right now of losing our democracy right here. The people who are running the world at present, very badly in many places, have the feeling that successfully controlled direction is the only answer. My feeling . . . is exactly the opposite. Global capitalism does not speak of a free market but of a controlled globe. It is alien to the creative possibilities that have not yet been tapped in legions of people who have never had a chance to be creative, who work and die without creative moments in their lives. . . . A man running a small business is living by his wits, but people enter corporations in order not to have to live by their instincts—or, most important—their fears. Only a few have to take responsibility. The corporation can be a relatively benign organization, but is still subtly totalitarian. And this is spreading. People at the top want to control the world because they're in terror that otherwise we are going to blow it up. My feeling is that if corporations take over the world, it will indeed blow apart because technology could end by violating too much of human nature. . . .

The Democratic Party needs to be renovated from top to bottom. . . . It may have to lose some twenty or thirty years rehabilitating itself. If it doesn't, it may always be the second party. Because they are linked to the corporation. Until they separate themselves, until they recognize that there's two kinds of capitalism—each opposed to the other—the capitalism of the corporation and that of small business. The latter is creative and the first is a totalitarian leviathan.

The Ruinous War of Political Extremes

My larger perspective contains a fear that we may not reach the end of this century. We've advanced enormously. By the measure of previous history, it's as if during my life span we've progressed not through four generations, but eight, even ten. As if we squeezed two to three centuries into the last fifty years. As a result, the world is vastly more powerful and yet more sensually deprived. More noise, more din, more interruption in the world. I feel as if we are losing the ability to concentrate. Everyone seems to suffer from a sense that they are getting dim in their memories. Yet more and more, we in the West are engaged in a race to conquer nature on our terms. That is undeniably a large and general remark, but it's as if back of everything, a great war is going on here, larger even than we realize, between the liberals and the conservatives. The conservatives are saying, in effect, "You guys are trying to wreck existence by becoming too vain, too Godless." And liberals are replying, "Your obsession that God is judgmental looks to force all of humanity into rigid patterns that won't work any longer." The worst of it is that they are both right. It's a war between extremes, and they are both right. . . . This serves to augment my gloominess. At its worst, my feeling is that we will be lucky to get to the year 2100. Over the last century, living with our fear of nuclear war, that became a prime worry. Would we even reach the next century? Well, we did. The Cold War ended in a most astonishing fashion. After all, given the paranoia that existed on both sides, it was remarkable how peacefully it ended. That could happen again. Life may well go on. But we are in greater danger than we ever were before because we have more power, and we just don't begin to know how to use it.

(The Big Empty)

The Right Wing in America . . . covers a spectrum of opinion as wide as the peculiarities one encounters on the Left. If we of the Left are a family of anarchists and Communists, socialists, pacifists, nihilists, beatniks, international spies, terrorists, hipsters and Bowery bums, secret agents, dope addicts, sex maniacs and scholarly professors, what indeed is one to make of the Right, which includes the president of a corporation or the Anglican headmaster of a preparatory school, intellectually attired in the fine ideas of Edmund Burke, down the road to the Eisenhower-is-a-Communist set of arguments, all the way down the road to an American Nazi like George Lincoln Rockwell, or to the sort of conservatives who attack property with bombs in California. . . .

But it is easy to mock the Right Wing. I would rather put the best face one can on it. I think there are any number of interesting adolescents and young men and women going to school now who find themselves drawn to the Right. Secretly drawn. Some are drawn to conservatism today much as they might have been attracted to the Left thirty years ago. They are the ones who are curious for freedom, the freedom . . . not only to make money, but the freedom to discover their own nature, to discover good and to discover—dare I say it?—evil. At bottom they are ready to go to war with an already-made world which they feel is stifling them. I hope it is evident that I do not see the people in the Right Wing as a simple group of fanatics, but rather as a contradictory stew of reactionaries and individualists, of fascists and libertarians. It could be said that most Right Wingers don't really know what they want.... The politics of the Right in America reflects an emotion more than an insight....

The moral well may be that certain distinctions have begun to disappear. The average experience today is to meet few people who are authentic. Our minds belong to one cause, our hands manipulate a machine which works against our cause. We are not our own masters. We work against ourselves. We suffer from a disease. It is a disease which afflicts almost all of us by now, so prevalent, insidious and indefinable that I choose to call it a plague. I think somewhere, at some debatable point in history, it is possible man caught some unspeakable illness of the psyche, that he betrayed some secret of his being and so betrayed the future of his species. I could not begin to trace the beginning of this plague, but whether it began early or late, I think it is accelerating now at the most incredible speed, and I would go so far as to think that many of the men and women who belong to the Right Wing are more sensitive to this disease than virtually any other people in this country. I think it is precisely this sensitivity which gives power to the Right Wing's passions.

Face to face with a danger they cannot name, there are still many people on the Right Wing who sense that there seems to be some almost palpable conspiracy to tear life away from its roots. There is a biological rage at the heart of much Right Wing polemic. They feel as if somebody, or some group—in New York no doubt—are trying to poison the very earth, air and water of their existence. In their mind, this plague is associated with collectivism, and I am not so certain they are wrong. The essence of biology seems to be challenge and response, risk and survival, war and the lessons of war. It may be biologically true that life cannot have beauty without its companion, danger. Collectivism promises security. It spreads security the way a knife spreads margarine. Collectivism may well choke the pores of life....

But there is a contradiction here. Not all of the Right Wing, after all, is individual and strong. Far from it. The Right Wing knows better than I would know how many of them are collectivists in their own hearts, how many detest questions and want answers, loathe paradox, and live with a void inside themselves, a void of fear, a void of fear for the future and for what is unexpected.... The Right Wing often speaks of freedom when what it desires is iron law, when what it really desires is collectivism managed by itself. If the Right Wing is reacting to the plague, too many of the powerful people on the Right are helping to disseminate the plague....

Now this plague appears to us as a sickening of our substance, an electrification of our nerves, a deterioration of desire, an apathy about the future, a detestation of the present, an amnesia of the past. Its forms are many, its flavor is unforgettable: It is the disease which destroys flavor. Its symptoms appear everywhere: in architecture, medicine, in the deteriorated quality of labor, the insubstantiality of money, the ravishment of nature, the impoverishment of food, the manipulation of emotion, the emptiness of faith, the displacement of sex, the deterioration of language, the reduction of philosophy, and the alienation of man from the product of his work and the results of his acts....

Even twenty-five years ago architecture, for example, still told one something about a building and what went on within it. Today, who can tell the difference between a modern school and a modern hospital, between a modern hospital and a modern prison, or a prison and a housing project. The airports look like luxury hotels, the luxury hotels are indistinguishable from a modern corporation's home office, and the home office looks like an air-conditioned underground city on the moon. In medicine, not so long ago ... there still used to be diseases. Diphtheria, smallpox, German measles, scarlet fever. Today there are allergies, viruses, neuroses, incurable diseases. Surgery may have made some mechanical advances, but sickness is more mysterious than ever. No one knows quite what a virus is, nor an allergy, nor how to begin to comprehend an incurable disease. We have had an avalanche of antibiotics, and now we have a rampage of small epidemics with no name and no distinctive set of symptoms. Nature is wounded in her fisheries, her forests. Airplanes spray insecticides. Species of insects are removed from the chain of life. Crops are poisoned just slightly. We grow enormous tomatoes which have no taste. Food is raised in artificial circumstances, with artificial nutrients, full of alien chemicals and foreign bodies. Our emotions are turned like television dials by men in motivational research. Goods are not advertised to speak to our needs but to our secret itch. Our secondary schools have a curriculum as interesting as the wax paper on breakfast food. Our educational system teaches us not to think, but to know the answer. Faith is half-empty. Until the churches can offer an explanation for Buchenwald, or Siberia, or Hiroshima, they are only giving solace to the unimaginative. They are neglecting the modern crisis. For all of us live today as divided [souls]. Our hope for the future must be shared with the terror that we may go exploding into the heavens at the same instant 10,000,000 other souls are being exploded beside us. Not surprising, then, if many people no longer look to sex as an act whose final purpose is to continue the race. Language is drowning in jargons of mud. Philosophy is in danger of becoming obsolescent. Metaphysics disappears, logical positivism arises. The mass ... begins to have respect not for those simple ideas which are mysteries, but on the contrary for those simple ideas which are certitudes. Soon a discussion of death will be considered a betrayal of philosophy. Finally, there is a vast alienation of man from responsibility. [Over] one hundred years ago Marx was writing about the alienation of man from his tools and the product of his work. Today that alienation has gone deeper. Today we are alienated from our acts.

(The Presidential Papers)

Patriotism, Free Speech, and the Cure

I've always had the fear that America would go totalitarian, and it may yet—there's nothing guaranteed about a democracy—but I didn't understand democracy, the ways in which it is very dialectical. So when you think one tendency is going to overtake everything in American life, a countertendency arises. In that sense, we've kept going back and forth, back and forth for the last fifty years. . . .

I'm not concerned with being a good American. That kind of idea has been spoiled for us. You know, all the worst people are good Americans. "Patriotism is the last refuge of the scoundrel," H. L. Mencken said. It isn't that I don't want to be American, I do. I feel very

American. When I'm in a foreign country, I'm amazed at how American I am in my reactions. And if there's one thing I love about this country, and I do love it, it's the absolute sense of freedom that I've had all my life to say what I think. Now, you know, you pay a price for saying what you think, but it's not a crippling price. It's not a mortal price. I've felt free to think in this country. In a certain sense, all the intellectual faults of America have made it easier for me to think.... I certainly do have affection for the absolute sense of intellectual freedom that exists as a live nerve, a live wire right through the center of American life. Every time I get totally discouraged with this country, I remind myself, "No. The fact is that we can really say what we think." And some extraordinary things come out of that. I mean, when before did a great empire give up on a horrible war, Vietnam, because a large minority of the citizens protested? Now that's a distortion of how the war ended, but nonetheless, it was freedom of speech in America that ended the war in Vietnam, arguably, more than any other single factor.

(Dreams and Nightmares: Mailer's America)

Art, free inquiry, and the liberty to speak may be the only cure against the plague.

(The Presidential Papers)

1

THE GENERAL'S LECTURE

(THE NAKED AND THE DEAD, 1948)

The word "democracy" does not appear in the following excerpt from Mailer's bestselling first novel, but his awareness of the incipient threats to it are apparent in the sharp exchange between two of the novel's most important characters: Edward Cummings, a two-star general who is attempting, in late 1943, to defeat an entrenched Japanese force on a South Pacific island, and Robert Hearn, his aide, a Harvard-educated, left-leaning second lieutenant. Cummings selected Hearn as his aide because he needs an audience, someone sufficiently intelligent to appreciate the nuances of his authoritarian political philosophy, fascism with an American twist. Disgusted with one of the general's lectures, Hearn mashes out his cigarette on the floor of the general's tent prior to this scene.

"I'm going to give you a lecture, Robert." Until now Cummings had had no idea of how he would proceed. He had trusted his instincts to direct him. And this was the way. Put it on the intellectual frame, let Hearn slip into it, be unaware that there was going to be an end product today.

Hearn lit a cigarette, "Yes, sir?" He was still holding the match in his hand, and they both looked at it. There was a quite perceptible pause while Hearn fingered it, and then leaned forward to drop it in an ashtray.

"You're remarkably neat," Cummings said sourly.

Hearn's eyes lifted, searched his for an instant, wary, judging his answer. "Family upbringing," he said shortly.

"You know, it seems to me there are things, Robert, you could have learned from your father."

"I didn't know you knew him," Hearn said quietly.

"I'm familiar with the type." Cummings stretched. Now the other question while Hearn was unready for it. "Have you ever wondered, Robert, why we're fighting this war?"

"Do you want a serious answer, sir?"

"Yes."

Hearn kneaded his thighs with his large hands. "I don't know, I'm not sure. With all the contradictions, I suppose there's an objective right on our side. That is, in Europe. Over here, as far as I'm concerned, it's an imperialist toss-up. Either we louse up Asia or Japan does. And I imagine our methods will be a little less drastic."

"Is that your contribution?"

"I don't pretend to read history in advance. I'll be able to give you the real answer in a century probably." He shrugged. "I'm surprised that you want my opinion, General." His eyes had become lazy, again, studiedly indifferent. Hearn had poise. That was undeniable.

"It seems to me, Robert, you can do a little better than that."

"All right, I can. There's an osmosis in war, call it what you will, but the victors always tend to assume the ... the, eh, trappings of the loser. We might easily go Fascist after we win, and then the answer's really a problem." He puffed at his cigarette. "I don't go in for the long views. For want of a better idea I just assume it's a bad thing when millions of people are killed because one joker has to get some things out of his system."

"Not that you *really* care, Robert."

"Probably not. But until you show me some other idea to replace it, I'll hold to this one."

Cummings grinned at him. His anger had subsided to a cold effective resolve. Hearn was fumbling now, he had noticed that in him. Whenever Hearn had to search his ideas he was obviously uncomfortable, obviously trying to avoid the other conclusions.

Hearn seemed absorbed for just a moment. "We're moving toward greater organization, and I don't see how the left can win that battle in America. There're times when I think it's Gandhi who's right."

Cummings laughed out loud. "You know you couldn't have picked a more unperceptive man. Passive resistance, eh. You'd be good in that role. You and Clellan [Cummings's enlisted aide] and Gandhi."

Hearn sat up a little straighter in his chair. The noon sun, harsh now that the overcast had blown away, glinted cruelly over the bivouac, threw into bold relief the shadows under the flaps of the tent. About a hundred yards away, on a downhill slope through the sparse foliage, Cummings watched the chow line, two hundred and fifty men long, trudge slowly forward.

"It seems to me," Hearn said, "Clellan's more in your line. And while we're on that you might tell him that the flowers are your idea."

Cummings laughed again. That had taken effect then. He opened his eyes widely, conscious of the effect their bald white surfaces would give, and then he slapped this thigh in a facsimile of mirth. "Are you getting enough liquor, Robert?" Of course, that was why he had crushed the cigarette on the floor.

Hearn made no answer, but his jaws quivered just perceptibly.

Cummings sat back, enjoying himself. "We're wandering a little far afield. I was going to explain the war to you."

"Yes, if you would." Hearn's sharp voice, slightly unpleasant, was exhibiting the least bit of irritation.

"I like to call it a process of historical energy. There are countries which have latent powers, latent resources, they are full of potential energy, so to speak. And there are great concepts which can unlock that, express it. As kinetic energy a country is organization, coordinated effort, your epithet, fascism." He moved his chair slightly. "Historically the purpose of this war is to translate America's potential into kinetic energy. The concept of fascism, far sounder than communism if you consider it, for it's grounded firmly in men's actual natures, merely started in the wrong country, in a country which did not have enough intrinsic potential power to develop completely. In Germany with that basic frustration of limited physical means there were bound to be excesses. But the dream, the concept was sound enough." Cummings wiped his mouth. "As you put it, Robert, not too badly, there's a process of osmosis. America is going to absorb that dream, it's in the business of doing it now. When you've created power, materials, armies, they don't wither of their own accord. Our vacuum as a nation is filled with released power, and I can tell you that we're out of the backwaters of history now."

"We've become destiny, eh?" Hearn said.

"Precisely. The currents that have been released are not going to subside. You shy away from it, but it's equivalent to turning your back on the world. I tell you I've made a study of this. For the past century the entire historical process has been working toward greater and greater consolidation of power. Physical power for this century, an extension of our universe, and a political power, a political organization to make it possible. Your men of power in America, I can tell you, are becoming conscious of their real aims for the first time in our history. Watch. After the war our foreign policy is going to be far more naked, far less hypocritical than it has ever been. We're no longer going to cover our eyes with our left hand while our right is extending an imperialist paw."

Hearn shrugged. "You think it's going to come about as easily as that? Without resistance?"

"With much less resistance than you think. In college the one axiom you seem to have carried away is that everyone is sick, everyone is corrupt. And it's reasonably true. Only the innocent are healthy, and the innocent man is a vanishing breed. I tell you nearly all of humanity is dead, merely waiting to be disinterred."

"And the special few?"

"Just what do you think man's deepest urge is?"

Hearn grinned, his eyes probing Cummings. "A good piece of ass probably."

The answer grated, made Cummings's flesh tingle. He had been absorbed in the argument, temporarily indifferent to Hearn, concerned only with unfolding his thesis, and the obscenity stirred little swirls of apprehension in him. His anger returned again.

For the moment, however, he ignored Hearn. "I doubt it."

Hearn shrugged once more, his silence unpleasantly eloquent.

There was something unapproachable and unattainable about Hearn which had always piqued him, always irritated him subtly. The empty pit where there should be a man. And at the moment he desired, with an urgency that clamped his jaws together, to arouse some emotion in Hearn. Women would have wanted to excite some love from him, but for himself—to see Hearn afraid, filled with shame if only for an instant.

Cummings went on talking, his voice quiet and expressionless. "The average man always sees himself in relation to other men as either inferior or superior. Women play no part in it. They're an index, a yardstick among other gauges, by which to measure superiority."

"Did you arrive at that all by yourself, sir? It's an impressive analysis."

Hearn's sarcasm riled him again. "I'm quite aware, Robert, that you've worked out the ABC's of something like that, but you don't carry it any further. You stop there, go back to your starting point, and take off again. The truth of it is that from man's very inception there has been one great vision, blurred first by the exigencies and cruelties of nature, and then, as nature began to be conquered, by the second great cloak—economic fear and economic striving. That particular vision has been muddied and diverted, but we're coming to a time when our techniques will enable us to achieve it." He exhaled his smoke slowly. "There's that popular misconception of man as something between a brute and an angel. Actually man is in transit between brute and God."

"Man's deepest urge is omnipotence?"

"Yes. It's not religion, that's obvious, it's not love, it's not spirituality, those are all sops along the way, benefits we devise for ourselves when the limitations of our existence turn us away from the other dream. To achieve God. When we come kicking into the world, we *are* God, the universe is the limit of our senses. And when we get older, when we discover that the universe is not us, it's the deepest trauma of our existence."

Hearn fingered his collar. "I'd say *your* deepest urge is omnipotence, that's all."

"And yours too, whether you'll admit it or not."

Hearn's sharp voice softened a little with irony. "What moral precepts am I supposed to draw from all this?"

Cummings's tension altered. There had been a deep satisfaction in expounding this, a pleasure apart from all the other concerns of this discussion with Hearn. "I've been trying to impress you, Robert, that the only morality of the future is a power morality, and a man who cannot find his adjustment to it is doomed. There's one thing about power. It can flow only from the top down. When there are little surges of resistance at the middle levels, it merely calls for more power to be directed downward, to burn it out."

Hearn was looking at his hands. "We're not in the future yet."

"You can consider the Army, Robert, as a preview of the future."

Hearn looked at his watch. "It's time to go to chow." Outside the tent the earth was almost white in the glare of the overhead sun.

"You'll go to chow when I release you."

"Yes, sir." Hearn scraped his foot slowly against the floor, stared at him quietly, a little doubtfully.

"You threw that cigarette on my floor today, didn't you?"

Hearn smiled. "I figured that was going to be the point of all this talk."

"It was simple enough for you, wasn't it? You resented some of my actions, and you indulged a childish tantrum. But it's the kind of thing I don't care to permit." The General held his half-smoked ciga-rette in his hand, and waved it slightly as he spoke. "If I were to throw this down on the floor, would you pick it up?"

"I think I'd tell you to go to hell."

"I wonder. I've indulged you too long. You really can't believe I'm serious, can you? Supposed you understood that if you didn't pick it up, I would court-martial you, and you might have five years in a prison stockade."

"I wonder if you have the power for that?"

"I do. It would cause me a lot of difficulty, your court-martial would be reviewed, and after the war there might be a *bit* of a stink, it might even hurt me personally, but I would be upheld. I would have to be upheld. Even if you won eventually, you would be in prison for a year or two at least while it was all being decided."

"Don't you think that's a bit steep?"

"It's tremendously steep, it has to be. There was the old myth of divine intervention. You blasphemed, and a lightning bolt struck you. That was a little steep too. If punishment is at all proportionate to the offense, then power becomes watered. The only way you generate the proper attitude of awe and obedience is through immense and disproportionate power. With this in mind, how do you think you would react?"

Hearn was kneading his thighs again. "I resent this. It's an unfair proposition. You're settling a difference between us by . . ."

"You remember when I gave that lecture about the man with the gun?"

"Yes."

"It's not an accident that I have this power. Nor is it that you're in a situation like this. If you'd been more aware, you wouldn't have thrown down that cigarette. Indeed, you wouldn't have if I were a blustering profane General of the conventional variety. You don't quite believe I'm serious, that's all."

"Perhaps I don't."

Cummings tossed his cigarette at Hearn's feet. "All right, Robert, suppose you pick it up," he said quietly.

There was a long pause. Under his breastbone, Cummings could feel his heart grinding painfully. "I hope, Robert, that you pick it up. For your sake." Once more he stared into Hearn's eye.

And slowly Hearn was realizing that he meant it. It was apparent in his expression. A series of emotions, subtle and conflicting, flowed behind the surface of his face. "If you want to play games," he said. For the first time Cummings could remember, his voice was unsteady. After a moment or two, Hearn bent down, picked up the cigarette, and dropped it in an ashtray. Cummings forced himself to face the hatred in Hearn's eyes. He was feeling an immense relief.

"If you want to, you can go to chow now."

"General, I'd like a transfer to another division." Hearn was lighting another cigarette, his hands not completely steady.

"Suppose I don't care to arrange it?" Cummings was calm, almost cheerful. He leaned back in his chair, and tapped his foot slowly. "Frankly, I don't particularly care to have you around as my aide any longer. You aren't ready to appreciate this lesson yet. I think I'm going to send you to the salt mines. Suppose after lunch you report over to Dalleson's section, and work under him for a while."

"Yes, sir." Hearn's face had become expressionless again. He started toward the exit of the tent, and then paused, "General?"

"Yes?" Now that it was over, Cummings wished that Hearn would leave. The victory was losing its edge, and minor regrets, delicate little reservations, were cloying him.

"Short of bringing in every man in the outfit, all six thousand of them, and letting them pick up your cigarettes, how are you going to impress them?"

This was the thing that had sullied his pleasure. Cummings realized it now. There was still the other problem, the large one. "I'll manage that, Lieutenant. I think you'd better worry about your own concerns."

After Hearn had gone, Cummings looked at his hands. "When there are little surges of resistance, it merely calls for more power to be directed downward." And that hadn't worked with the line troops. Hearn he had been able to crush, any single man he could manage, but the sum of them was different still, resisted him still. He exhaled his breath, feeling a little weary. There was going to be a way, he would find it. There had been a time when Hearn had resisted him too.

And his elation, suppressed until now, stimulated him, eased to some extent the sores and frustrations of the past few weeks.

Hearn returned to his own tent, and missed lunch. For almost an hour he lay face down on his cot, burning with shame and self-disgust and an impossible impotent anger. He was suffering an excruciating humiliation which mocked him in its very intensity. He had known from the moment the General had sent for him that there would be trouble, and he had entered with the confidence that he wouldn't yield.

And yet he had been afraid of Cummings, indeed, afraid of him from the moment he had come into the tent. Everything in him had demanded that he refuse to pick up the cigarette and he had done it with a sick numbed suspension of his will.

"The only thing to do is to get by on style." He had said that once, lived by it in the absence of anything else, and it had been a working guide, almost satisfactory until now. The only thing that had been important was to let no one in any ultimate issue ever violate your integrity, and this had been an ultimate issue. Hearn felt as if an immense cyst of suppuration and purulence had burst inside him, and was infecting his bloodstream now, washing through all the conduits of his body in a sudden violent flux of change. He would have to react or die, effectively, and for one of the few times in his life he was quite uncertain of his own ability. It was impossible; he would have to do something, and he had no idea what to do. The moment was intolerable, the midday heat fierce and airless inside the tent, but he lay motionless, his large chin jammed into the canvas of his cot, his eyes closed, as if he were contemplating all the processes, all the things he had learned and unlearned in his life, and which were free now, sloshing about inside him with the vehemence and the agony of anything that has been suppressed for too long.

I never thought I would crawfish to him.

That was the shock, that was the thing so awful to realize.

2

To Beatrice Mailer

(AUGUST 8, 1945, *SELECTED LETTERS OF NORMAN MAILER*, 2014)

Mailer's army unit in the Philippines would have been part of General MacArthur's million-man invasion force had Japan not surrendered after atomic bombs were dropped on Hiroshima and Nagasaki. Mailer spent eight months in occupied Japan, returning to the United States in April 1946, after twenty-five months of active duty. His lifelong wariness of technology is noted in this letter to his wife, Beatrice.

Sweet Baby,

The news of the atom bomb has created more talk out here than the news of V-E day, and as much as President Roosevelt's death. I feel very confused about it. (this is written after just the barest communique. I don't know what it's done.) I'm understanding now how the bonds of self-interest affect thought. A good part of me approves anything which will shorten the war and get me home sooner, and this is often antagonistic to older more basic principles. For instance I hope the peace time draft is passed because if it's not, there may be an agonizingly slow demobilization. In the same sense I approve of an instrument that will kill under optimum conditions many people in one instant.

But really what a terrifying perspective this is. We've always talked of humanity destroying itself, but now it seems so near a thing, so much a matter of decades, of a very easily counted number of bombs. This atom smashing business is going to herald the final victory of the machine. It had always been no more than pleasurable calculation in the physics I studied, a remotely attainable dream, and even then a terrible one, for the atomic energy in a mass the size of a pea is enough to drive a locomotive so many fantastic times about the earth.

I think our age is going to mark the end of such concepts as man's will and mass determination of power. The world will be controlled by a few men, politicians and technicians—Spengler's men of the late West-European-American civilization. Much as he stimulates me, I'm no Spenglerian. In the alternatives of doing the necessary or nothing, I prefer nothing if the necessary is unpalatable.

Really, darling, the vista is horrifying. There will be another war, if not in twenty years, then in fifty, and if half of mankind survives, then what of the next war—I believe that to survive the world cities of tomorrow will be built a mile beneath the earth. Man then will have escaped his animal heritage—the insects will no longer bother him, and Scarr-like in searching for heaven, he will have descended a thousand fathoms nearer to Hell.

You know I am becoming as pathological about machines as mother is about Jack Maher. (In my outer life this consists of such things as turning down a jeep drivers job (one of the Recon vehicles)—much to everyone's amazement and disgust).

And I have contempt for sailors and flyers. What really do they know of war. Somehow the sailors I talked to on the ship coming here seemed so naive. They disliked the surly, odiously besored, sullen men they transported. When they heard of the mud and nausea and horror, they clucked sympathetically and uncomprehendingly. What did they know of (Gwaltney's phrase) work, misery, death? Theirs is an uneventful routine life, filled with the bondage and benefits of serving a machine. When death comes to them it is in storm claps—acts of God. They have no intimacy with it and therefore its final connotations are nightmarish in character, and as unreal as peacetime disasters. They cannot comprehend because the machine is so deceptive a fellow, so benign for so long that they forget it has a fuse. They have not experienced death as a daily element, as an emotional constant about on the level of opening a can of cold greasy K-ration hash when your belly is hot and roiled from too many hills in a cruel wet sun. They do not know the kind of fatigue that makes you tread upon a three week corpse because you have not the strength to step over it. And flyers are the same way as sailors. They fight too in an abstract way in an abstract fluid. Their lives are also comfortable, lonely and horny, and again death is the devastating, incomprehensible thunder clap. Those are lives with no other stench than the smell of gas and metal and lubricating oil. They do not know that latrines and bodies and swamps are something hard to differentiate.

And the personification they give their machines nauseates me. It is the substitute for the loneliness and horniness, but it is also so frightening. *We have come to the age when we love machines and hate women.* The next step is religious awe, and the atom bomb looks like the last deity, the final form line of entelechy.

So little of love in this, but I am a little soul-sick tonight. The more I think about these things, the more frightening they become. What combination can beat the alloy of mechanism with sentimentality.

3

HITLER ON MY MIND

(INTERVIEW WITH J. MICHAEL LENNON, *PROVINCETOWN ARTS*, 2008)

Both of Mailer's parents, Fanny ("Fan") and Isaac Barnett ("Barney"), were born in Lithuania in 1891, but they did not know each other there. They met in Long Branch, New Jersey, in January 1920. Norman Kingsley Mailer was born there on January 31, 1923.

Hitler has been on my mind since I was nine years old. By 1932, my mother was already sensitive, and intensely so, to the dangers he presented. After Hitler came to power in 1933, everything that happened in Nazi Germany used to cause my mother pain. It was as if she knew in advance what was going to occur. She'd grown up with a knowledge of the anti-Semitism her father had had to face in Lithuania. Then, as a child going to school in Long Branch, New Jersey, kids on the street would call her "Christ killer"—no surprise, then, if Hitler was immensely real to her. Finally, he took over a portion of my existence. Many people have little comprehension of what it means to lose half of the millions of people who dwell in your fold of humanity. The Irish have some sharp sense of that considering what they suffered in the potato famine. The Armenians have it. But generally speaking, the average Wasp or well-established Catholic in America does not really understand the depth of the effect. In the main, they do feel antipathetic by now to anti-Semitism, and it is true that any prominent politician who uttered an anti-Semitic remark today would probably see his political career seriously injured. Yet, this is not necessarily equal to understanding how deep a negative presence was Hitler to the Jews of my parents' generation and to mine as well.

4

FRONTIERS OF VIOLENCE

(DREAMS AND NIGHTMARES: MAILER'S AMERICA, 2000)

In 1890, the US Census Bureau announced that the American frontier was officially closed. Mailer's comment at the end of this excerpt about Blacks' deeper appreciation of life is a restatement of the same point in his seminal 1957 essay, "The White Negro," which is excerpted in this collection.

There's a certain savagery on the shoulders of American life, but not on the main highways. Quite the opposite. The main highways are almost too safe, but off on the shoulders, by byroads, the back alleys of America, there's violence and there's a lot. The only reason violence in America is interesting to people in Europe is that America is so advanced a nation, and yet it still has violence comparable to the violence in Third World countries. The violence in America comes out of the bad conscience of America to a degree, but it also comes out of the most powerful tradition in America, which is that we crossed a continent, we built a country. This is taught to us with our school books when we're six years old. It's not taught to us heavily. It just is implicit. You know, the idea that this is a good country. It's a good country, filled with good people. They're full of energy, full of adventure, full of creativity, and they do things. And then our frontier was closed. Finally, we go to California and that was the end of the frontier. So new frontiers began. Space became a frontier; Hollywood became a frontier; madness became a frontier. For us in Greenwich Village in New York, sexual exploration became a frontier back in the sixties. People in America grow up with a concept of a frontier.

Now in France, how can one conceive of a frontier? The country's been settled for hundreds of years. It's frontiers that create the violence. Don't forget America was founded on violence. The people who left other countries to come to America were forced immigrants in a way. They left because they weren't wanted in their country. So to begin with they were angry people. And then we had Blacks who had been taken from their own country and enslaved and sent over in the slave ships, and worked as slaves for generation after generation. So, given all that, it would be amazing if we weren't violent. The roots are violent. This country came into existence because people had a violent desire to escape from where they were, or were ripped out of where they were and thrust into a new place without being asked whether they would choose it or not. So there's violence all over the place in this country. And then, the Black and white question, of course, is searing. It'll never quiet down until it's resolved one way or another. There's a powerful envy on both sides. Whites envy Blacks. Blacks envy whites. It's taken for granted that Blacks envy whites, but what's not understood is that whites also envy Blacks because Blacks have more of an appreciation of the very existence of life than whites do, and so they envy them.

5

RUSSIA, THE PROGRESSIVE PARTY, AND HENRY LUCE

(DREAMS AND NIGHTMARES: MAILER'S AMERICA, 2000)

Mailer made more than two dozen campaign speeches for Henry A. Wallace (1888–1965), the former Democratic vice president (1940–44) and 1948 presidential candidate of the Communist-infiltrated Progressive Party. Mailer believed that a Wallace presidency would halt the drift toward a war with Russia. "Wallace is the only national figure," he said during the campaign, "who is an obstacle to fascism in America." Mailer had nothing but scorn for Cold War warrior Henry R. Luce (1898–1967), the founder of the Time-Life media empire. Winston Churchill (1874–1965) made his "Iron Curtain" speech at Westminster College in Missouri on March 5, 1946.

To understand the background of the Progressive Party under whose banner Henry Wallace ran for president in 1948, you have to know that there had been an enormous amount of positive writing in American newspapers and magazines about the Soviet Union during the war. About how brave they were, how strong they were, what great fighters they were, how they were resisting Nazism. Here and there you'd find people who said, "No. Russia is a bad country. It's a horrible place. It's communism," but generally speaking, it was the honeymoon. Those were the great years between America and the Soviets. Joseph Stalin was "Uncle Joe." "He's a wonderful fella," all of that. And right after the war, Churchill made his Fulton, Missouri, speech saying there was an Iron Curtain separating Europe into two halves, and everything in the media changed, changed almost overnight. Suddenly, Stalin was a monster, which indeed he was, but now everyone was saying it. The Soviet Union was a horrible country.

They were looking to take over the world, on and on, they were our enemy and we had to stand up to them. That's the key phrase always in America. "We have to stand up to 'em." Now there were a great many of us who had fallen in love with the Soviet Union because of all that propaganda that had been sent our way by the American media. We thought they were a wonderful country. They'd fought a brave war, a much tougher war than we had fought. It would have been almost impossible for America to have defeated Germany without the help of the Soviet Union. So there was a sense of outrage among many of us, particularly all of us on the left felt that this was a madness to destroy the Soviet Union at all costs while they were weak and wounded. So that was the background for the Progressive Party. Now the Communists in America had always been semi-comic because they'd been nothing but a hair on the tail of the dog of the Soviet Union. So they were sort of comic to us, but, nevertheless, they were very well organized. And so they began to take over the Progressive Party. We sort of knew that the Communists were running a lot of the Progressive Party, but we didn't care. We wanted to oppose what was going on in America. *Life* magazine and *Time* magazine in those years were creatures of its founder, Henry Luce, who was a great believer in the American Century. Luce's idea was that America was a great country and that Communism was something to be stopped at all costs, no matter how. Fair play was no longer a criterion, because you couldn't be fair with people who weren't playing fair. Some of the worst excesses of the Cold War in American were encouraged by Luce. Luce, for the Progressive Party, was the enemy.

6

ROOTS AND PARANOIA

(DREAMS AND NIGHTMARES: MAILER'S AMERICA, 2000)

Mailer often noted that a great deal of his writing unfolds beneath the over-hang of the Cold War, the standoff between the Communist bloc, led by the Soviet Union, and the western bloc of NATO nations that endured from 1947 to 1991.

We soldiers had an attitude that couldn't have been more incorrect, but we all believed it. We believed that we would come back, there'd be no jobs, there'd be a terrible depression. There had been a depression when the war started. It was replaced by the war, which brought a certain sort of fevered prosperity to a great many people, but probably two-thirds to three-quarters of the people in America assumed that again we'd be in a depression when the war was over. So to come back and discover that one was wrong, affected the people of America profoundly for the next ten years. You see, my generation and the generation before me had grown up with the idea that they were going to have a very tough life. All through the thirties I remember my father was out of work for periods and things were very tough. People assumed that life would be hard. And, instead, there was a prosperity after the war. The Cold War, in my opinion, created that prosperity. We traded World War II for the Cold War. The Cold War kept all the armaments factories functioning in one way or another. They kept the idea of a large army intact. It did a lot of things, the Cold War. But the main thing it did is it kept America prosperous. So we had a peculiar situation because hardly anyone expected to be doing well after the war, and now they were. And they had no habits for it. They had grown up with the habits of a Depression generation. They expected to have a hard life and now they were having a relatively easy one. It made everyone nervous. It was a little bit like a poor man winning a sweepstakes. I would go so far as to say that after the Second World War America suffered from a collective shift of identity and everyone felt uncomfortable.

The Cold War filled that discomfort perfectly, from the point of view of the establishment, because it gave us an enemy again and Americans function best—we're team players to an extraordinary extent—against an opponent. And so the big game became the Cold War. There was Russia, absolutely wiped out by the war, but suddenly they were this dangerous enemy who had to be stopped at all costs because of the godless materialism, and it fit the uneasiness of America. We now had an enemy that we could see as dangerous. It mobilized—all the loose forces in America, you might say. It gave encouragement to American paranoia, which is always present. It's a constant factor in American life. America is never more unhappy and more uncomfortable than when it doesn't have something to be paranoid about. And the reason for that is that we're all weeds. There's hardly an American alive who wasn't transplanted. They were pulled out of Europe, Africa, or Asia, and they came to America. Ninety-five percent of the people in America can't trace the family back three or four generations. Or if they can trace the family back five or six generations, they're usually Black because they were brought over as slaves. So there's no real rootedness that Europeans have. It's why Europeans, in my opinion, have such huge difficulty understanding Americans. You know, they always have theories about us, but the theories usually don't cover enough of the complexity. The root of the matter is that we do not have roots.

7

DEPRESSION, DESPERATION, FASCISM I

(DREAMS AND NIGHTMARES: MAILER'S AMERICA, 2000)

Mailer's family, like millions of others, had a difficult time during the Depression. His father, an accountant, was unemployed for long stretches. It was only through financial help given by a relative that Norman was able to go to Harvard, even though he graduated number two in a class of six hundred from Boys High School in Brooklyn.

The fear I've had for many, many years is what happens if we get into a truly terrible depression? There's very little in this country to hold it together. There were a lot of problems in the thirties in America during the Depression, but there was a warmth in America then that I remember from my childhood that does not exist today, because people were all in the soup together. There was a real feeling that "We're all suffering in this together. We're all without work," which a great many people were, or "We're afraid the very people we work for will collapse." People were supportive of the people they worked for because they didn't want them to collapse. If they collapsed, then they would too. There was a sense of collective responsibility, collective involvement in that frightening Depression. But if a depression came today, I don't know that warmth would be there. And if things get very bad, the first people that suffer will again be the Blacks. And if they do, then there could well be real trouble this time, real riots in the ghetto, real situations that have to be put down by armed force one way or another. And if that happens and a great many more people are arrested when the jails are already filled to overflowing, to bursting, filled to the point there's going to be barbed wire and encampments. And once you have barbed wire and encampments, the next step is that you really have to worry about the freedom of the press (that much-maligned medium) will become something to save because they won't be able to write real stories about it, and the country will be further divided at a time when people are getting desperate and fear that the country will not hold together. So what you have at a certain point is you have a de facto fascism. It won't be called that. That's the one thing I can guarantee. Whatever happens, it will never be called "fascism" in this country, but we'll be living in an essentially totalitarian environment and it could get worse and worse. This is my great fear for the country.

8

McLeod Tells All

(BARBARY SHORE, 1951)

Mailer's Cold War novel, set in a Brooklyn rooming house, centers on a series of cat-and-mouse conversations between William McLeod, a former high-level international Communist operative, and Leroy Hollingsworth, a feckless FBI agent, as reported by the narrator, Mickey Lovett, an amnesiac war veteran. In this scene, McLeod brilliantly exaggerates his crimes and treasons—to the chagrin of his interrogator—to the level of farce, Mailer's way of depicting the semi-hysterical fears of the American right wing in the postwar period.

McLeod started to yawn, but he did not finish.

For someone scratched upon the door.

It was one of the most curious sounds I had ever heard, light, rapid, and with a persistence that spoke of an animal's claw. McLeod revolved in his chair, his body stiffened, an attitude of intense concentration upon his features. What he expected I could not guess, but his reaction was extreme—all blood left his face. He sat transfixed for many seconds while the scratching repeated.

With what effort he replaced his eyeglasses, adjusted them upon his nose. "It is Hollingsworth then," he whispered incomprehensibly. And all his will and all his strength apparently necessary for the next action, he straightened himself in the chair, and froze his face into a surface composure, his lips supporting a mild distaste. "Come on in," he called suddenly in an even voice.

Hollingsworth proffered his polite smile as a token of admission. He eddied toward us, dressed in his tidy fashion, a clean shirt, light summer pants, and for the jaunty note, a pair of black-and-white sport shoes. "I'm awfully sorry to disturb you," he said in his remote voice, "but I heard people talking, and I thought that I might share in whatever you're saying." To me he nodded. "How do you do Mr. Lovett? It's nice to see you again."

"Take a chair," McLeod told him.

He sat down after hoisting his trousers carefully, and for over a minute we gazed judiciously at one another in unavoidable proximity. Except McLeod. He consumed Hollingsworth with his stare.

I wondered if Hollingsworth had left his place in the same clutter I had seen it last, the clothing upon the floor, the bureau drawers jammed and overflowing. I could see him giving a last survey, and then convinced everything was in order, turning the key, pausing to listen to us, and scratching for entrance.

He cleared his throat now, and leaned forward, his hands cupped over his knees, the palms arched to avoid deranging the crease of his pants. "If you fellows don't mind," he said without preamble, "I wonder if we could discuss politics."

McLeod grinned, but weakly. "Anything we can clear up for you in a couple of minutes?"

He considered this seriously. "It's hard to say. I've noticed that political discussions have a way of becoming very long and drawn out if you know what I mean." When we did not respond to this, he said, "It's mainly about the Bolshevists I'd like to talk. I heard Mr. Wilson and Mr. Court discussing them at the office the other day, and I realized I have a great deal to learn on the subject." With modesty, his opaque blue eyes upon us, he added, "I have to keep well informed on all subjects, and it makes a fellow hop sometimes."

"What makes you think I know anything about it?" McLeod asked. Color was returning to his face, but he was still pale.

In the ingenuous voice of a child, Hollingsworth said simply, "Well, you're a Bolshevist, aren't you, Mr. McLeod?"

"Do you mean a Communist?"

Hollingsworth looked perplexed. "They're the same thing, aren't they?"

McLeod yawned violently. "Call it the egg and the dinosaur," he said, closing his lips in a cryptic smile.

"That's an interesting way of putting it," Hollingsworth said. "And you'd say you're both?"

Once again McLeod could dissect him with his eyes. There was a pause, and behind the impassivity of their faces, I could sense the rapidity with which their minds were working. "Yes, both," McLeod said. "Yes, absolutely both. Absolutely."

His face was impassive, his body draped carelessly upon the chair, but like a safety valve shrilling its agitation, his foot—so disconnected from him—tapped ever more rapidly, ever more nervously upon the floor.

"Well, then you can answer some of my questions," Hollingsworth said pleasantly.

"Possibly I can," McLeod admitted. "Yet first let me ask one. What made you decide to do it this way?"

Hollingsworth looked puzzled. His eyes seemed to pinch the thin flanks of his nose as he pondered, and his answer was not exactly responsive. "Oh, I couldn't say. You talk sort of differently." He glanced about the room. "And the other time I was here when we talked about the bathroom—I'm awfully sorry we've never been able to work out a schedule for that—I noticed you had so many big books on the shelf." He had withdrawn a tiny pad of paper from his jacket, and this he balanced on his knee, his pencil playing over it in the motions of a man sketching idly. "Would you say then that you're an atheist?" he asked politely.

"Yes." The pencil flicked lightly upon the pad.

McLeod, a grin cemented to his jaw, murmured, "As a matter of fact, I'm more than that. I've been head of the church dynamiting section in my time. We've knocked over several in the past."

"And you're against free enterprise?"

"Completely." As if passing from acceptance of the game to active encouragement, McLeod delivered himself of a long exposition, his voice never altering from the acrid tone with which he began. "You might say that I am against free enterprise because it sucks the workers dry, turns man upon his brother, and maintains the inequities of a class society. This poison may only be met with poison, violence with violence. A campaign of vigorous terrorism must be undertaken to wrest the seats of power from the buh-geoisie. The president must be assassinated, and congressmen imprisoned. The State Department and Wall Street must be liquidated, libraries must be burned, and the filthy polluted South must be destroyed nigh unto the last stone with the exception of the Negroes." McLeod halted, and lit a cigarette for himself. The first match went out, and he struck another one, brought it to the tip, his hands cupped in an excess of care. "Do you have any more questions?" he asked.

Hollingsworth scratched his head. "Well, you've given me a great deal to think about. This is all extremely interesting I should say." Carefully he brushed a cowlick from his forehead. "Oh, yes." He leaned forward, phrased the next question diffidently. "Would you feel that your first allegiance is not to the Stars and Stripes, but to a foreign power?"

McLeod betrayed no humor. "I would admit that is generally correct." He stared at his hands in a curious way, as if resigning himself to whatever he saw portrayed there. After a moment he looked up. "Does this conclude the political discussion?" he asked.

Hollingsworth nodded. "I must say you have it all at your finger tips."

"I've prepared it," McLeod said. "For years."

"I appreciate your co-operativeness."

McLeod leaned toward him. "Wall Street is interesting, isn't it?" he asked in an amiable tone.

"Oh, yes. Very much so. I really feel as if it's an education."

Subtly, perhaps unconsciously, McLeod was parodying him. "Yes, that could be said." With a sudden motion, he reached forward and flipped the pad from Hollingsworth's knee. "Don't mind if I look at this, do you?" he asked.

But Hollingsworth performed the ritual of a man who obviously did mind. He started in his chair, his arm extended in pursuit of the pad, his fingers closed and opened to articulate his frustration. Slowly his tongue licked over his lips. "Do you think a fellow ought to play that kind of trick on one?" he asked me quietly, his neutral voice washed faintly by righteousness.

I was watching McLeod. He sat back in his chair and studied what Hollingsworth had written. From time to time he chuckled without amusement. Then he passed me the pad, and I read it with my heart beating stupidly. Hollingsworth had made the following list:

Admits to being a Bolshevist.
Admits to being Communist.
Admits to being atheist.
Admits to blowing up churches.
Admits to being against free enterprise.
Admits to encouraging violence.
Advocates destruction of the South.
Advocates use of poison.
Advocates rise of the colored people.
Admits allegiance to a foreign power.
Is against Wall Street.

Silently, I handed the pad back to McLeod. In a flat voice, not without mockery, he said to Hollingsworth, "You made a mistake. I never advocate the use of poison."

Hollingsworth had recovered. Diffidently, but not without firmness, he shook his head. "I'm sorry, I don't like to disagree with a fellow, but you did say that. I heard you."

McLeod shrugged. "All right, leave it in." He took a long puff at his cigarette. "Tell me, old man," he drawled, "is there anything else I can do for you?"

"Why yes." Hollingsworth adjusted the belt of this trousers. He leaned forward again, and his face which had been in shadow entered the cone of light cast by the bulb hanging from the ceiling. Upon his mouth he exhibited his apologetic smile.

But there was little apology in his other movements. Firmly, he pointed to the pad. "I wonder if you would affix a signature to this," he said formally. "I would like to keep it as one of my souvenirs, and that would"—he searched for a word—"enhance the value thereon."

"Sign it?"

"Yes. If you don't mind."

McLeod smiled, tapped the pad upon his knee for a moment, and then to my astonishment, took a pen from the breast pocket of his shirt, scribbled a few words, and scratched his signature. He read aloud, "Transcript of remarks made by William McLeod—signed—William McLeod. Does that do?"

"Oh, that's fine," Hollingsworth said. "It's nice to meet people who are so co-operative." When neither of us replied, he looked at his watch with great seriousness. "My, I've stayed longer than I thought." He stood up, and took the notes which McLeod extended to him. "Well, I'd like to thank you fellows for being so nice about it all."

"Any time we can help you, any time," McLeod nodded.

Hollingsworth still remained at the door, fingering the pad. With a certain gentleness, he ripped off the top sheet on which they had written, and tore it in two. "You know," he said, "on second thought perhaps I really don't want this souvenir."

"It is valueless," McLeod drawled again.

"Yes, so it is." He dropped the pieces to the floor, and was gone.

When the door had closed, McLeod rested his head on his hands and laughed wearily. Upon his head beat the glare of the light bulb, seeming to burn through the frail thin hair at the peak of his scalp, and thrusting beyond him across the floor a distorted shadow of himself, elongated and bent, eloquent in its shadowed head and emaciated forearms. I became aware that the shades were down, and in this stifling room, nothing moved, nothing stirred, the books along the wall in silent witness beside myself. He raised his head and stared at the light as if he must excoriate himself like a fakir searing his vision into the sun.

With what seemed an intense effort, he tore his eyes from the light, and looked at his hands. "You ever wait for anybody?" he asked quietly.

I did not understand at first what he meant, but from some recess of my mind leaped again the image of the stranger, the door opening, the obscured face hovering above my bed. "I don't know," I said.

He stood up and leaned against the bookcase, the end of his cigarette still pinched against his fingers. When he looked at me there was small recognition in his eyes. "One thing I'd like to find out," he said. "Which team does he come from?"

"I don't follow you," I said.

Something flickered in his stare. Perhaps he was aware of me again. "That's right, you wouldn't know, would you, Lovett?" And then for an instant he grasped my wrist. "Of course it's one of the techniques to leave the innocent behind, and he's the one who carries away the valuable piece." But as I met his look, he relaxed his grip upon me. "No, you're not in it, I'm certain of that." He snickered. "I suppose I have to be."

I stammered out a question and McLeod made no response. Instead, he laughed again to himself. "I'll tell you, Lovett," he said, "I'm tired. Do you mind leaving here? I want to think for a while."

I went away with McLeod sitting in the chair in the middle of the room, the light bulb above his head, his eyes looking without expression at the peeling plaster upon his wall. I had the impression he would remain in this position for hours.

9

To Arthur Miller

(EARLY SEPTEMBER, 1950; *SELECTED LETTERS OF NORMAN MAILER*, 2014)

Mailer and playwright Arthur Miller (1915–2005), the author of Death of a Salesman *(1949), lived in the same Brooklyn building in the late 1940s but never became close friends. Both, however, were supporters of the Hollywood Ten, a group of writers, directors, and producers who were subpoenaed to testify before Congress in 1947 about their purported Communist Party affiliations and were subsequently imprisoned for refusing to answer any questions.*

Dear Art,

I got a letter a few weeks ago from you about the Hollywood Ten and a statement, and have been meaning to answer it ever since.

Here's the statement:

America moves ever more rapidly to war, to state capitalism, and to the suppression of all individual liberty. In this process the imprisonment of the Hollywood Ten has its obvious significance. That the same fate would befall writers like myself in the Soviet Union—the classic representative of state capitalism— merely underlines the irony of being martyred in support of one exploitative system against another.

I'll be looking forward to seeing the advertising proof.

10

THE DEPTHS OF DEMOCRATIC STRENGTH

(DREAMS AND NIGHTMARES: MAILER'S AMERICA, 2000)

In the early 1950s, a right-wing faction led by Senator Joseph McCarthy (1908–57) investigated and accused many government employees thought to have Communist Party associations, however insubstantial or unproven. Lolita (1955), a brilliant, controversial novel by Vladimir Nabokov (1899–1977), explores the intimate relationship between a twelve-year-old girl and a middle-aged man.

The early fifties were very patriotic, very much "In God We Trust," "Under God," all those phrases. It was the period of Senator Joe McCarthy. Everyone was afraid of their shadow. There was a feeling of totalitarianism growing in the country. People—many people, responsible, serious, calm people—were terribly worried that America was going to become totalitarian. I, who was out ahead of the pack, was convinced we were going to become totalitarian. You know, part of my grudging respect for the depths of democracy comes because I've been wrong so many times about how we were going to become totalitarian. We never did. We came within range of it more than a few times. Certainly during the war in Vietnam, there were people, again, responsible people, who feared we would end up totalitarian. Those are the two periods of quasi-totalitarianism in America, the early fifties and second half of the sixties with the war in Vietnam. But in neither case did we go in that direction. We never did, ultimately. There were very powerful forces, democratic forces, that still exist in this country. And I never had enough understanding of the depth of those democratic forces, which is why I was always so pessimistic. But to go back to it, there were two things going on at once. There was the deep belief in God that was being promulgated by the authority, by the establishment. One of the reasons they were doing it is they were frightened by the increasing sexuality of America. The Second World War had opened up sex for a great many people. People who would normally have married and had a conventional married life and perhaps never cheated on one another at all, were suddenly separated from two to five years by the war. And in that period, there were young men and there were young women who had affairs, a good many of them. And when they came back, it was never the same. Marriage was never the same after the Second World War. And the powers that be, the church fathers and high government officials who were monitoring mores and the morals of the country, were worried about the increasing intensification of sexuality. *Lolita* is a very good example of that. But, at any rate, there were two processes going on at once and they've been going on in America all these fifty years. The forces of repression and the forces of liberation, to speak in programmatic terms, were each working overtime. Sometimes one would be stronger. Sometimes the other would be stronger. Certainly in the late sixties the forces of liberation, if you will, were all over the place and the forces of repression were in retreat. During other years, the reverse was true. Certainly in the early fifties, the reverse was true. So this war has been going on, and each side has had its excesses. You know, the forces of liberation have now become the forces in many places of political correctness, which is a disaster as far as I'm concerned.

11

EITEL TELLS ALL

(THE DEER PARK, 1955)

Mailer's Hollywood novel, written in the aftermath of the conviction of the Hollywood Ten, culminates in the coerced testimony of a left-wing director, Charles Eitel, to investigators from the House Un-American Activities Committee (HUAC). In this scene, Eitel replays his interrogation for his protégé, Sergius O'Shaughnessy, a former US Air Force pilot. Teppis and Munshin, who pressured Eitel to testify, are executives at Supreme Pictures.

When Eitel finished telling the story, we continued to sit in the living room with the litter of a dozen half-filled cartons and several pieces of luggage. "Do you want me to help you pack?" I said at last.

He shook his head. "No, somehow I enjoy doing it myself. It's the last opportunity I'll have to be alone for some time."

I guessed what he meant. "Everything's been set for you to testify?"

Eitel shrugged. "You may as well know. You'll be reading about it in the newspapers soon enough."

"What will I read?"

He did not answer the question directly. "You see, after Elena left," he said, "I couldn't stand to stay here. Not for the first few days. I drove into the capital early that morning, and I went to see my lawyer. There's no use giving you all the bits and pieces. I must have talked to a dozen people. The amazing thing is how complicated it is."

"Then you're going to have your secret session?"

"No." Eitel looked away while he lit a cigarette. "They're not letting me off that easy. You see, those people are artists. If you admit that you're ready for a secret session, they know that you'll testify in public session, too. They get down to bed-rock, don't you see?" Eitel smiled pensively. "Oh, I gave them a bit of trouble. I walked out of a conference when they told me the session would have to be public, and I went to my lawyer's office, and I raved, and I ranted, but all the time I knew I was going to give them what they wanted." He took a careful swallow of his drink. "If I had had something to return to in Desert D'Or—well, in that case, I don't know, I won't look for excuses. The fact is I didn't have anything. All I could do was admit to how clever they are. They know you win an empire by asking for an acre at a time. After we'd agreed on a public session, there came the business of the names." He gave a little laugh. "Oh, the names. You have no idea how many names there are. Of course I never belonged to *that* political party, and so it was obvious right along that I could never be the sort of witness who qualifies for Stool Of The Year. Still they knew ways to use me. I had several conferences with two detectives Crane uses for his investigations. They looked like an All-American guard and tackle posing for a photograph. They knew so much more about me than I knew about them. I never realized how many papers a man could put his name to in ten years. Who asked me, they wanted to know, to sign the petition against the exploitation of child labor in the salt mines of Alabama? That sort of thing. A hundred, two hundred, four hundred signatures. I could just as well have been on a couch coughing up my childhood. A little word at this cocktail party with that dangerous political operator—some fool of a writer, mind you, who liked to think of himself as a liberal with muscles—he had given me a paper to sign." Eitel felt his bald spot as though to learn how many hairs he had lost in the process. "I found it confusing for a while. There were certain people they wanted me to accuse, and there were others, particularly a couple of movie stars I know at Supreme and Magnum whom they were absolutely disinterested in. When I began to understand what sort of arrangement existed between the Committee and the studios we began to make progress. You see they had a list of fifty people prepared for me. Seven of those people I could swear I never met in my life but it seems I'm wrong. There were so many big parties after all, and my two football players knew all about them. 'You were both in the same room on such and such a night at so-and-so's party,' they would let me know, and eventually I would produce the sort of political conversation that one might have had. Toward the end, they got friendly. One of them took the trouble to tell me he liked a picture I had made, and we even made a bet on a fight. Finally, it seemed to me as if I liked my detectives just as much as some of the people whose names I'm going to give. For that matter, half the names on my list have repulsive personalities." Eitel smiled wearily. "The interrogation took two days. Then Crane was back and I went to see him. He was very pleased, but it seems there were still more things to be asked of me. I hadn't done enough."

"Not enough?" I said.

"There were still a few acres to be picked. Crane called my lawyer in, and they took the trouble to tell me that I ought to have a statement to release to the newspapers after I testified. Crane had written it for me. Of course I was free to use different wording, but he had thought, he said, to show me the sort of thing which was probably best. Later my lawyer gave me another suggestion. Everybody seemed to think it would be practical to take out a paid advertisement in the trade papers to explain how proud I was to have testified, and how I hoped that others in my position would do their duty in the same way. Do you care to see the statement I'm giving to the newspapers next week?"

"I'd like to see it," I said.

I glanced over a few lines:

"It has taken me a year of wasted and misplaced effort to recognize the useful and patriotic function of the Committee, and I testify today without duress, proud to be able to contribute my share to the defense of this country against all infiltration and subversion. With a firm knowledge of the democratic heritage we share, I can only add that it is the duty of every citizen to aid the Committee in its work with whatever knowledge he may possess."

"It goes about par for the course," I said.

Eitel was off on other subjects. "You ought to know," he remarked, "that Crane keeps his word. While I was in his office he called up people at different studios, and said a word or two for me. It was the one part of the process I found surprising. My mind's too subtle. I didn't expect he would pick up the phone in front of me."

"What about your script?" I asked. I had a headache.

"That's the funny part, Sergius. You know when I started to feel ashamed? It was at the idea of double-crossing Collie Munshin. I felt I ought to see him first, and I told Collie that I intended to sell the script as my own. He didn't even get angry. I think he was expecting it. Collie just said he was glad I would be back, and he talked me into staying with him. Do you know, I realized that he does care about me, and I was very touched by that. We worked out a new contract. Collie and I will split evenly if he's able to talk Teppis into letting me direct the film. Tomorrow, when I get in, everything will be settled. All I have to do is approve the galley-sheet on my advertisement."

"Yes, but how do you *feel*?" I asked suddenly, not able to listen to him anymore.

The ironic disciplined expression on his face gave way for an instant to something vulnerable behind it.

"How do I feel?" Eitel asked. "Oh, nothing so extraordinary, Sergius. You see, after a while, I knew they had me on my knees, and that if I wasn't ready to take an overdose of sleeping pills, I would have to let myself slide through the experience, and not try to resist it. So for the first time in my life I had the sensation of being a complete and total whore in the world, and I accepted every blow, every kick, and every gratuitous kindness with the inner gratitude that it could have been a good deal worse. And now I just feel tired, and if the truth be told, pleased with myself, because believe me, Sergius, it was *dirty* work." He lit a cigarette and held it away from his mouth. "In the end that's the only kind of self-respect you have. To be able to say to yourself that you're disgusting."

12

Eisenhower and Corporate Power

(DREAMS AND NIGHTMARES: MAILER'S AMERICA, 2000)

In his January 1961 farewell address to the nation, President Dwight D. "Ike" Eisenhower, a former five-star general, warned of the growing danger of the axis between the Pentagon and the defense industry. Mailer harbored a lifelong abhorrence for the many ways large corporations exercise control over American life. He believed that such economic behemoths undercut personal initiative and creativity and, ultimately, encourage conformity.

The fifties, in a sense, started in 1952 with Eisenhower. He was much beloved. The two presidents that have probably been loved the most since Franklin Delano Roosevelt have been Eisenhower and Reagan. Eisenhower gave a great feeling of security to the country and he was much beloved. He didn't stand for much and he was terribly conventional and life was pretty stultifying for me in the early fifties. As the fifties warmed up, it got more and more interesting and more and more exciting. Finally, we were on the edge of radical times by the end of the fifties. And Eisenhower himself changed a little bit, because, after all, there's that famous last speech he made warning us to watch out and worry about the military–industrial complex. Now when a general says that, that's significant. And that's one of the last remarks he made. On the other hand, like Reagan, he may have been getting a little old in the top of his head by the time he came to the end of his presidency. And we on the left did not think too much of Eisenhower. Looking back on him, I think maybe America was lucky to have had him because if we'd had someone who was a little bit more like Joe McCarthy, we could have gone in very bad directions. Eisenhower kept the balance in the country. Looking back on it, it was a time when the American corporation began to take huge strides toward controlling America. By now, in the 1990s, the corporation runs America. . . .

It used to be—let's take a working man—it used to be that, let's say, in the thirties and the forties, he worked in a factory. Yes, a corporation was running the factory, and the working man belonged to a labor union. He lived in a period of excitement about the developing labor unions. And, he saw the boss as his enemy. What happened is that the corporation very slowly and subtly over these decades has been giving people the idea that the corporation is the place to be, that you're lucky working for a corporation, that it's an agreeable place to be, that they take care of you. It's relatively true in certain places and hardly at all true in other places, but—but they have succeeded in brain-washing America, then and now. And in the fifties, the idea that the corporation was the place to be, that you lived a good life if you worked for the corporation, you lived a clean life. It was a great encouragement to mediocrity. You see, if you were a loyal, but mediocre person, you could thrive in the corporation. It was like a benign version of Sovietism, if you will.

13

JACKIE ROBINSON AND BLACK RAGE

(DREAMS AND NIGHTMARES: MAILER'S AMERICA, 2000)

Jackie Robinson (1919–72), All-Star professional baseball player and member of the Baseball Hall of Fame, broke the color barrier in 1947 with the Brooklyn Dodgers, the same year he was Rookie of the Year. He went on to be the National League's Most Valuable Player and led the Dodgers to a World Series victory in 1955. Mailer saw Robinson play many times at Ebbets Field, the Dodgers' home park. He believed Robinson to be one of the reasons for hope that the divisions between Blacks and whites in America—which he saw as the fundamental threat to American democracy—might be healed.

The most positive aspect of American life in the fifties was that relations between Blacks and whites were opening up. Blacks were finally gaining more equality in major league baseball, which had been as tightly closed as a bank. Everybody knew that if you get a Black man in there and he did well, the doors were going to open, because it was a competitive sport and if one team was prospering with a Black man, the other teams would want to do that too. So Jackie Robinson was chosen, and the animosity toward him by many white players was immense. He played for the Brooklyn Dodgers, and I had been a Brooklyn Dodger fan ever since the thirties. They were a weak baseball team, a comic baseball team. We'd always finish sixth or seventh out of eight teams. Then we began to get better and better, and by the time he came along, the Dodgers were a good team. And what was wonderful about that team was that the white ball players on that team liked Robinson and supported him against other teams who hated Robinson because he was a Black man. By 1950 he was an accepted star, but the courage it took that man for a couple of years to be able to play in that league under all the pressure was huge. He was a dynamic player who was cautioned not to be too dynamic his first year or two. In other words, he was wonderful at base stealing, but for the first year or two they told him it would really infuriate white ball players if he kept stealing bases on them. So he couldn't do the things he was best at. He had to hold his temper. He had to show he was a model gentleman; he had to show that he was extraordinarily cool. Well, it's hard to be a baseball player if you have to hold in all your impulses all the time. So his feat was huge.

Jackie Robinson brought Blacks and whites together. More Black people began to come to the games. Let's say Robinson got a hit and you'd be standing up cheering and there'd be a Black man standing up cheering next to you, each of you doing it individually. And then you became aware of each other cheering the same thing. For Blacks, white people cheering a Black man warmed some of the old sores. It was a time when Blacks and whites were coming together.

One of the saddest things that's happened in America is the huge division that exists now between white and Black. But it is unavoidable. The forces that were set loose were too enormous. Blacks were carrying ten generations of anger from the time they'd come from Africa. They couldn't play nice-nice for too long. Their anger rose to the surface. But once the anger rose to the surface, then the Southern mentality in America took over, which is: "These people are very difficult, full of rage. Keep 'em down on the farm. Don't give 'em too much liberty. You'll regret it." This was the Southern attitude. When Northerners would argue with Southerners, this was the form the argument would take in the forties and fifties. In the army, I remember we used to have that argument because we used to watch Black platoons marching and they could march far better than we could, with real style and éclat. We used to go "One-two-three-four," and they'd go, "Hut-oo-ee-fo-hah-had-out-the-door." It was like full of rhythm and marvelous cadence and extraordinary. We were fighting this war for democracy and we had separate-color units. This was no democracy. Blacks suffered the rotten end of that democracy for a century and more. So when Black Power came into being, everything began to fall apart because a lot of white liberals were shocked at the depth of the problem. They thought it was an easy problem to solve. All it took was some friendliness back and forth. They were well intentioned. When the Black rage began to express itself, I was less surprised than a lot of liberals, but I also was very depressed because I knew that nothing good was going to come of it. I could see the Black point of view. They had to express that anger.

I do not have the answer. When I ran for mayor of New York in 1969, I ran on the theme of power to the neighborhoods. In other words, to make New York, the city, the fifty-first state, and in that state people could form little cities, hamlets, villages, towns on whatever basis they chose. And if you had Black communities that wished to be Black communities as such, they had that right. You see, I felt that for democracy truly to function, people must be able to find a common denominator within a manageable group. Now whether the idea would have worked or not, I don't have a clue, frankly.

14

JAZZ AND THE WHITE NEGRO

(DREAMS AND NIGHTMARES: MAILER'S AMERICA, 2000)

Mailer's fourth wife, Beverly Bentley (1930–2018), had an extended rela-tionship with jazz trumpeter Miles Davis (1926–91), and Mailer used him as a model for the jazz singer Shago Martin, a character in his 1965 New York City novel, An American Dream. *Mailer saw the brilliance of Black jazz as another reason for optimism about the continuance of democracy.*

Back in the mid-fifties after I discovered marijuana, I had some Black friends at the time. I used to go up to Harlem quite a bit. We used to have parties there. It was altogether different. Relations between Blacks and whites couldn't have been more different in those years because there was a great deal more optimism. The whites were dis-covering all the wonders of the Black psyche, the Black way of life, the Black love of life, which we, as whites, felt we had less of. They might be poor, but they had a love of life that we didn't have. And Blacks on their side felt that they were getting closer to whites, so there was less antagonism back and forth. So there was a period— you might call it a window—from 1955 into the early sixties where Blacks and whites were coming together. But that ended very dra-matically by the middle of the sixties when Black Power came along and then the gulf between whites and Blacks began to get wider until finally, relations between Blacks and whites tended to be much more arbitrary and constructed than real. There's much more distrust on both sides.

During that open period there were a great many whites who began to understand all sorts of values in Black life. And they began to love the free Black man, as they saw it. It was very sentimental, very romantic, very over-dramatized in our lives. We didn't understand all the horrors of Black life. What we saw was the positive side of it, and so there were a great many white people who began to try to live like Black people. The core idea that I used for it was that you follow your orgasm, which infuriated a great many Black people at the time. "How dare he say that—he's reducing us to animals. How dare he say that we follow our orgasm and whites don't." But I do think there was a certain truth to it, all the same, whether they like it or not, which was that the objective correlative in the white man's life was how well did he do in his job, how well he did in society. For a great many Black people, who had no real future, very often the objective correlative was how their body was feeling, better or worse. And I began to feel there were a great many white men who were doing that also.

So I coined this phrase "the white Negro." It seemed to me this characterized what were then called hipsters. At the time, I thought a great deal was going to happen with hipsters. I was wrong, as I often am, at least 50 percent of the time, on declarations. The idea dwindled away and yet became part of the American culture at the same time. So there are elements of Black sensuality in a great many aspects of American life now. Black music was fabulous. In the fifties and sixties you could go to a jazz club like the Five Spot down near the Bowery or a little later, the Jazz Gallery, and you'd hear this incredible music, you know, wonderful, creative jazz music night after night. You'd hear Thelonious Monk and Sonny Rollins. Once in a while you'd hear Miles Davis in these places. Any number of other people, Ahmad Jamal, John Coltrane, Charlie Mingus. You began to see the extraordinary creativity that existed in Black life.

Listening to Black people improvise was an incredible experience because it was so creative and rich and structured and full of stuff. The idea that Black people had no real inner culture was absurd when you started listening to jazz. And that music, of course, has generated rap, which is also an improvisational kind of music. It has its merits, but compared to the great jazzmen, I see very little merit in all the forms, including rock 'n' roll and the Black aspects of rock 'n' roll. It seems to me that popular music had gotten noisier and thinner and, of course, there are no lyrics any longer. There's not a melodic line with the richness and variations that you used to have. . . .

The best jazz had the power to change people's minds. You could get white people who would come and hear jazz and they began to understand what was going on in that music, began to under-stand how rich the creativity was and how much actually was being achieved by the jazz, creatively speaking, aesthetically speaking. . . . There's no question in my mind that jazz was the most fertile and creative aesthetic experience I had in those years of the late fifties, early sixties. Meant much more to me for that short period than literature.

15

"THE WHITE NEGRO"

(ADVERTISEMENTS FOR MYSELF, 1959)

In this excerpt from Mailer's endlessly reprinted essay, he connects three of the most monstrous horrors of the twentieth century: the bombing of Hiroshima and Nagasaki, the Nazi Holocaust, and the continuing miseries of American Blacks resulting from centuries of slavery and violent discrimination. James Baldwin criticized the essay for misunderstanding Black sexuality, while Eldridge Cleaver and Allen Ginsberg praised it. The debate continues.

Probably, we will never be able to determine the psychic havoc of the concentration camps and the atom bomb upon the unconscious mind of almost everyone alive in these years. For the first time in civilized history, perhaps for the first time in all of history, we have been forced to live with the suppressed knowledge that the smallest facets of our personality or the most minor projection of our ideas, or indeed the absence of ideas and the absence of personality, could mean equally well that we might still be doomed to die as a cipher in some vast statistical operation in which our teeth would be counted, and our hair would be saved, but our death itself would be unknown, unhonored, and unremarked, a death that could not follow with dignity as a possible consequence to serious actions we had chosen, but rather a death by *deus ex machina* in a gas chamber or a radioactive city; and so in the midst of a civilization founded upon the Faustian urge to dominate nature, our psyche was subjected to the intolerable anxiety that death being causeless, life was causeless as well, and time deprived of cause and effect had come to a stop.

The Second World War presented a mirror to the human condition that blinded anyone who looked into it. For if tens of millions were killed in concentration camps out of the inexorable agonies and contractions of super-states founded upon the always insoluble contradictions of injustice, one was then obliged also to see that no matter how crippled and perverted an image of man was the society he had created, it was nonetheless his creation, his collective creation (at least his collective creation from the past) and if society was so murderous, then who could ignore the most hideous of questions about his own nature?

Worse. One could hardly maintain the courage to be individual, to speak with one's own voice, for the years in which one could complacently accept oneself as part of an elite by being a radical were forever gone. A man knew that when he dissented, he gave a note upon his life that could be called in any year of overt crisis. No wonder then that these have been the years of conformity and depression. A stench of fear has come out of every pore of American life, and we suffer from a collective failure of nerve. The only courage, with rare exceptions, that we have been witness to has been the isolated courage of isolated people.

It is on this bleak scene that a phenomenon has appeared: the American existentialist—the hipster, the man who knows that if our collective condition is to live with instant death by atomic war, relatively quick death by the State as *l'univers concentrationnaire*, or with a slow death by conformity with every creative and rebellious instinct stifled (at what damage to the mind and the heart and the liver and the nerves no research foundation for cancer will discover in a hurry), if the fate of twentieth-century man is to live with death from adolescence to premature senescence, why then the only life-giving answer is to accept the terms of death, to live with death as immediate danger, to divorce oneself from society, to exist without roots, to set out on that uncharted journey into the rebellious imperatives of the self. In short, whether the life is criminal or not, the decision is to encourage the psychopath in oneself, to explore that domain of experience where security is boredom and therefore sickness, and one exists in the present, in that enormous present which is without past or future, memory or planned intention, the life where a man must go until he is beat, where he must gamble with his energies through all those small or large crises of courage and unforeseen situations that beset his day, where he must be with it or doomed not to swing. The unstated essence of Hip, its psychopathic brilliance, quivers with the knowledge that new kinds of victories increase one's power or new kinds of perception; and defeats, the wrong kind of defeats, attack the body and imprison one's energy until one is jailed in the prison air of other people's habits, other people's defeats, boredom, quiet desperation, and muted icy self-destroying rage. One is Hip or one is Square (the alternative that each new generation coming into American life is beginning to feel), one is a rebel or one conforms, one is a frontiersman in the Wild West of American night life or else a Square cell, trapped in the totalitarian tissues of American society, doomed willy-nilly to conform if one is to succeed.

A totalitarian society makes enormous demands on the courage of men, and a partially totalitarian society makes even greater demands, for the general anxiety is greater. Indeed if one is to be a man, almost any kind of unconventional action often takes disproportionate courage. So it is no accident that the source of Hip is the Negro, for he has been living on the margin between totalitarianism and democracy for two centuries. But the presence of Hip as a working philosophy in the sub-worlds of American life is probably due to jazz, and its knifelike entrance into culture, its subtle but so penetrating influence on an avant-garde generation—that postwar generation of adventurers who (some consciously, some by osmosis) had absorbed the lessons of disillusionment and disgust of the twenties, the depression, and the war. Sharing a collective disbelief in the words of men who had too much money and controlled too many things, they knew almost as powerful a disbelief in the socially monolithic ideas of the single mate, the solid family, and the respectable love life. If the intellectual antecedents of this generation can be traced to such separate influences as D. H. Lawrence, Henry Miller, and Wilhelm Reich, the viable philosophy of Hemingway fit most of their facts. In a bad world, as he was to say over and over again (while taking time out from his parvenu snobbery and dedicated gourmandise), in a bad world there is no love nor mercy nor charity nor justice unless a man can keep his courage, and this indeed fitted some of the facts. What fitted the need of the adventurer even more precisely was Hemingway's categorical imperative that what made him feel good became therefore The Good.

So no wonder that in certain cities of America, in New York, of course, and New Orleans, in Chicago and San Francisco and Los Angeles, in such American cities as Paris and Mexico, D.F., this particular part of a generation was attracted to what the Negro had to offer. In such places as Greenwich Village, a ménage-à-trois was completed—the bohemian and the juvenile delinquent came face-to-face with the Negro, and the hipster was a fact in American life. If marijuana was the wedding ring, the child was the language of Hip, for its argot gave expression to abstract states of feeling that all could share, at least all who were Hip. And in this wedding of the white and the black it was the Negro who brought the cultural dowry. Any Negro who wishes to live must live with danger from his first day, and no experience can ever be casual to him, no Negro can saunter down a street with any real certainty that violence will not visit him on his walk. The cameos of security for the average white—mother and the home, job and the family—are not even a mockery to millions of Negroes; they are impossible. The Negro has the simplest of alternatives: live a life of constant humility or ever-threatening danger. In such a pass where paranoia is as vital to survival as blood, the Negro had stayed alive and begun to grow by following the need of his body where he could. Knowing in the cells of his existence that life was war, nothing but war, the Negro (all exceptions admitted) could rarely afford the sophisticated inhibitions of civilization, and so he kept for his survival the art of the primitive. He lived in the enormous present, he subsisted for his Saturday night kicks, relinquishing the pleasures of the mind for the more obligatory pleasures of the body, and in his music he gave voice to the character and quality of his existence, to his rage and the infinite variations of joy, lust, languor, growl, cramp, pinch, scream, and despair of his orgasm. For jazz is orgasm, it is the music of orgasm, good orgasm and bad, and so it spoke across a nation. It had the communication of art even where it was watered, perverted, corrupted, and almost killed. It spoke in no matter what laundered popular way of instantaneous existential states to which some whites could respond. It was indeed a communication by art, because it said, "I feel this, and now you do too."

So there was a new breed of adventurers, urban adventurers who drifted out at night looking for action with a black man's code to fit their facts. The hipster had absorbed the existentialist synapses of the Negro, and for practical purposes could be considered a white Negro.

16

J. Edgar Hoover and Stalin

(DREAMS AND NIGHTMARES: MAILER'S AMERICA, 2000)

Irv Kupcinet (1912–2003), longtime columnist for the Chicago Sun-Times, *hosted a television talk show from 1959 to 1986. J. Edgar Hoover (1895–1972), the director of the FBI from 1935 until his death, was criticized for harassing leftist political dissidents.*

There was a radio show in Chicago in 1958 or '59, *At Random*. Irv Kupcinet used to do it. What he would do is start at midnight and would go to three or four in the morning. It went as long as it went. And it was live, absolutely live. And you had different kinds of experts on, whoever was in Chicago for that weekend was invited to the show. I was on one night with about twelve people, everything from a black police officer from Ghana who was studying at the FBI, to a reporter who'd traveled with Eisenhower, to [singer and actress] Dinah Shore, to some guy who raised money for Jewish charities. We got into a discussion about the FBI and J. Edgar Hoover. And I said, "In my opinion, J. Edgar Hoover has done more harm to America than Joseph Stalin." Well, every hand shot up, except Dinah Shore's, to say they disagreed with me. They had call-ins and I thought, "Well, it's going to be fifty to five on the call-ins," fifty opposed to me, five for me. Instead, it was forty-eight opposed to me and forty for me, and you had to leave your name and address. I thought if forty people dared to side with me, then something profound has happened in America. And I was right. It was the beginning of the sixties. People were fed up with the restrictions and the congealed attitudes of the Cold War. It was one of the braver things I've done in my life, because everyone was so afraid of J. Edgar Hoover. He could destroy your life. Years later I saw my FBI file. There were three hundred pages in my file. Eighty of them were devoted to that one evening on television, eighty pages, and there were all sorts of attitudes. It was fascinating to get this cross-section of opinion on the FBI. Hoover was absolutely infuriated that someone could say something like that. But I love the remark. To this day I believe it's true that J. Edgar Hoover did much more harm to American than Joseph Stalin ever did. He poisoned our minds. He made us afraid to speak our piece. He was an enemy of democracy. Stalin we knew was no good, but Stalin was never a threat to us. We didn't live in fear of Stalin. We lived in fear of J. Edgar Hoover.

17

"Superman Comes to the Supermarket"

(ADVERTISEMENTS FOR MYSELF, 1959)

Mailer claimed, not unreasonably, that his Esquire *portrait of presidential candidate John F. Kennedy and the 1960 Democratic National Convention in Los Angeles, which appeared about six weeks before the election, was one of several key factors contributing to JFK's razor-thin victory over the Republican candidate, Richard M. Nixon. His essay, excerpted below, represents a radical change in the way American political life was reported. Mailer's vote for JFK was his first in a presidential election since 1948.*

Since the First World War Americans have been leading a double life, and our history has moved on two rivers, one visible, the other underground; there has been the history of politics which is concrete, factual, practical and unbelievably dull if not for the consequences of the actions of some of these men; and there is a subterranean river of untapped, ferocious, lonely and romantic desires, that concentration of ecstasy and violence which is the dream life of the nation.

The twentieth century may yet be seen as that era when civilized man and underprivileged man were melted together into mass man, the iron and steel of the nineteenth century giving way to electronic circuits which communicated their messages into men, the unmistakable tendency of the new century seeming to be the creation of men as interchangeable as commodities, their extremes of personality singed out of existence by the psychic fields of force the communicators would impose. This loss of personality was a catastrophe to the future of the imagination, but billions of people might first benefit from it by having enough to eat—one did not know—and there remained citadels of resistance in Europe where the culture was deep and roots were visible in the architecture of the past.

Nowhere, as in America, however, was this fall from individual man to mass man felt so acutely, for America was at once the first and most prolific creator of mass communications, and the most rootless of countries, since almost no American could lay claim to the line of a family which had not once at least severed its roots by migrating here. But, if rootless, it was then the most vulnerable of countries to its own homogenization. Yet America was also the country in which the dynamic myth of the Renaissance—that every man was potentially extraordinary—knew its most passionate persistence. Simply, America was the land where people still believed in heroes: George Washington; Billy the Kid; Lincoln, Jefferson; Mark Twain, Jack London, Hemingway; Joe Louis, Dempsey, Gentleman Jim; America believed in athletes, rum-runners, aviators; even lovers, by the time Valentino died. It was a country which had grown by the leap of one hero past another—is there a county in all of our ground which does not have its legendary figure? And when the West was filled, the expansion turned inward, became part of an agitated, overexcited, superheated dream life. The film studios threw up their searchlights as the frontier was finally sealed, and the romantic possibilities of the old conquest of land turned into a vertical myth, trapped within the skull, of a new kind of heroic life, each choosing his own archetype of a neo-renaissance man, be it Barrymore, Cagney, Flynn, Bogart, Brando or Sinatra, but it was almost as if there were no peace unless one could fight well, kill well (if always with honor), love well and love many, be cool, be daring, be dashing, be wild, be wily, be resourceful, be a brave gun. And this myth, that each of us was born to be free, to wander, to have adventure and to grow on the waves of the violent, the perfumed, and the unexpected, had a force which could not be tamed no matter how the nation's regulators—politicians, medicos, policemen, professors, priests, rabbis, ministers, *idéologues*, psychoanalysts, builders, executives and endless communicators—would brick-in the modern life with hygiene upon sanity, and middle-brow homily over platitude: the myth would not die. Indeed a quarter of the nation's business must have depended upon its existence. But it stayed alive for more than that—it was as if the message in the labyrinth of the genes would insist that violence was locked with creativity, and adventure was the secret of love.

Once, in the Second World War and in the year or two which followed, the underground river returned to earth, and the life of the nation was intense, of the present, electric; as a lady said, "That was the time when we gave parties which changed people's lives." The Forties was a decade when the speed with which one's own events occurred seemed as rapid as the history of the battlefields, and for the mass of people in America a forced march into a new jungle of emotion was the result. The surprises, the failures, and the dangers of that life must have terrified some nerve of awareness in the power and the mass, for, as if stricken by the orgiastic vistas the myth had carried up from underground, the retreat to a more conservative existence was disorderly, the fear of communism spread like an irrational hail of boils. To anyone who could see, the excessive hysteria of the Red wave was no preparation to face an enemy, but rather a terror of the national self: free-loving, lust-looting, atheistic, implacable—absurdity beyond absurdity to label communism so, for the moral products of Stalinism had been Victorian sex and a ponderous machine of material theology.

Forced underground again, deep beneath all *Reader's Digest* hospital dressings of Mental Health in Your Community, the myth continued to flow, fed by television and the film. The fissure in the national psyche widened to the danger point. The last large appearance of the myth was the vote which tricked the polls and gave Harry Truman his victory in '48. That was the last. Came the Korean War, the shadow of the H-bomb, and we were ready for the General. Uncle Harry gave way to Father, and security, regularity, order, and the life of no imagination were the command of the day. If one had any doubt of this, there was Joe McCarthy with his built-in treason detector, furnished by God, and the damage was done. In the totalitarian wind of those days, anyone who worked in Government formed the habit of being not too original, and many a mind atrophied from disuse and private shame. At the summit there was benevolence without leadership, regularity without vision, security without safety, rhetoric without life.

The ship drifted on, that enormous warship of the United States, led by a Secretary of State [John Foster Dulles, 1888–1959] whose cells were seceding to cancer, and as the world became more fantastic—Africa turning itself upside down, while some new kind of machine man was being made in China—two events occurred which stunned the confidence of America into a new night: the Russians put up their Sputnik, and Civil Rights—that reluctant gift to the American Negro, granted for its effect on foreign affairs—spewed into real life at Little Rock. The national Ego was in shock: the Russians were now in some ways our technological superiors, and we had an internal problem of subject populations equal conceivably in its difficulty to the Soviet and its satellites. The fatherly calm of the General began to seem like the uxorious mellifluences of the undertaker.

Underneath it all was a larger problem. The life of politics and the life of myth had diverged too far, and the energies of the people one knew everywhere had slowed down. Twenty years ago a post-Depression generation had gone to war and formed a lively, grousing, by times inefficient, carousing, pleasure-seeking, not altogether inadequate army. It did part of what it was supposed to do, and many, out of combat, picked up a kind of private life on the fly, and had their good time despite the yaws of the military system. But today in America the generation which respected the code of the myth was Beat, a horde of half-begotten Christs with scraggly beards, heroes none, saints all, weak before the strong, empty conformisms of the authority. The sanction for finding one's growth was no longer one's flag, one's career, one's sex, one's adventure, not even one's booze. Among the best in this newest of the generations, the myth had found its voice in marijuana, and the joke of the underground was that when the Russians came over they could never dare to occupy us for long because America was too Hip. Gallows humor. The poorer truth might be that America was too Beat, the instinct of the nation so separated from its public mind that apathy, schizophrenia, and private beatitudes might be the pride of the welcoming committee any underground could offer.

Yes, the life of politics and the life of the myth had diverged too far. There was nothing to return them to one another, no common

danger, no cause, no desire, and, most essentially, no hero. It was a hero
America needed, a hero central to his time, a man whose personality
might suggest contradictions and mysteries which could reach into
the alienated circuits of the underground, because only a hero can
capture the secret imagination of a people, and so be good for the
vitality of his nation; a hero embodies the fantasy and so allows each
private mind the liberty to consider its fantasy and find a way to
grow. Each mind can become more conscious of its desire and waste
less strength in hiding from itself. Roosevelt was such a hero, and
Churchill, Lenin and De Gaulle; even Hitler, to take the most odious
example of this thesis, was a hero, the hero-as-monster, embodying
what had become the monstrous fantasy of a people, but the horror
upon which the radical mind and liberal temperament foundered was
that he gave outlet to the energies of the Germans and so presented
the twentieth century with an index of how horrible had become the
secret heart of its desire. Roosevelt is of course a happier example of
the hero; from his paralytic leg to the royal elegance of his geniality
he seemed to contain the country within himself; everyone from the
meanest starving cripple to an ambitious young man could expand
into the optimism of an improving future because the man offered an
unspoken promise of a future which would be rich. The sexual and
the sex-starved, the poor, the hard-working and the imaginative well-
to-do could see themselves in the President, could believe him to be
like themselves. So a large part of the country was able to discover its
energies because not as much was wasted in feeling that the country
was a poisonous nutrient which stifled the day.

Too simple? No doubt. One tries to construct a simple model.
The thesis is after all not so mysterious; it would merely nudge the
notion that a hero embodies his time and is not so very much better than his time, but he is larger than life and so is capable of giving direction to the time, able to encourage a nation to discover the
deepest colors of its character. At bottom the concept of the hero is
antagonistic to impersonal social progress, to the belief that social
ills can be solved by social legislating, for it sees a country as all-but-
trapped in its character until it has a hero who reveals the character
of the country to itself. The implication is that without such a hero

the nation turns sluggish. Truman for example was not such a hero, he was not sufficiently larger than life, he inspired familiarity without excitement, he was a character but his proportions came from soap opera: Uncle Harry, full of salty common-sense and small-minded certainty, a storekeeping uncle.

Whereas Eisenhower has been the anti-Hero, the regulator. Nations do not necessarily and inevitably seek for heroes. In periods of dull anxiety, one is more likely to look for security than a dramatic confrontation, and Eisenhower could stand as a hero only for that large number of Americans who were most proud of their lack of imagination. In American life, the unspoken war of the century has taken place between the city and the small town: the city which is dynamic, orgiastic, unsettling, explosive and accelerating to the psyche; the small town which is rooted, narrow, cautious and planted in the life-logic of the family. The need of the city is to accelerate growth; the pride of the small town is to retard it. But since America has been passing through a period of enormous expansion since the war, the double-four years of Dwight Eisenhower could not retard the expansion, it could only denude it of color, character, and the development of novelty. The small-town mind is rooted—it is rooted in the small town—and when it attempts to direct history the results are disastrously colorless because the instrument of world power which is used by the small-town mind is the committee. Committees do not create, they merely proliferate, and the incredible dullness wreaked upon the American landscape in Eisenhower's eight years has been the triumph of the corporation. A tasteless, sexless, odorless sanctity in architecture, manners, modes, styles has been the result. Eisenhower embodied half the needs of the nation, the needs of the timid, the petrified, the sanctimonious, and the sluggish. What was even worse, he did not divide the nation as a hero might (with a dramatic dialogue as the result); he merely excluded one part of the nation from the other. The result was an alienation of the best minds and bravest impulses from the faltering history which was made. America's need in those years was to take an existential turn, to walk into the nightmare, to face into that terrible logic of history which demanded that the country and its people must become more extraordinary and more adventurous, or else perish, since the only alternative was to offer a false security in the power and the panacea of organized religion, family, and the FBI, a totalitarianization of the psyche by the stultifying techniques of the mass media which would seep into everyone's most private associations and so leave the country powerless against the Russians even if the denouement were to take fifty years, for in a competition between totalitarianisms the first maxim of the prizefight manager would doubtless apply: "Hungry fighters win fights." . . .

One had the opportunity to study Kennedy a bit in the days that followed. His style in the press conferences was interesting. Not terribly popular with the reporters (too much a contemporary, and yet too difficult to understand, he received nothing like the rounds of applause given to [FDR's wife] Eleanor Roosevelt, [Adlai] Stevenson, [Senator Hubert H.] Humphrey, or even Johnson), he carried himself nonetheless with a cool grace which seemed indifferent to applause, his manner somehow similar to the poise of a fine boxer, quick with his hands, neat in his timing, and two feet away from his corner when the bell ended the round. There was a good lithe wit to his responses, a dry Harvard wit, a keen sense of proportion in disposing of difficult questions—invariably he gave enough of an answer to be formally satisfactory without ever opening himself to a new question which might go further than the first. Asked by a reporter, "Are you for Adlai as vice president" the grin came forth and the voice turned very dry, "No, I cannot say we have considered Adlai as a vice president." Yet there was an elusive detachment to everything he did. One did not have the feeling of a man present in the room with all his weight and all his mind. Johnson gave you all of himself, he was a political animal, he breathed like an animal, sweated like one, you knew his mind was entirely absorbed with the compendium of political fact and maneuver; Kennedy seemed at times like a young professor whose manner was adequate for the classroom, but whose mind was off in some intricacy of the PhD thesis he was writing. Perhaps one can give a sense of the discrepancy by saying that he was like an actor who had been cast as the candidate, a good actor, but not a great one—you were aware all the time that the role was one thing and the man another—they did not coincide, the actor seemed a touch too aloof (as, let us say, Gregory Peck is usually too aloof) to become the part. Yet one had little sense of whether to value this elusiveness, or to beware of it. One could be witnessing the fortitude of a superior sensitivity or the detachment of a man who was not quite real to himself. And his voice gave no clue. When Johnson spoke, one could separate what was fraudulent from what was felt, he would have been satisfying as an actor the way Broderick Crawford or Paul Douglas are satisfying; one saw into his emotions, or at least had the illusion that one did. Kennedy's voice, however, was only a fair voice, too reedy, near to strident, it had the metallic snap of a cricket in it somewhere, it was more impersonal than the man, and so became the least-impressive quality in a face, a body, a selection of language, and a style of movement which made up a better-than-decent presentation, better than one had expected.

With all of that, it would not do to pass over the quality in Kennedy which is most difficult to describe. And in fact some touches should be added to this hint of a portrait, for later (after the convention), one had a short session alone with him, and the next day, another. As one had suspected in advance the interviews were not altogether satisfactory, they hardly could have been. A man running for President is altogether different from a man elected President: the hazards of the campaign make it impossible for a candidate to be as interesting as he might like to be (assuming he has such a desire). One kept advancing the argument that this campaign would be a contest of personalities, and Kennedy kept returning the discussion to politics. After a while one recognized this was an inevitable caution for him. So there would be not too much point to reconstructing the dialogue since Kennedy is hardly inarticulate about his political attitudes and there will be a library vault of text devoted to it in the newspapers. What struck me most about the interview was a passing remark whose importance was invisible on the scale of politics, but was altogether meaningful to my particular competence. As we sat down for the first time, Kennedy smiled nicely and said that he had read my books. One muttered one's pleasure. "Yes," he said, "I've read—" and then there was a short pause which did not last long enough to be embarrassing in which it was yet obvious no title came instantly to his mind, an omission one was not ready to mind altogether since a man in such a position must be obliged to carry a hundred thousand facts and names in his head, but the hesitation lasted no longer than three seconds or four, and then he said, "I've read *The Deer Park* and the others," which startled me for it was the first time in a hundred similar situations, talking to someone whose knowledge of my work was casual, that the sentence did not come out, "I've read *The Naked and the Dead* and the others." If one is to take the worst and assume that Kennedy was briefed for this interview (which is most doubtful), it still speaks well for the striking instincts of his advisers.

18

LIVING LIKE COCKROACHES

(DREAMS AND NIGHTMARES: MAILER'S AMERICA, 2000)

The powerful influence of his essay "Superman Comes to the Supermarket" encouraged Mailer to seek a seat in President Kennedy's kitchen cabinet. Here, Mailer reflects on his motives.

I wanted to be a presidential adviser. There were years when I wanted to be an adviser to any number of powerful people. I felt that I might have a certain talent for it. Looking back on it, it was a folly. I had this romantic notion that the impossible was attainable. It died hard in me. It took a long time to die. And I didn't begin to give up on it until about ten years ago.

Let me try to explain it a little more carefully. There's a dream life in America, and Kennedy and Mrs. Kennedy were closer to that dream life than the Eisenhowers, for example, or than Richard Nixon would be. Movie stars, you see, are more than icons to Americans. They're like gods. To the degree that Americans are still pagan, movie stars are our pagan gods. Now at that time I was very much oriented toward the pagan. In other words, what was pagan in my mind was good because it would free the spirit. I had the feeling in the fifties that America's heading right toward what I used to call Cancer Gulch. Everything was full of propriety. You couldn't express yourself. You couldn't have fun. If you wanted to have fun, you lived on the fringe. I began to have a sense of what life was like, and I realized that life, in its imminence, in its presence, in its resonance, once you could feel it, was extraordinary, but that we were all living like cockroaches, scurrying here and there and not having that life. And so that became my, if you will, my sermon, that I was preaching for the next ten-fifteen-twenty years: let's get back to instinctive life. Let's get back to a life where we can feel what's going on in ourselves. And I felt that Kennedy and his wife, precisely because of their youth and their good looks, were going to encourage an opening in America, a return to the pagan, the sense of one's self as a human animal who lived in a field of senses. And I felt that we needed that very badly in America. I still think I was right on that, by the way. I think there's a tendency in America to shut the senses down all the time. They open the senses and they shut them down. It's a very complex country. So in a certain sense there's a wildness, almost a formalized wildness in America now. In places like Las Vegas we have a night life of sorts. But, on the other hand, what we also have are superhighways. We have hotel rooms where you can't open the window. In other words, there's a war that goes on in America between the instinctive sentient life and the controlled life. Life controlled by others. It's just the stakes have changed, and now it goes on more intensely. And at that time, I felt that Jack Kennedy and Jacqueline Kennedy were going to accelerate, willy-nilly, the instinctive side of life.

19

"The Existential Heroine: Jackie Kennedy"

(*THE PRESIDENTIAL PAPERS,* 1963)

Mailer's essay on the president's wife was not received favorably—political commentators of that era generally avoided even marginally negative comments about the family of US presidents. In later years, when she worked as an editor at Viking Press, she and Mailer became friendly again and saw each other often as prominent members of the New York literary scene.

A few of you may remember that on February 14 [1962], last winter, our First Lady gave us a tour of the White House on television. For reasons to be explained in a while, I was in no charitable mood that night and gave Mrs. Kennedy a close scrutiny. Like anybody else, I have a bit of tolerance for my vices, at least those which do not get into the newspapers, but I take no pride in giving a hard look at a lady when she is on television. Ladies are created for an encounter face-to-face. No man can decide a lady is trivial until he has spent some minutes alone with her. Now while I have been in the same room with Jackie Kennedy twice, for a few minutes each time, it was never very much alone, and for that matter I do not think anyone's heart was particularly calm. The weather was too hectic. It was the Summer of 1960, after the Democratic Convention, before the presidential campaign had formally begun, at Hyannis Port, site of the Summer White House—those of you who know Hyannis ("Highanus," as the natives say) will know how funny is the title—all those motels and a Summer White House too: the Kennedy compound, an enclosure of three summer homes belonging to [JFK's father] Joe Kennedy, Sr., RFK [JFK's brother, Robert Francis Kennedy], and JFK, with a modest amount of lawn and beach to share among them. In those historic days the lawn was overrun with journalists, cameramen, magazine writers, politicians, delegations, friends and neighboring gentry, government intellectuals, family, a prince, some Massachusetts state troopers, and red-necked hard-nosed tourists patrolling outside the fence for a glimpse of the boy. He was much in evidence, a bit of everywhere that morning, including the lawn, and particularly handsome at times as one has described elsewhere (*Esquire*, November, 1960), looking like a good version of Charles Lindbergh at noon on a hot August day. Well, Jackie Kennedy was inside in her living room sitting around talking with a few of us, [historian] Arthur Schlesinger, Jr. and his wife Marian, Prince [Stanislaw] Radziwill [husband of Lee Radziwill, Jackie Kennedy's sister], Peter Maas the writer, Jacques Lowe the photographer, and [JFK's press secretary] Pierre Salinger. We were a curious assortment indeed, as oddly assembled in our way as some of the do-gooders and real baddies on the lawn outside. It would have taken a hostess of broad and perhaps dubious gifts ... to have woven some mood into this occasion, because pop! were going the flashbulbs out in the crazy August sun on the sun-drenched terrace just beyond the bay window at our back....

I had the impression that Jackie Kennedy was almost suffering in the flesh from their invasion of her house, her terrace, her share of the lands, that if the popping of the flashbulbs went on until midnight on the terrace outside she would have a tic forever in the corner of her eye. Because that was the second impression of her, of a lady with delicate and exacerbated nerves. She was no broad hostess, not at all; broad hostesses are monumental animals turned mellow: hippopotami, rhinoceri, plump lion, sweet gorilla, warm bear. Jackie Kennedy was a cat, narrow and wild, and her fur was being rubbed every which way. This was the second impression. The first had been simpler. It had been merely of a college girl who was nice. Nice and clean and very merry. I had entered her house perspiring—talk of the politician, I was wearing a black suit myself, a washable, the only one in my closet not completely unpressed that morning, and I had been forced to pick a white shirt with button-down collar: all the white summer shirts were in the laundry. What a set-to I had had with

Adele Morales [Mailer's second wife] at breakfast. Food half-digested in anger, sweating like a goat, tense at the pit of my stomach for I would be interviewing Kennedy in a half hour, I was feeling not a little jangled when we were introduced, and we stumbled mutually over a few polite remarks, which was my fault I'm sure more than hers for I must have had a look in my eyes— I remember I felt like a drunk marine who knows in all clarity that if he doesn't have a fight soon it'll be good for his character but terrible for his constitution.

She offered me a cool drink—iced verbena tea with sprig of mint no doubt—but the expression in my face must have been rich because she added, still standing by the screen in the doorway, "We do have something harder of course," and something droll and hard came into her eyes as if she were a very naughty eight-year-old indeed. More than one photograph of Jackie Kennedy had put forward just this saucy regard—it was obviously the life of her charm. But I had not been prepared for another quality, of shyness conceivably. There was something quite remote in her. Not willed, not chilly, not directed at anyone in particular, but distant, detached as the psychologists say, moody and abstracted the novelists used to say. As we sat around the coffee table on summer couches, summer chairs, a pleasant living room in light colors, lemon, white and gold seeming to predominate, the sort of living room one might expect to find in Cleveland, may it be, at the home of a fairly important young executive whose wife had taste, sitting there, watching people go by, the group I mentioned earlier kept a kind of conversation going. Its center, if it had one, was obviously Jackie Kennedy. There was a natural tendency to look at her and see if she were amused. She did not sit there like a movie star with a ripe olive in each eye for the brain, but in fact gave conversation back, made some of it, laughed often. We had one short conversation about Provincetown, which was pleasant. She remarked that she had been staying no more than fifty miles away for all these summers but had never seen it. She must, I assured her. It was one of the few fishing villages in America which still had beauty. Besides it was the Wild West of the East. The local police were the Indians and the beatniks were the poor hard-working settlers. Her eyes turned merry. "Oh, I'd love to see it," she said. But how did one go? In three black limousines and fifty police for escort, or in a sports car at four a.m. with dark glasses? "I suppose now I'll never get to see it," she said wistfully.

She had a keen sense of laughter, but it revolved around the absurdities of the world. She was probably not altogether unlike a soldier who has been up at the front for two weeks. There was a hint of gone laughter. Soldiers who have had it bad enough can laugh at the fact some trooper got killed crossing an open area because he wanted to change his socks from khaki to green. The front lawn of this house must have been, I suppose, a kind of no-man's-land for a lady. The story I remember her telling was about Stash, Prince Radziwill, her brother-in-law, who had gone into the second-story bathroom that morning to take a shave and discovered, to his lack of complete pleasure, that a crush of tourists was watching him from across the road. Yes, the house had been besieged, and one knew she thought of the sightseers as a mob, a motley of gargoyles, like the horde who riot through the last pages in [Nathanael West's 1939 Hollywood novel] *The Day of the Locust.*

Since there was an air of self-indulgence about her, subtle but precise, one was certain she liked time to compose herself. While we sat there she must have gotten up a half-dozen times, to go away for two minutes, come back for three. She had the exasperated impatience of a college girl. One expected her to swear mildly. "Oh, Christ!" or "Sugar!" or "Fudge!" And each time she got up, there was a glimpse of her calves, surprisingly thin, not unfeverish. I was reminded of the legs on those adolescent Southern girls who used to go out together and walk up and down the streets of Fayetteville, North Carolina, in the Summer of 1944 at Fort Bragg. In the petulant Southern air of their boredom many of us had found something luminous that summer, a mixture of languor, heat, innocence and stupidity which was our cocktail vis-à-vis the knowledge we were going soon to Europe or the other war. One mentions this to underline the determinedly romantic aura in which one had chosen to behold Jackie Kennedy. There was a charm this other short Summer of 1960 in the thought a young man with a young attractive wife might soon become President. It offered possibilities and vistas; it brought a touch of life to the

monotonies of politics, those monotonies so profoundly entrenched
into the hinges and mortar of the Eisenhower administration. It was
thus more interesting to look at Jackie Kennedy as a woman than as
a probable First Lady. Perhaps it was out of some such motive, such a
desire for the clean air and tang of unexpected montage, that I spoke
about her in just the way I did later that afternoon.

"Do you think she's happy?" asked a lady, an old friend, on the
beach at Wellfleet.

"I guess she would rather spend her life on the Riviera."

"What would she do there?"

"End up as the mystery woman, maybe, in a good murder case."

"Wow," said the lady, giving me my reward.

It had been my way of saying I liked Jackie Kennedy, that she was
not at all stuffy, that she had perhaps a touch of that artful madness
which suggests future drama.

My interview the first day had been a little short, and I was
invited back for another one the following day. Rather nicely, Senator
Kennedy invited me to bring anyone I wanted. About a week later I
realized this was part of his acumen. You can tell a lot about a man by
whom he invites in such a circumstance. Will it be a political expert
or the wife? I invited my wife. The presence of this second lady is not
unimportant, because this time she had the conversation with Jackie
Kennedy. While I was busy somewhere or other, they were introduced. Down by the Kennedy family wharf. The Senator was about
to take Jackie for a sail. The two women had a certain small general
resemblance. They were something like the same height, they both
had dark hair, and they had each been wearing it in a similar style
for many years. Perhaps this was enough to create a quick political
intimacy. "I wish," said Jackie Kennedy, "that I didn't have to go on
this corny sail, because I would like very much to talk to you, Mrs.
Mailer." A stroke. Mrs. M. did not like many people quickly, but Jackie
now had a champion. It must have been a pleasant sight. Two attractive witches by the water's edge.

20

To *Playboy*

(DECEMBER 21, 1962; *SELECTED LETTERS OF NORMAN MAILER*, 2014)

Mailer's September 1962 debate with William F. Buckley, Jr., the editor of the conservative journal National Review, *was published in* Playboy *in January 1963. Mailer disliked being called a liberal because many of his political beliefs were closer to conservative values.*

Dear Sir:

I wish you hadn't billed the debate between William Buckley and myself as a meeting between a conservative and a liberal. I don't care if people call me a radical, a rebel, a red, a revolutionary, an outsider, an outlaw, a Bolshevik, an anarchist, a nihilist, or even a left conservative, but please don't ever call me a liberal.

21

A Long Season of Dread

(THE PRESIDENTIAL PAPERS, 1963)

This Esquire *column is a reflection on the Cuban Missile Crisis of October 1962, when the world trembled on the brink of a nuclear war. Mailer uses the situation as a meditation on freedom and our alienation from nature.*

The rite of spring is in the odor of the air. The nerve of winter which enters one's nose comes a long far way like a scythe from the peak of mountains. To the aged it can feel like a miasma up from the midnight corridors of a summer hotel, empty and out of season. Winter breath had the light of snow when the sun is on it, or the bone chill of a vault. But the spring air comes up from the earth—at worst it can be the smell of new roots in bad slimy ground, at best the wine of late autumn frost is released from the old ice. Intoxication to the nostril, as if a filbert of fine sherbet had melted a sweet way into the tongue back of the throat down from the teeth. Spring is the season which marks the end of dread—so it is the season of profound dread for those who do not lose their fear.

Looking back on the winter and fall, one thinks of a long season of dread. There was that week toward the end of October when the world stood like a playing card on edge, and those of us who lived in New York wondered if the threat of war was like an exceptional dream which would end in a happy denouement (as indeed it did) or whether the events of each day would move, ante raised on ante, from boats on a collision course to invasions of Cuba, from threat of nuclear reprisal to the act itself, the Götterdämmerung of New York. Or would the end come instantly without prevision or warning, we would wonder as well, were we now heroes in a movie by Charlie Chaplin, was our house at the edge of the cliff, would we open the door and step in an abyss? There was dread that week. One looked at the buildings one passed and wondered if one was to see them again. For a week everyone in New York was like a patient with an incurable disease—would they be dead tomorrow or was it life for yet another year?

We sat that week in New York thinking of little. When movies are made of the last week on earth, the streets thrive with jazz, the juveniles are unrestrained, the adults pillage stores, there is rape, dancing, caterwauling laughter, sound of sirens and breaking glass, the roller coaster of a brave trumpet going out on its last ride. But we sat around. All too many watched television. Very few of us went out at night. The bars were half empty. The talk was quiet. One did not have the feeling great lovers were meeting that week, not for the first time nor for the last. An apathy came over our city. A muted and rather empty hour which lasted for a week. If it all blew up, if it all came to so little, if our efforts, our loves, our crimes added up to no more than a sudden extinction in a minute, in a moment, if we had not even time before the bomb (as civilians did once) to throw one quick look at some face, some trinket, some child for which one had love, well, one could not complain. That was our fate. That was what we deserved. We did not march in the street or shake our fists at the sky. We waited in our burrow like drunks in the bullpen pacing the floor of our existence, waiting for court in the morning while the floor was littered with the bile that came up in our spit and the dead butts of our dying lung's breath. Facing eternity we were convicts hanging on the dawn. There was no lust in the streets nor any defiance with which to roar at eternity. We were guilty.

We gave our freedom away a long time ago. We gave it away in all the revolutions we did not make, all the acts of courage we found a way to avoid, all the roots we destroyed in fury at that past which still would haunt our deeds. We divorced ourselves from the materials of the earth, the rock, the wood, the iron ore; we looked to new materials which were cooked in vats, long complex derivatives of urine which we called plastic. They had no odor of the living or of what once had lived, their touch was alien to nature. They spoke of the compromise of incompatibles. The plastic which had invaded our bathrooms, our kitchens, our clothing, our toys for children, our tools, our containers, our floor coverings, our cars, our sports, the world of our surfaces was the simple embodiment of social cowardice. We had tried to create a world in which all could live even if none could breathe. There had been a vast collective social effort in the twentieth century—each of us had tried to take back a critical bit more from existence than we had given to it.

There was a terror to contemplate in the logic of our apathy. Because if there was a God and we had come from Him, was it not the first possibility that each of us had a mission, one of us to create, another to be brave, a third to love, a fourth to work, a fifth to be bold, a sixth to be all of them. Was it not possible that we were sent out of eternity to become more than we had been?

That is why we did not roar into the street and shout that it was unnatural for mankind to base its final hope on the concealed character of two men, that it was unnatural to pray that Kennedy and Khrushchev taken together were more good than evil. What an ignoble suppliant hope for civilization to rest its security on two men, no more, two men. What had happened to the dream of the world's wealth guarded by the world's talent, the world's resource?

We sat in apathy because most of us, in the private treacherous dialogues of our sleep, had turned our faith away from what was most vital in our mind, and had awakened in depression. We had drawn back in fright from ourselves, as if in our brilliance lay madness, and beyond the horizon dictated by others was death. We had been afraid of death as no generation in the history of mankind has been afraid.

22

MARCH ON WASHINGTON FOR JOBS AND FREEDOM

(*ESQUIRE*, DECEMBER 1963)

In this column, Mailer recalls the March after which Martin Luther King gave his celebrated "I Have a Dream" speech, August 28, 1963, at the Lincoln Memorial. The March is widely credited to have enhanced the passage of the landmark Civil Rights Act of 1964.

Now, almost three months after 200,000 Negroes and whites made their March on Washington, the reports I remember best were the ones I read in *The Village Voice* (September 5, 1963). There was . . . a political analysis by Robert Levin with which I disagreed, but thought to the point. In fact it established where the point could be found. Let me quote from it:

> The March almost happened during that brief period when . . . tens of thousands of people walked down Constitution Avenue, from the Washington Monument to the Lincoln Memorial, singing spirituals. That part was very moving, but it did not last for very long and it did not culminate in anything more than a four-hour platitude. Perhaps one had no right to expect anything else. What the limitations of the demonstration were going to be had been decided by the President and the Negro leaders, and widely publicized weeks before the fact. The demonstration was neutralized in the very nature and process of its organization.
>
> It was designed and ordered in such a way as to disturb the psyche of no one. How could any mass demonstration the style of which the New York *Daily News* and the *Times* were

able to condone have any real significance? It complied with the very terms and standards that had fostered the necessity of revolution . . . If the Negro energy is going to make a revolution that would achieve something more than the dubious right to dream the American Dream too—and it must want more than that if this country is going to survive the cost of its hideous ambition—then violence must be risked. Had the demonstrators invaded halls of Congress in the manner in which many of them had invaded Southern lunchrooms, there might indeed have been violence. Probably in such a confrontation, there would have been an explosion. But just possibly the fear of confrontation, that fear, in effect, of life stuck like a rock in the American gut, serving the nerve and paralyzing the sensibilities . . . that fear just might have been exorcised. At least the falling atoms of the consciousness might have settled in a new and different pattern. So the Congressmen as well as the demonstrators were cheated, and the American air was no less free of the toxic breath of total-itarianism on Thursday morning than it had been on Tuesday. . . .

Let me make it clear that one does not argue with Robert Levin's description of the sensuous aspects of the March. The best part was indeed the walk—it was quiet, it was solemn, it was rich. It was the rarest American experience: a fruition. There was a collective emotion which was the magnification of the particular emotion a middle-aged couple of immigrant stock might feel on the day their first son graduates from college. Deeds of abnegation, of selflessness, of thrift, years of planning had resulted in a successful issue. That was the mood of the March—you wished it had been five miles long rather than one.

And the four hours of speeches which followed *were* anticlimactic. The collective mood shifted. While it was pleasant to a point, while it was not inaccurate to say—as nearly everyone did—that the atmosphere was reminiscent of a huge Sunday picnic, a church picnic, there was also an air of subtle depression, of wistful apathy which existed in many—one felt a little of the muted disappointment which attacks a crowd in the seventh inning of a very important baseball game when the score has gone eleven-to-three. The home team is ahead, but the tension is broken: one's concern is no longer noble. It was an agreeable afternoon, but it had a touch of the cancerous to it—"the toxic air of Totalitarianism." Because two hundred thousand people had come down, some in fear, some in all courage, but they had come with the memory of the summer behind them, that historic summer of television when revolution for the first time had been created in part by the indignation of all those millions who had seen Bull Connor's police using firehoses on Negro children, yes, a revolution created in part by television, that instrument of social control which had been used since its inception precisely to dull and/or end forever the possibility of revolution. Yes, the seed of dialectics was stirring again, the shade of Marx, the ghost of Lenin. Many, maybe most of those two hundred thousand people came to Washington expecting danger, looking secretly for an historic issue that day.

And they were disappointed. Considering the heat and the depressed fury of the history which had created this March, it was probably the most peaceful large assemblage in the history of the Republic. Never had one seen people so polite to one another. The iron word had gone out: No violence today! And there was none. That took its toll. That put the hint of a powerful depression into the agreeableness of the afternoon.

Yet I think the leaders were right to do it the way they chose to do it, and I think Robert Levin, for all the pertinence of his comment, is still wrong. Because a revolution is broken if it cannot move on two feet—one of Lenin's favorite notions—and the Negro had already demonstrated to the collective psyche of America that they had the greatest potential for violence of any political body in our American world; now, on this afternoon, they chose to show that they also possessed the finest capacity for order and discipline in the nation. Could one dream of bringing together two hundred thousand whites steaming with bitterness and the hot heart of injustice on a hot summer day with no riot breaking forth? Impossible. A deep blues went out from Washington in those hours: a revolutionary force existed in the land; it could move with violence, and it could move with discipline. No invasion of Congress, no sit-down in the halls could have thrust the message so far into the fifty million or hundred million Americans who are neither for nor against this revolution. Indeed, a violent demonstration could have alienated them. The Capitol Building is one of the altars of the Republic—a sit-down inside Congress on that day would have made [Alabama] Governor Wallace [1919–1998] a candidate for President in a new party. To the average American it would have been equal to stomping on the flag. A revolution withers if it is afraid of creating outrage, but it is killed in ambush if it accepts and attacks each and every possibility for outrage presented to it. There was revolutionary genius in bringing off the March on Washington, for it created the second leg of the movement. The price—that air of violence gone deeper, that touch of cancer—may not have been too great. The horror of a revolution is that the brave and the half-brave pay with diseases of the flesh and nausea of the spirit for the compromises, hypocrisy, and evasion of the past.

23

"THE LEADING MAN": REVIEW OF *J.F.K.:* *THE MAN AND THE MYTH* BY VICTOR LASKY

(CANNIBALS AND CHRISTIANS, 1966)

In this review, Mailer reiterates his fundamental uncertainty about JFK's moral nature: hero, opportunist, or both? Despite his question, Mailer came to believe that electing JFK, a young, intelligent, and magnetic figure, as president was a major and positive turning point in American democracy.

Victor Lasky has now written a giant political biography of John Fitzgerald Kennedy.... It is close to being a monumental study of Jack Kennedy's stops and starts, dips and swoops, turns to Right and Left as he advanced along his political life, and the work becomes an indispensable if not altogether trustworthy reference to anyone who would study the peculiar logic of political success, the practical details in the art of the possible.

Lasky has done an impressive amount of work. He has hunted down a thousand anecdotes in newspapers and magazines (half of them sufficiently apocryphal to be worthless, we can suspect), he has talked to everyone who knew Kennedy and would agree to talk to Lasky, he has come up with much of the goods and a hundred goodies. Did Jack Kennedy ever kiss a baby in the congressional campaign of 1946 and turn to a friend to say, "Kissing babies gives me asthma"? Well, you may be certain Lasky has found the item and put it in. *J.F.K.: The Man and the Myth* is a book which will give pleasure to every Kennedy-hater who reads it—they will feel as if they are dipping into a box of creamy chocolate. Indeed, at his best and worst, Lasky is

reminiscent of [political columnists Jack] Lait and [Lee] Mortimer—
he could have called his job *John F. Kennedy—Confidential*.

And there is value in such an undertaking: a man is responsible for
his past. It is not fitting that Jack Kennedy should get away with all of
it. The Republicans will employ these pages as a running handbook
for the '64 campaign, and it will be of inestimable use to them, good
use and dirty use, but ideally the book can be worth even more for
liberal Democrats, since their chronic disease is hero worship, and
Lasky's pages are effective antitoxin. For example:

> In 1950, John F. Kennedy made a personal contribution to
> Richard M. Nixon in his Senate campaign against the Califor-
> nia Congresswoman [Helen Gahagan Douglas]. Like any other
> contribution it was turned over to the Nixon Senate Campaign
> Committee in California.

On the preceding page is one of numerous references to the President's not unfavorable attitude towards [Senator Joseph] McCarthy
in the early Fifties: "he thought he 'knew Joe pretty well, and he may
have something.'"

But then the Kennedy of 1948 was making these sorts of head-
lines in the *Boston Herald*: "Kennedy says Roosevelt sold Poland to
Reds." F.D.R. had done this "because he did not understand the Russian mind." So had gone a modest speech Congressman Kennedy had
given to the Polish-American Citizens Club in Roxbury. . . .

A speech made in one city does not have the same magic when it
is read about in another city. A promise made in private to a politician
will not interfere with a contradictory promise made to another politician. When the time comes to fulfill the promise, one can reward
the man who did the most for you, or is strongest, or indeed one can
break both promises and make a deal with a third politician. One can
promise the Negro his rights in the North while giving intimations
to the South that one is secretly sympathetic to their fears. The art is
to practice duplicity and double-dealing with a sense of moderation,
taste, and personal style; the secret is to remain alert to the subtler
shifting realities of mass communication: what sort of news in this

season is likely to become national, which oratory will happily or unhappily remain local.

These are some of the lessons to be elucidated from the political career of John Fitzgerald Kennedy. If Lasky's work had been an objective study, if Kennedy had been considered merely the first among equals, if it had been understood that such men as Barry Goldwater, Hubert Humphrey, and Dick Nixon are all in their way equally adept as political operators—if Lasky's work had risen into an unbiased exploration of political mendacity in general and President Kennedy in particular, there might have been a hard remaining substance to the book. He could have left us with a classic in political biography. (A badly written classic, be it said—the prose is left without comment.) Instead, Lasky's pretense to be objective, which keeps the first half of his book interesting, begins even as pretense to disappear about the time Jack Kennedy begins to work for his nomination. Lasky's bias shows itself. He is, we discover, a Nixon man, an all-out Nixon man. The moral judgments slide over into propaganda. Nixon is invariably presented as honest, self-effacing, put upon, unjustly rejected; Kennedy grows into a villain of the first proportions. So a work which might have reminded us that we take the politician too seriously is replaced by Lasky's more specific objective—which is to stitch up a campaign flag for the return of Richard M. Nixon; so a work which could have reminded Jack Kennedy that there is still a public conscience becomes instead a campaign tract to be overpraised by Republicans and damned by Democrats. That is the crime of commission in *J.F.K.: The Man and the Myth*.

The void of omission is more grave. For, with all his documentation of Jack Kennedy's political life, the large disappointment in the book is that Lasky has no intimation of the curious depths in the President's nature. J.F.K. is a divided man, and only half his nature is political. Even through the lenses of his bias, Lasky understands that half very well—that half-man comes through the pages as one of the most consummate political animals in the history of America. But the half omitted is more crucial. For Jack Kennedy is a new kind of political leader, and a study of his past political sins will not help us to comprehend his future. The likelihood is that our President is a new kind of Commander-in-Chief. He is not a father, nor a god, nor a god-figure, nor an institution, nor a symbol. He is in fact—permit the literary conceit—a metaphor. Which is to say that Jack Kennedy is more like a hero of uncertain moral grandeur: is his ultimate nature tragic or epic? Is he a leading man or America's brother? . . .

J.F.K.: The Man and the Myth is an irritating, frustrating, and finally disappointing book because it offered the promise of becoming a first-rate job, and was spoiled—this spoliation being a first-rate loss— by Lasky's incapacity to entertain a poetic concept of his subject. Jack Kennedy is somewhat more and considerably less after all than a hero or a villain—he is also an empty vessel, a man of many natures, not all of them necessarily rooted in granite. He is, it must be said, a Kierkeg-aardian hero. One can assume that in the private stricken moments of his life, those moments all of us know at rare and best-forgotten times, it is impossible for him to be certain of his moral bedrock. Kierkeg-aard was probably the first Western mind to have an intimation that either the nature of man was changing or had never been properly understood, that it was just as natural for man to be flooded with sensations of goodness when he was most evil as it was for him to taste his evil, and that a man in the act of being good could equally be depressed with an awareness of his profound evil. In this sense one did not have a nature which was formed already—on the contrary, one created one's nature by the depth or power of one's acts. Kierkegaard had divined that there was probably no anguish on heaven or earth so awful as the inability to create one's nature by daring, exceptional, forbidden, or socially impossible acts.

This impulse—to create and forever re-create his nature—has been the President's dominant passion. There is no other way to com-prehend him. From the Hairbreadth Harry of his P.T. boat exploits through the political campaigns with their exceptional chances (who could beat [Massachusetts Senator Henry] Cabot Lodge in Massachu-setts in 1952?) through the lively bachelordom, through the marriage to the impossibly beautiful and somewhat madcap wife, the decision to run for President, a decision worthy of Julien Sorel, the adventure in Cuba, the atomic poker game with Khrushchev last October when the biggest bluff in the history of the world was called—yes, each is a panel of scenes in the greatest movie ever made.

The President is not a great mind, and it may be that he will prove ultimately not to be a good man—those who are forever re-creating their personalities can end with a mediocre nature even more naturally than a great one—but he had genius in one respect. Jack Kennedy understood that the most important, probably the only dynamic culture in America, the only culture to enlist the imagination and change the character of Americans, was the one we had been given by the movies. Therefore a void existed at the center of American life. No movie star had the mind, courage or force to be national leader, and no national leader had the epic adventurous resonance of a movie star. So the President nominated himself. He would fill the void. He would be the movie star come to life as President. That took genius. For Jack Kennedy grew up in the kind of milieu which was so monumental with finance and penurious with emotion that everybody's breath smelled like they had been swallowing pennies and you were considered mentally disturbed if you did not bet on the New York Yanks. He had a character thus created of the most impossible ingredients for his venture: over-weening ambition and profound political caution—he had been taught never to commit himself to a political idea since ideas often pass, weaken, and die long before the men who believed in them.

Yes, John F. Kennedy was without principles or political passions except for one. He knew the only way he could re-create the impoverished circuits which lay between himself and the depths of his emotions was to become President. *He* was his own idea, and he had the luck to have a powerful father who agreed entirely with his venture. So he combined the two halves of his nature, the Faustian adventurer and the political opportunist, and behind him left a record of deceits, evasions, broken promises, Congressional absenteeism, political pusillanimities, after-dinner clichés, amoral political negotiations and a complete absence on the record of a single piece of important legislation. Or the utterance of a single exciting political idea. He didn't have to. He was on the trail of something else and the people who gathered to his support were in quest of something else.

His impulse, that profound insight into the real sources of political power in America, came from a conscious or unconscious cognition that the nation could no longer use a father; it was Kennedy's genius to appreciate that we now required a leading man. The contradictions of our national character had become so acute that no symbol of authority could satisfy our national anxiety any longer. We had become a Kierkegaardian nation. In the deep mills of our crossed desires, in the darkening ambiguities of our historic role, we could know no longer whether we were good or evil as an historic force, whether we should prosper or decline, whether we were the seed of freedom or the elaboration of a new tyranny. We needed to discover ourselves by an exploration through our ambiguity. And that precise ambiguity is embodied in the man we chose for our President. His magnetism is that he offers us a mirror of ourselves, he is an existential hero, his end is unknown, it is even unpredictable, even as our end is unpredictable, and so in this time of crisis he is able to perform the indispensable psychic act of a leader, he takes our national anxiety so long buried and releases it to the surface—where it belongs.

Now we must live again as a frontier nation, out on a psychic frontier without the faith of children or the security of answers. So the country for better or for worse, is now again on the move, and the President is the living metaphor of our change. It is this power in him to excite—whether he desires it or no—our change, our discord, and our revolt, which Victor Lasky has failed most resolutely to comprehend. He does not see that Kennedy is the agent of our ferment and that we now go forth into the future ignorant of whether the final face of the Presidency and America shall prove to be Abraham Lincoln or Dorian Gray.

24

To Mickey Knox

(DECEMBER 17, 1963; *SELECTED LETTERS OF NORMAN MAILER,* 2014)

Mailer met Knox in Hollywood in 1948, and they remained lifelong friends. A voice coach and actor who appeared in more than eighty films, Knox was black-listed during the McCarthy era and spent decades working in Paris and Rome. President John F. Kennedy was assassinated by Lee Harvey Oswald on November 22, 1963, and two days later Oswald was shot to death by Jack Ruby.

Dear Mickey,

The Kennedy thing hit very hard here. Women were crying in the streets (mainly good-looking women), a lot of middle-aged Negroes looked sad and very worried, and then we all sat around in gloom and watched the television set for the next seventy-two hours. Altogether it was one of three events having something profoundly in common: Pearl Harbor day and the death of Roosevelt being the other two. And the Ruby-Oswald stuff was just too much on top of it. I haven't felt like writing a word about the whole thing, I've been too fucking depressed every which way. The main loss I think was a cultural one. Whether he wanted to or not Kennedy was giving a great boost to the arts, not because Jackie Kennedy was inviting Richard Wilbur to the White House, but somehow the lid was off, and now I fear it's going to be clamped on tight again.

As for Oswald and Ruby, I don't know what was going on, but I don't have the confidence we'll ever know. I'd like to believe that the FBI had a sinister hand in all of this, but somehow I doubt it. I suspect the real story is that two lonely guys, all by themselves, put more grit in the gears than anyone ever succeeded in doing before, and it's just a mess, a dull miserable mess.

25

Ike's GOP Convention Speech, 1964

(CANNIBALS AND CHRISTIANS, 1966)

During Eisenhower's eight years in office, from 1953 to 1961, Mailer found him to be dull, plodding, and resistant to changes in civil rights and free speech. Later, he softened his opinion, largely because Eisenhower shared his consternation about powerful corporations.

First major event of the convention was [former President] Eisenhower's appearance at the Cow Palace [in Daly City, California] to give a speech on Tuesday afternoon. The arena was well-chosen for a convention. Built in the Thirties when indoor sports stadiums did not yet look like children's nurseries, the Cow Palace offered echoes—good welterweights and middleweights had fought here, there was iron in the air. And the Republicans had installed the speaker's platform at one end of the oval; the delegates sat therefore in a file which was considerably longer than it was wide, the speaker was thus installed at the handle of the sword. (Whereas the Democrats in 1960 had put the speaker in the middle of the oval.) But this was the party after all of Republican fathers rather than Democratic mothers. If there were any delegates to miss the psychic effect of this decision, a huge banner raised behind the speaker confronted them with the legend: Of the people, By the people, For the people. "Of the people" was almost invisible; "By the people" was somewhat more clear; "For the people" was loud and strong. This was a party not much "of the people" but very much "for the people," it presumed to know what was good for them.

And for fact, that had always been Ike's poor lone strength as a speaker, he knew what was good for you. He dipped into his speech, "here with great pride because I am a Republican," "my deep dedication to Republicanism"—he had not been outward bound for five minutes before the gallery was yawning. Ike had always been a bore, but there had been fascination in the boredom when he was President—this, after all, was the man. Now he was just another hog wrassler of rhetoric; he pinned a few phrases in his neat determined little voice, and a few phrases pinned him back. Ike usually fought a speech to a draw. It was hard to listen. All suspense had ended at Monday morning's press conference. Ike would not come out in support of Scranton. So the mind of the Press drifted out with the mind of the gallery. If Ike said a few strong words about the Civil Rights Bill—"Republicans in Congress to their great credit voted far more overwhelmingly than did our opponents to pass the Civil Rights Bill"—it meant nothing. The Moderates tried to whoop it up, the Goldwater delegations looked on in ranked masses of silence. Ike went on. He gave the sort of speech which takes four or five columns in the *New York Times* and serves to clot the aisles of history. He was still, as he had been when he was President, a cross between a boy and an old retainer. The boy talked, earnest, innocent, a high-school valedictorian debating the affirmative of, Resolved: Capitalism is the Most Democratic System on Earth; and the old retainer quavered into the voice, the old retainer could no longer live without love.

Ike had bored many a crowd in his time. He had never bored one completely—he had always known how to get some token from a mob. Ever since 1952, he had been giving little pieces of his soul to draw demonstrations from the mob. You could always tell the moment. His voice shifted. Whenever he was ready to please the crowd, he would warn them by beginning to speak with a brisk little anger. Now it came, now he said it. "Let us particularly scorn the *divisive* efforts of those outside our family, including sensation-seeking columnists and commentators [beginning of a wild demonstration] because," said Ike, his voice showing a glint of full spite, "I assure you that these are people who couldn't care less about the good of our party." He was right, of course. That was not why he said it, however; he said it to repay the Press for what they had said about him these last three weeks; the sensation they had been seeking was—so far as

he was concerned—to arouse needles of fury in an old man's body—
he said what he said for revenge. Mainly he said it to please the Goldwater crowd, there was the hint of that in his voice. The Goldwater
delegations and the gallery went into the first large demonstration of
the convention. Trumpets sounded, heralds of a new crusade: cockroaches, columnists, and Communists to be exterminated. There were
reports in the papers next day that delegates shook their fists at news-
papermen on the floor, and at the television men with their micro-
phones. The mass media is of course equipped for no such war. Some
of the men from the mass media looked like moon men: they wore
red helmets and staggered under the load of a portable camera which
must have weighed fifty pounds and was packed on their back; others
of the commentators had portable mikes and hats with antennae. To
the delegates they must have looked like insects grown to the size of
a man. Word whipped in to the delegation from the all-call telephone
in the office trailer of the Goldwater command post back of the Cow
Palace. Cut the demonstration, was the word from F. Clifton White.
The demonstration subsided. But the Press did not, the rest of the
mass media did not. They remain in a state of agitation: if Ike was
ready to accuse anyone could serve as hangman.

26

Goldwater: Sincere Demagogue

(CANNIBALS AND CHRISTIANS, 1966)

Mailer wrote about presidential candidate Arizona senator Barry Goldwater in this excerpt from a long essay, "In the Red Light," about the July 1964 Republican National Convention in Daly City, California. Goldwater was in part responsible for broadening the base of the Republican Party that year, despite his overwhelming loss to Lyndon Johnson in the election. The 1964 election exposed deep divisions in the country. Behind the slogans and election-eering and beneath the declaration that candidate Goldwater's acceptance speech is famous for, "Extremism in defense of liberty is not a vice," Mailer diagnoses a nation "in disease" and foresees the "wars" and "revolution" that will ensue.

Now, as for Goldwater, he had dimensions. Perhaps they were no more than contradictions, but he was not an easy man to comprehend in a hurry. His wife, for example, had been at the Gala, sitting with some family and friends, but at one of the less agreeable tables on the floor, off to the side and sufficiently back of the stage so that you could not see the entertainer. It seemed a curious way for the Establishment to treat the wife of the leading contender, but I was assured by the young lady who brought me over for the introduction that Mrs. Goldwater preferred it that way. "She hates being the center of attention," I was told. Well, she turned out to be a shy attractive woman with a gentle not altogether happy but sensual face. There was something nice about her and very vulnerable. Her eyes were moist, they were luminous. It was impossible not to like her. Whereas her daughters were attractive in a different fashion. "I want the best ring in this joint, buster," I could hear them say.

Goldwater's headquarters, however, were at a remove from the ladies. Occupying the fourteenth and fifteenth floors of the Mark Hopkins, they were not easy to enter. The main elevators required a wait of forty-five minutes to go up. The alternate route was off the mezzanine through a pantry onto a service car. A half-filled twenty-gallon garbage can stood by the service-elevator door. You went squeezed up tight with high and low honchos for Goldwater, plus waiters with rolling carts working room service. . . . They had something in common—professional workers for Goldwater—something not easy to define. They were not like the kids out in the street, nor did they have much in common with the old cancer-guns in the lobby; no, the worst of these workers looked like divinity students who had been expelled from the seminary for embezzling class funds and still felt they were nearest to J.C.—there was a dark blank fanaticism in their eyes. And the best of the Goldwater professionals were formidable, big rangy men, some lean, some flabby, with the hard distasteful look of topflight investigators for fire-insurance companies, field men for the F.B.I., or like bright young district attorneys, that lean flat look of the hunter, full of moral indignation and moral vacuity. But the total of all the professional Goldwater people one saw on the fourteenth and fifteenth floors was directly reminiscent of a guided tour through the F.B.I. in the Department of Justice Building in Washington, that same succession of handsome dull faces for guide, hair combed straight back or combed straight from a part, eyes lead shot, noses which offered nothing, mouths which were functional, good chins, deft moves. . . . The faces in these rooms were the cream of the tourists and the run of the F.B.I.; there was a mood like the inside of a prison: enclosed air, buried urgency. But that was not altogether fair. The sense of a prison could come from the number of guards and the quality of their style. . . . That was Headquarters. One never got to see Goldwater in the place.

There was opportunity, however, to come within three feet of him later that day, once at the caucus of the Florida delegation in the Beverly Plaza. Barry sat in the front, a spotlight on him, a silver film of perspiration adding to his patina, and the glasses, those black-framed glasses, took on that odd life of their own, that pinched severity, that uncompromising idealism which made Goldwater kin to the tight-mouthed and the lonely. Talking in a soft modest voice, he radiated at this moment the skinny boyish sincerity of a fellow who wears glasses but is determined nonetheless to have a good time. Against all odds. It was not unreminiscent of Arthur Miller: that same mixture of vast solemnity and unspoiled boyhood, a sort of shucks and aw shit in the voice. "Well, you see," said Goldwater, talking to the Florida delegation, "if I was to trust the polls right now, I'd have to say I didn't have a chance. But why should I trust the polls? Why should any of us trust the polls? They've been wrong before. They'll be wrong again. Man is superior to the machine. The thing to remember is that America is a spiritual country, we're founded on belief in God, we may wander a little as a country, but we never get too far away. I'm ready to say the election is going to give the Democrats a heck of a surprise. Why, I'll tell you this," Goldwater said, sweating mildly, telling the folks from Florida just as keen as if he was alone with each one of them, each one of these elderly gents and real-estate dealers and plain women with silver-rimmed eyeglasses, "tell you this, I'm doing my best not to keep this idea a secret, but I think we're not only going to give the Democrats a heck of a surprise, I think we're going to win. (Applause, cheers.) In fact I wouldn't be in this if I didn't think we were going to win. (Applause.) Why, as I sometimes tell my wife, I'm too young to retire and too old to go back to work." (Laughter, loud cheers.) Goldwater was done. He smiled shyly, his glasses saying: I am a modest man, and I am severe on myself. As he made his route to the door, the delegates were touching him enthusiastically.

At the Hotel Clift he talked to the Washington delegates. We were definitely back in high school. That was part of Goldwater's deal—he brought you back to the bright minted certitudes of early patriotism when you knew the U.S. was the best country on earth and there was no other. Yes, his appeal would go out to all the millions who were now starved and a little sour because some part of their life had ended in high school, and the university they had never seen. But then Barry had had but one year of college—he had indeed the mind of a powerful freshman. "I want to thank you folks from Washington for giving me this warm greeting. Of course, Washington is the name of a place I often like to get the heck out of, but I'm sure I won't confuse the two right here." (Laughter.) He was off, a short political speech. In the middle, extremism. "I don't see how anybody can be an extremist who believes in the Constitution. And for those misguided few who pretend to believe in the Constitution, but in secret don't, well they may be extremists, but I don't see any necessity to legislate against them. I just feel sorry for them." (Cheers. Applause. Happiness at the way Barry delivered anathemas.) At a certain point in the speech, he saw a woman in the audience whom he recognized, and stopped in the middle of a phrase. "Hi, honey," he sang out like a traveling sales-man, which brought a titter from the delegation, for his voice had shifted too quickly . . . Something skinny, itchy, hard as a horselaugh, showed—he was a cannoneer with a hairy ear. Goldwater went on, the good mood continued; then at the end, speech done, he turned down a drink but said in his best gee-whizzer, "I'm sorry I have to leave because gosh I'd like to break a few with you." Laughter, and he took off head down, a little modest in the exit, a little red in the neck.

There was entertainment at the Republican Gala on Sunday night. The climax was a full marching band of bagpipers. They must have been hired for the week since one kept hearing them on the fol-lowing days, and at all odd times, heard them even in my hotel room at four a.m., for a few were marching in the streets of San Francisco, sounding through the night, giving off the barbaric evocation of the Scots, all valor, wrath, firmitude, and treachery—the wild complete treachery of the Scots finding its way into the sound of the pipes. They were a warning of the fever in the heart of the Wasp. There are sounds which seem to pass through all the protective gates in the ear and reach into some nerve where the eschatology is stored. Few parents have failed to hear it in the cry of their infant through the morning hours of a bad night—stubbornness, fury, waste, and the promise of revenge come out of a flesh half-created by one's own flesh; the knowledge is suddenly there that seed is existential, no paradise resides in seed, seed can be ill-inspired and go to a foul gloomy end. Some find their part of the truth in listening to jazz—it is moot if any white who had no ear for jazz can know the passion with which some whites become attached to the Negro's cause. So, too, listening to the bagpipes, you knew this was the true music of the Wasps. There was something wild and martial and bottomless in the passion, a pride which would not be exhausted, a determination which might never end, perhaps should never end, the Faustian rage of a white civilization was in those Highland wails, the cry of a race which was born to dominate and might never learn to share, and never learning, might be willing to end the game, the end of the world was in the sound of the pipes. Or at very least the danger one would come closer to the world's end. So there was a vast if all-private appeal in listening to the pipes shrill out the herald of a new crusade, something jagged, Viking, of the North in the air, a sense of breaking ice and barbaric shields, hunters loose in the land again. And this had an appeal which burrowed deep, there was excitement at the thought of Goldwater getting the nomination, as if now finally all one's personal suicides, all the deaths of the soul accumulated by the past, all the failures, all the terrors, could find purge in a national situation where a national murder was being planned (the Third World War) and one's own suicide might be lost in a national suicide. There was that excitement, that the burden of one's soul (always equal to the burden of one's personal responsibility) might finally be lifted—what a release was there! Beauty was inspired by the prospect. For if Goldwater won, and the iron power of the iron people who had pushed him forth—as echoed in the iron of the Pinkertons on the fourteenth and fifteenth floor now pushed forth over the nation an iron regime with totalitarianism seizing the TV in every frozen dinner, well then at last a true underground might form; and liberty at the thought of any catalyst which could bring it on.

Yes, the Goldwater movement excited the depths because the apocalypse was brought more near, and like millions of other whites, I had been leading a life which was a trifle too pointless and a trifle too full of guilt and my gullet was close to nausea with the endless compromises of an empty liberal center. So I followed the four days of the convention with something more than simple apprehension. The country was taking a turn, the colors were deepening, the knives of the afternoon were out, something of the best in American life might now be going forever; or was it altogether to the opposite? and was the country starting at last to take the knots of its contradictions up from a premature midnight of nightmare into the surgical terrains of the open skin? Were we in the beginning, or turning the middle, of our worst disease? One did not know any longer, you simply did not know any longer, but something was certain: the country was now part of the daily concern. One worried about it for the first time, the way you worried about family or work, a good friend or the future, and that was the most exceptional of emotions. . . .

Nixon made the speech of introduction for Goldwater [at the 1964 Republican Convention]. In the months ahead, when the bull in Barry swelled too wild and he gave promise of talking again of Negro assailants getting Medals of Honor, they would send in Nixon to calm him down. The Eastern Establishment, hydra head, was not dead after all; they still had Nixon. He was the steer to soothe the bull. Poor Barry. He had tried to lose Nixon in Cleveland, he had said, "He's sounding more like Harold Stassen every day." Nixon however was as easy to lose as a plain wife without prospects is easy to divorce.

"My good friend and great Republican, Dick Nixon . . . " was how Goldwater began his historic acceptance speech. It had come after a rich demonstration of happiness from the delegates. A boxcar of small balloons was opened in the rafters as Goldwater came down the ramp with his wife, his sons, his daughters. The balloons tumbled in thousands to the floor where (fifty balloons being put out each second by lighted cigarettes) a sound like machine-gun fire popped its way through the cheers. Fourth of July was here once more. He looked good, did Goldwater. Looking up at him from a position just beneath the speaker's stand, not twenty feet away, it was undeniable that Barry looked as handsome as a man who had just won the five-hundred-mile race in Indianapolis, had gone home to dress, and was now attending a party in his honor. He was even, protect the mark, elegant.

Then he began his speech. Today, the voice for large public gatherings had dignity. It was not a great voice, as Churchill's voice was great; there were no majesties nor storms of complexity, no war of style between manner and the obligation to say truth; but it was a balanced manly voice that would get votes. His speech was good in its beginning.

Now my fellow Americans, the tide has been running against freedom. Our people have followed false prophets. . . . We must, and we shall, set the tide running again in the cause of freedom. . . . Every breath and every heartbeat has but a single resolve, and that is freedom. . . . Tonight there is violence in our streets, corruption in our highest offices, aimlessness among our youth, anxiety among our elderly . . . despair among the many who look beyond material success toward the inner meaning of their lives.

As the speech went on, the mind went out again on a calculation that this candidate could win. . . . Goldwater was a demagogue—he permitted his supporters to sell a drink called Gold Water, twenty-five cents a can for orange concentrate and warm soda—let no one say it went down like piss—he was a demagogue. He was also sincere. That was the damnable difficulty. Half Jew and blue-eyed—if you belonged in the breed, you knew it was manic-depressive for sure: a man who designed his own electronic flagpole to raise Old Glory at dawn, pull her down at dusk—he had an instinct for the heart of the disease—he knew how to bring balm to the mad, or at least to half the mad; Goldwater would have much to learn about Negroes. But one thing was certain: he could win. He would be breadwinner, husband and rogue to the underprivileged of the psyche, he would strike a spark in many dry souls for he offered release to frustrations deeper than politics. Therefore, he could beat Lyndon Johnson, he could beat him out of a variety of cause, out of natural flood or hurricane, in an epidemic of backlash, or by an epidemic of guilt—how many union workers fed to the nose with exhortations that Johnson was good for take-home pay might rise and say to themselves, "I've been happy with less." Indeed I knew Goldwater could win because something in me leaped at the thought; a part of me, a devil, wished to take that choice. For if Goldwater were President, a new opposition would form, an underground—the time for secret armies might be near again. And when in sanity I thought, Lord, give us twenty more years of Lyndon Johnson, nausea rose in some cellar of the throat, my stomach was not strong enough to bear such security; and if true for me, true for others, true perhaps for half or more of a nation's vote. Yet what of totalitarianism? What of war? But what of war? And the answer came back that one might be better a little nearer to death than the soul dying each night in the plastic encirclements of the new architecture and the new city, yes better, if death had dimension and one could know the face of the enemy and leave a curse. What blessing to know the face of the enemy by the end of the second third of the twentieth century. . . .

The country was in disease. It had been in disease for a long time. There was nothing in our growth which was organic. We had never solved our depression, we had merely gone to war, and going to war had never won it, not in our own minds, not as men, no, we had won it but as mothers, sources of supply; we did not know that we were equal to the Russians. We had won a war but we had not really won it, not in the secret of our sleep. So we had not really had a prosperity, we had had fever. *Viva-Olé.* We had grown rich because of one fact with two opposite interpretations: there had been a cold war. It was a cold war which had come because Communism was indeed a real threat to freedom, or it had come because capitalism would never survive without an economy geared to war; or was it both—who could know, who could really know? The center of our motive was the riddle wrapped in the enigma—was the country extraordinary or accursed? No, we had not even found our Communist threat. We had had a secret police organization and an invisible government large enough by now to occupy the moon, we had hunted Communists from the top of the Time-Life Building to the bottom of the Collier mine; we had not found that many, not that many, and had looked like Keystone cops. We had even had a Negro Revolution in which we did not believe. . . . So we were never too authentic. No.

We had had a hero. He was a young good-looking man with a beautiful wife, and he had won the biggest poker game we ever played, the only real one—we had lived for a week ready to die in a nuclear war. Whether we liked it or not. But he had won. It was our one true victory in all these years, our moment; so the young man began to inspire a subtle kind of love. His strength had proved stronger than we knew. Suddenly he was dead, and we were in grief. But then came a trial which was worse. For the assassin, or the man who had been arrested but was not the assassin—we would never know, not really—was killed before our sight. In the middle of the funeral came an explosion on the porch. Now, we were going mad. It took more to make a nation go mad than any separate man, but we had taken miles too much. . . .

If Goldwater were elected, he could not control the country without moving to the center; moving to the center he would lose a part of the Right, satisfy no one, and be obliged to drift still further Left, or moving back to the Right would open schisms across the land which could not be closed. Goldwater elected, America would stand revealed, its latent treacheries would pop forth like boils; Johnson elected, the drift would go on, the San Francisco Hiltons would deploy among us. Under Goldwater, the odds were certainly greater that nuclear war would come, but under Johnson we could move from the threat of total war to war itself with nothing to prevent it; the anti-Goldwater forces which might keep the country too divided to go to war would now be contained within Johnson. Goldwater promised to lead the nation across the edge of a precipice, Johnson would walk us through the woods, perchance to quicksand itself. Goldwater would open us to the perils of our madness, Johnson would continue our trip into the plague. Goldwater could accelerate the Negro Revolution to violence and disaster—Johnson might yet be obliged to betray it from within. And what a job could be done! Who in such a pass should receive the blessing of a vote—the man who inspired the deepest fear, or the man who encouraged us to live in a lard of guilt cold as the most mediocre of our satisfied needs?

Still, the more Goldwater talked, the less impressive became his voice. When he went on too long, his voice grew barren. One could never vote for him, one could not vote for a man who made a career by crying Communist—that was too easy: half the pigs, bullies, and cowards of the twentieth century had made their fortune on that fear. I had a moment of rage at the swindle. I was tired of hearing about Barry Goldwater's high fine courage. Yesterday, on the floor, talking to a young delegate from Indiana, I had said, "Did it ever occur to you that Fidel Castro might have more courage than Barry Goldwater?"

"Yes, but Castro is a criminal mentality," said the boy.

I had cut off the argument. I was too close to losing my temper. Would the best of the young in every hick town, washed by the brainwater of the high school and the Legion, come to join this conservative crusade because Goldwater made an appeal to freedom, to courage, to change? What a swindle was in the making, what an extinction of the best in Conservative thought. They were so righteous, these Republicans. Goldwater might end with more warfare, security, and statism than any Democrat had ever dared; as a conservative, he would fail altogether (doubtless!) but certain he was to do one thing: he would march into Cuba. That was too much. One could live with a country which was mad, one could even come to love her (for there was agony beneath the madness), but you could not share your life with a nation which was powerful, a coward, and righteously pleased because a foe one-hundredth our size had been destroyed. So one got up to leave at this—we would certainly be strong enough to march into Cuba.

Then Goldwater uttered his most historic words: "Extremism in the defense of liberty is no vice. Moderation in the pursuit of justice is no virtue," and I sat down and took out my notebook and wrote in his words, since I did not know how famous they would become. And thought; Dad, you're too much. You're really too much. You're too hip, baby. I have spent my life seeking to get four-letter words into U.S. magazines, and now you are ready to help me. And as I left the arena, there was a fire engine and the cry of a siren and the police with a gaunt grim look for the end of the week. There had been a fire burning, some small fire.

On the way out, outside the Cow Palace, a wet fog was drifting and out beyond the exits, demonstrators from CORE were making a march. They had been out there every day of the convention: Monday, Tuesday, Wednesday, and Thursday now, each day had demonstrated, carrying their placards, marching in a circle two abreast, singing "We Shall Overcome," shouting, "Goldwater Must Go," marching round and round like early Christians in the corrals waiting to be sent to the arena, while about them, five, six, ten deep, was a crowd of the Republican curious, some with troubled faces, some with faces troubled by no more than appetite, hounds staring at the meat, these white girls and Negro boys walking side by side, the girls pale, no lipstick, unlike, disdainful, wearing denim shirts and dungarees; the Negroes tall and sometimes handsome, not without dignity, bearded almost all, the wild Negro girl in the center screaming savage taunts at the watching crowd, rude as Cassius Clay [Clay changed his name to Muhammad Ali in March 1964, just before Mailer wrote this essay] with a high-yaller mouth, and the crowd dreaming of an arena where lions could be set on these cohabiting blacks and whites, and the black and whites in the marching circle with their disdainful faces. Yes, kill us, says the expression on the face of the nun-like girl with no lipstick, you will kill us but you will never digest us: I despise you all. And some of the old Wasps are troubled in their Christian heart, for the girl is one of theirs, no fat plain Jewess with a poor nose is this one, she is part of the West, and so their sense of crisis opens and they know like me that America has come to a point from which she will never return. The wars are coming and the deep revolutions of the soul.

27

TO EIICHI YAMANISHI

(APRIL 17, 1964; *SELECTED LETTERS OF NORMAN MAILER*, 2014)

Yamanishi was Mailer's Japanese translator. They exchanged ideas about government and politics from the late 1940s through the early 1970s.

Dear Eiichi,

Let me congratulate you on what must have been the Herculean labor of translating [Leo] Deutsch's trilogy on [Leon] Trotsky [Soviet leader and theoretician, 1879–1940]. I only read excerpts of that book, but it impressed me very much, as indeed Deutsch's work always does. And I think it is heroic of you to have accomplished this translation in the midst of all the other work you take on. As for Trotsky, it is not that I feel antipathetic to him, indeed I think he is one of the few great figures of the twentieth century, and I've always felt sympathetically close to him, but the Trotsky movement in America is unspeakably arid and hidebound. Indeed one hardly hears of their existence any longer. Besides, there are political phenomena in America which Marx could never have contemplated, for the continued survival of capitalism displaced the economic imbalance into a psychic imbalance which corrupts the very being of people's lives here. Indeed, it is almost profitable to conceive of America as one vast horde of psychic totalitarians ruled by an establishment which is exceptionally self-contradictory; for while on the one hand it pushes America toward totalitarianism, there are elements in the establishment which offer our greatest defense against the continuing totalitarianization of the masses. Kennedy, for all his contradictions, was probably a defense of that sort, whereas Johnson, who has almost virtually the same political program, encourages the drift toward totalitarianism by the vacuity of his personality. The key to the entire situation is the Negro revolution, I believe. If it fails, and it most certainly can, even via the route of the next Presidential election, then the legal counter-revolution is, I fear, in the making. America is like a sullen attic full of smoldering dull heats. We can go on like this for years, but then again the fire can break out in six months. For we are in a profound crisis psychologically, since the country as it sees itself was founded and prospered on ideas of faith and reason, and faith has now become shattered or authoritarian, or the average American has lost his confidence in reason. The assassination of Kennedy did untold harms. The assassination of Oswald multiplied the disaster many times again.

28

REVIEW OF *MY HOPE FOR AMERICA* BY LYNDON B. JOHNSON

(*CANNIBALS AND CHRISTIANS*, 1966)

Mailer lauded President Johnson's leadership in passing the Civil Rights Act of 1964 and the later creation of Medicare and Medicaid but believed that his unwillingness to end the Vietnam War, as well as the "abominable, damnable" rhythms of his prose, enhanced the authoritarian strain in American polity. Mailer's review appeared just before Johnson was elected to his first full term in November 1964.

In 20 years it may be taken for granted that 1964 was the year in which a major party nominated a major pretender to conservatism. It was a loss, and it was conceivably a horror, for 1964 was also a year in which a real conservative still had a great deal to say to the nation. He could have demonstrated with no vast difficulty that America was under the yoke of a monstrous building boom whose architecture gave promise of being the ugliest in the history of man, that our labor unions had watered the value of labor until physical work had become as parasitical as white-collar work, and that our medicine had been overburdened beyond repair by a proliferation of wonder drugs whose side effects (with the notable exception of thalidomide) were still largely unknown—hence a delayed mass poisoning might yet be the fruit of this research. Our fruits, our vegetables, our cattle, had lost the opportunity to feed on native soil and organic food; the balance of nature, the fisheries, the economy of marine life, and the insect economies were being disrupted to the root by marinas and insecticides; our old neighborhoods and old homes were being—one could swear it—systematically demolished, and our educational system was glutted by a host of intellectual canapés: art appreciation, domestic economy, sexual efficiency, the modern novel, and so forth. . . .

But what a conservative came down the pike [in Goldwater]! Marooned in a hopeless traffic with hate groups and bigots, Southern bullies and oil pirates, offering a program of sinister hints that a Federal police force would protect the young ladies of our land on their walk through our streets at night; reasoning with all the homely assurance of a filthy sock that he would protect the past by destroying the present (as in those remarks about scorching the foliage in Vietnam in order to keep the guerrillas from concealing themselves); wasting the substance of his campaign in pointless technical arguments with the Pentagon; and boring reconciliations and new feuds with the stricken Moderates of his party—the alleged conservative candidate was perhaps no more than a demagogue of the Right with a manly Christian air, a sweet voice, eyeglasses, and total innocence of a sense of contradiction, a spirit so naturally conservative that on the grounds of his home he raised the American flag with an electronic flagpole. Up at dawn, down at dusk, commanded the photoelectric cells in the mast. Well, one couldn't vote for such a man. He pressed the wrong buttons.

The mandate would go therefore to Lyndon Johnson. So most of America had seemed to decide by the eve of election. But it was nonetheless a vote heavy with gloom, and stricken with a sense of possible bad consequence, for there was much about Johnson which appealed not at all, and some of the evidence was intimate. He had written a book. That is intimate evidence. *My Hope for America*, he had called it. Now, of course, a book written by a high official must not be judged by average standards, or one would be forced to say, for example, that Jack Kennedy was not a very good writer and that Bobby Kennedy, at last reading, wrote a dead stick's prose—his style almost as bad as J. Edgar Hoover's. But even at its worst, the prose style of Jack Kennedy (and his ghost writers) is to the prose style of L.B.J. (and his ghost writers) as De Tocqueville is to Ayn Rand. It is even not impossible that *My Hope for America* is the worst book ever written by any political leader anywhere.

The private personality of L.B.J., as reported by the authority of the best gossip, is different from his public presence. He is, one is told, not too unlike Broderick Crawford in *All the King's Men*, roaring, smarting, bellowing, stabbing fingers on advisers' chests, hugging his daughters, enjoying his food, mean and unforgiving, vindictive, generous, ebullient, vain, suddenly depressed, then roguish, then overbearing, suddenly modest again only to bellow once more. It is somewhat like the description of an early Renaissance prince, and if one looks hard at the photograph of the President on the cover of *My Hope for America*, a leader of *condottieri* stands forth—hard, greedy, exceptionally intelligent eyes whose cynicism is spiked by a fierce pride, big fleshy inquisitive (and acquisitive) nose, thin curved mouth (a boss mouth) and a slab of round hard jaw, deep dimple on the upper lip, deep dimple on the chin. It is not a bad face altogether, it is sufficiently worldly to inspire a kind of confidence that while no age of high ideals is close at hand, yet no martyrs are to be tortured, for there is small profit in that. It is a face and a concealed personality which could even, considering the Republican alternative, inspire a touch of happiness, if it were not for the public image—that boundless sea of overweening piety which collects here in this slim volume, this cove of Presidential prose whose waters are so brackish that a spoonful is enough to sicken the mind for hours. *My Hope for America* is an abominable, damnable book, and what makes it doubly awful is that nearly all of its ideas are blessed. It is in fact difficult to disagree with almost any one of them.

Who can argue on the side of poverty, or against justice, or against the idea of a Great Society? Let Barry Goldwater argue, not I. No, the ideals in this book are double-barreled, double-ringed, a double end of the cornucopia. More for the poor, more for the rich; more for peace, more for war; dedicatedly opposed to Communism, cautiously conciliatory; out to raise the income of poor nations, out to squash the economy of Cuba; all out for the Negro, all violence to be checked in city streets; all for the Democratic party, all for a party which includes Democrats and Republicans. There is even, and it is the achievement of this book, a curious sense of happiness running through its paragraphs. It is that happiness which is found at the end of the vision. It is as if the dream of Rousseau and Condorcet and Bakunin and Herzen and Marx and Lenin and Trotsky and John Dewey and the Webbs and Keynes and Roosevelt, Dreiser, and Darrow—name any of a hundred, any of that long stream of political engineers who dreamed of changing a material world by material means to make all men free and equal—had come down at the end to Little Ol' Lyndon, and hot damn, he had said, discovering Progressive religion in 1964, that's the ticket, that's the liver-eating ticket! And he was off to bring it off. And happy as a clam. That's the happiness which comes off this book. It is like a dream of heaven in a terminal ward.

For beneath this odd disembodied happiness is a prose more sinister than the most pious of Lyndon Johnson's misrepresentations of his own personality; it is a prose which stirs half-heard cries of the death by suffocation of Western Civilization, it is a prose almost so bad and so deadening as the Georgian catechisms Josef Stalin used to hammer out: "Why is the Communist Party the party of the Soviet people? The Communist Party is the party of the Soviet people because ..." It was enough at the time, reading Stalin, to keep from becoming a Communist. Now, reading Lyndon!—the horror is that one must still vote for him. But what a book is *My Hope for America.*

Examine it: 127 pages, a little more than 200 words to a page, most of the pages half pages or blank pages so that in bulk there are 17,000 words collected in 13 short chapters; they have titles like this: "President of All the People," "A President's Faith and Vision," "Building the Atlantic Partnership," "This Developing World," "Creative Federalism." Each page of each chapter is divided into paragraphs. Page 8 has 12 paragraphs; the average page has four or five with a generous space between each paragraph. This is not because the remarks have the resonant echo of Pascal's *Pensées*, rather—one idea does not lead to another. So the space must be there. It is useful for burying whichever infinitesimal part of the brain died in the gas of the preceding phrase.

Yet every altruistic idea and every well-tuned moderation which Lyndon Johnson's political experience has put together over the years

is somehow worked into the organum of his credo. It is impossible
to disagree with a single of its humanistic desires ("We know that we
can learn from the culture, the arts, and the traditions of other countries"); it is equally impossible to feel the least pleasure at the thought
these goods may yet come to be—just so bad and disheartening is the
style of this book:

> Reality rarely matches dream. But only dreams give nobility to
> purpose. This is the star I hope to follow—which I know most
> of you have seen, and which I first glimpsed many years ago in
> the Texas night.
>
> When the helpless call for help—the hearing must hear, the
> seeing must see, and the able must act.
>
> It is an America where every man has an equal chance for
> the well-being that is essential to the enjoyment of the freedom
> that we brag about.
>
> The Gulf of Tonkin may be distant Asian waters, but none
> can be detached about what happened there.

High-school students will be writing essays on these paragraphs.
One's stomach turns over. It is certain that if Barry Goldwater had
written the same book, everyone would be agreed his style was a
menace. Still, what is quoted up to here is still English, English more
or less. It is in the depth of the real prose articulated by Johnson and
his corps of ghost writers that the heart of the darkness resides. For
Johnson is not a writer and has no wish to be. He is a communications engineer. He uses words in interlocking aggregates which fence
in thoughts like cattle. At bottom, the style consists of nothing but
connectives and aggregate word—that is, political phrases five words
long which are one aggregate word and so should be hyphenated.
Example:

> And it is one-of-the-great-tasks-of-Presidential-leadership to
> make our people aware that they share-a-fundamental-unity-of-
> interest-and-purpose-and belief.

The essence of totalitarian prose is that it does not define, it does not deliver. It oppresses. It obstructs from above. It is profoundly contemptuous of the minds who will receive the message. So it does its best to dull this consciousness with sentences which are nothing but bricked-in power structures. Or alternately a totalitarian prose slobbers upon an audience a sentimentality so debauched that admiration for shamelessness is inspired. But then, sentimentality is the emotional promiscuity of those who have no sentiment:

> When I was a child, one of my first memories was hearing the powder go off on an anvil on Armistice Day. I remember the terror that flowed from the Lusitania. I remember seeing boys come marching home, and the welcome we gave them at our little schoolhouse. When Pearl Harbor was attacked—

There is one expanding horror in American life. It is that our long odyssey toward liberty, democracy and freedom-for-all may be achieved in such a way that utopia remains forever closed, and we live in freedom and hell, debased of style, not individual from one another, void of courage, our fear rationalized away. We will all have enough money and we will all have a vote. The money will buy appliances made of plastic, and the money will buy books just as bad as *My Hope for America* or *The Conscience of a Conservative.* . . .

"In the next forty years," writes Johnson, "we must rebuild the entire urban United States." But who will do it? Whose vision will prevail? Which head of horror may condemn generations not yet born to look at faceless buildings and roofless roofs, the totalitarianism stealing in from without, from the formless forms and imprisoned air of a new society which had lost the clue that a democracy could become equable only if it became great, that finally the world would continue to exist only by an act of courage and a search for style. Democracy flowers with style; without it, there is a rot of wet weeds. Which is why we love the memory so of F.D.R. and J.F.K. For they offered high style to the poor. And that is worth more than a housing project. That is the war against poverty.

Still, Lyndon Johnson must be given a vote. Because *My Hope for America* contains one good sentence, one more than Barry Goldwater could claim. This sentence reads: ". . . the wall between rich and poor is a wall of glass through which all can see." It inspires a corollary which is almost as good—the space between hypocrisy and honest manner may not forever insulate the powerful from the poor.

29

"A Speech at Berkeley on Vietnam Day"

(CANNIBALS AND CHRISTIANS, 1966)

Mailer spoke before an outdoor audience of ten thousand at the University of California, Berkeley, on Vietnam Day, May 21, 1965, a moment when public sentiment in favor of the Vietnam War had begun to sour. He said later that it was on this day that he received the longest standing ovation of his life.

President Johnson's motive in escalating the war in Vietnam may be psychic in nature. This assumes of course that the prime mover in the new war in Vietnam is precisely the President; it assumes that Vietnam is not the unhappy expression of vast inevitable historic forces too large for any man; to the contrary this premise supposes flat-out that there was a choice in Vietnam, and one man, balanced at the fulcrum of power between the Pentagon on one side and his liberal support on the other, decided to accelerate the war. So it is a thesis which would say that the mystery of Vietnam revolves around the mystery of Lyndon Johnson's personality.

To ferret one's way into the recesses of that mysterious and explosive personality is an activity which would give pause to many. It gives pause to me. He is after all a very intelligent man. He is doubtless more intelligent than you or me. He is certainly most intelligent about getting his way. He is also a complex man, and his sides are many. The only side of him which is evident to all is that he is famished for popularity.

At the Democratic Convention in Atlantic City in 1964, not one picture of the President was hung behind the speaker's rostrum, but two. They were each forty feet high. So said his public relations. These photographs, however, looked like they were eighty feet high, high as an eight-story motel.

They dominated every movement at the convention. They spoke of an ego that had the voracity of a beast.... But Johnson was intelligent enough to run a total land, he had vast confidence, no vision, and the heart to hold huge power, he had the vanity of a modern dictator. Under Johnson we could move from the threat of total war to war itself with nothing to prevent it; the anti-Goldwater forces might keep the country too divided to go to war which would now be contained within Johnson.

That was a final description of the Democratic convention, and it still missed the point. Because the final unhappy point was that Barry Goldwater had established Johnson's power with such total perfection that the man elected had come closer to total control of America than any President before him. What could increase the fear is that Johnson might not be a whole man so much as he was alienated, a modern man, a member in a most curious sense of a minority group.

Lyndon Baines Johnson a member of a minority group? It is an extraordinary forcing of category. It is obvious some other notion is intended than a description of a Negro, a Jew, a Mexican, a Nisei, or a Puerto Rican. Will it make sense if we say Lyndon Johnson is alienated? Alienated from what, you may ask ...

And I say to you in no disrespect and much uneasiness that it is possible he is alienated from his own clear sanity, that his mind has become a consortium of monstrous disproportions, of pictures of himself in duplicate forty feet high, eighty feet high. Lyndon Johnson is not alienated from power, he is the most powerful man in the United States, but he is alienated from judgment, he is close to an imbalance which at worst could tip the world from orbit.

The legitimate fear we can feel is vast. Because there was a time when Lyndon Johnson could have gotten out of Vietnam very quietly—the image had been prepared for our departure—we heard of nothing but the corruption of the South Vietnam government and the professional cowardice of the South Vietnamese generals. We read how a Viet Cong army of 40,000 soldiers was whipping a government army of 400,000. We were told in our own newspapers how the Viet Cong armed themselves with American weapons brought to them by deserters or captured in battle with government troops; we knew it was an empty war for our side, Lyndon Johnson made no attempt to hide that from us. He may even have encouraged the press in this direction for a time. Abruptly, he dropped escalation into our daily life.

There is fear we must feel. It was not the action of a rational man, but a man driven by need, a gambler who fears that once he stops; once he pulls out of the game, his heart will rupture from tension. You see, Lyndon Johnson is a member of a minority group and so he must have action. But now let me explain. A member of a minority group is—if we are to speak existentially—not a man who is a member of a category, a Negro or a Jew, but rather a man who feels his existence in a particular way. It is in the very form or context of his existence to live with two opposed notions of himself.

What characterizes a member of a minority group is that he is forced to see himself as both exceptional and insignificant, marvelous and awful, good and evil. So far as he listens to the world outside he is in danger of going insane. The only way he may relieve the unendurable tension which surrounds any sense of his own identity is to define his nature by his own acts; discover his courage or cowardice by actions which engage his courage; discover his judgment by judging; his loyalty by being tested; his originality by creating. A Negro or a Texan, a President or a housewife, is by this definition a member of a minority group if he contains two opposed notions of himself at the same time. What characterizes the sensation of being a member of a minority group is that one's emotions are forever locked in the chains of ambivalence—the expression of an emotion forever releasing its opposite—the ego in perpetual transit from the tower to the dungeon and back again. By this definition nearly everyone in America is a member of a minority group, alienated from the self by a double sense of identity and so at the mercy of a self which demands action and more action to define the most rudimentary borders of identity. It is a demand which will either kill a brave man or force him to grow, but when a coward is put in need of such action he tears the wings off flies.

The great fear that lies upon America is not that Lyndon Johnson is privately close to insanity so much as that he is the expression of the near insanity of most of us, and his need for action is America's need for action; not brave action, but action; any kind of action; any move to get the motors going. A future death of the spirit lies close and heavy upon American life, a cancerous emptiness at the center which calls for a circus.

Our country was fearful, half-mad, inauthentic—it needed a war or it needed a purge. Bile was stirring in the pits of the national conscience and little to oppose it but a lard of guilt cold as the most mediocre of our needs. We took formal public steps toward a great society, that great society of computers and pills, of job aptitudes and bad architecture, of psychoanalysis, superhighways, astronauts, vaccinations, and a Peace Corps, that great society where nothing but frozen corn would be sold in the smallest towns of Iowa, where censorship would disappear but every image would be manipulated from birth to death.

Something in the buried animal of modern life grew bestial at the thought of this Great Society—the most advanced technological nation of the civilized world was the one now closest to blood, to shedding the blood and burning the flesh of Asian peasants it had never seen. The Pentagon had been kept on a leash for close to twenty years. Presidents so mediocre in their talents as Truman and Eisenhower had kept the military from dominating the nation.

But Johnson did not . . . Johnson was in accord. The body of a consummate politician took recognition as it slept that the nation was in disease and its only cure—out where the drums were beating and the fires would not cease—was to introduce us to the first anxieties of a war whose end might be limitless. Miserable nation cursed with a computer for its commander-in-chief, a computer with an ego so vain it could not bear the memory of his predecessor and the power he had had for a week when the world was on the edge of nuclear war.

Yet, there still remains the largest question of them all. It is the question of fighting Communism. Look, you may say, is it not possible that with all our diseases admitted, we are still less malignant than the Communists, we are the defense of civilization and they, not us, are the barbarians who would destroy it? If that is true, then—as some of you may argue the logic must be faced, the Chinese must be stopped, we must bomb their bomb. And I would argue in return that neither capitalism nor Communism is the defense of civilization but that they are rather each—in their own way—malignancies upon the spirit of honest adventure and open inquiry which developed across the centuries from primitive man to the Renaissance, and that therefore there is no man alive who can say at this point which system will perpetrate the greater harm upon mankind. But this I do know: existence alters the nature of essence. An unjust war, an unnatural war, an obscene war brutalizes what is best in a nation and encourages every horror to rise from its sewer. . . .

The grimmest truth may be that half of America at least must be not unwilling to have a war in Vietnam. Otherwise Lyndon Johnson could not have made his move, since Lyndon Johnson never in his life has dreamed of moving against a majority.

Let us then insist on this—it is equally visionary, but it is at least visionary in a military way and we are talking to militarists—let us say that if we are going to have a war with the Viet Cong, let it be a war of foot soldier against foot soldier. If we wish to take a strange country away from strangers, let us at least be strong enough and brave enough to defeat them on the ground. Our Marines, some would say, are the best soldiers in the world. The counter-argument is that native guerrillas can defeat any force of a major power man to man.

Let us, then, fight on fair grounds. Let us say to Lyndon Johnson, to Monstrous McNamara, and to the generals on the scene—fight like men, go in man to man against the Viet Cong. But first, call off the Air Force. They prove nothing except that America is coterminous with the Mafia. Let us win man to man or lose man to man, but let us cease pulverizing people whose faces we have never seen.

But of course we will not cease. Nor will we ever fight man to man against poor peasants. Their vision of existence might be more ferocious and more determined than our own. No, we would rather go on as the most advanced monsters of civilization pulverizing instinct with our detonations, our State Department experts in their little bow ties, and our bombs.

Only, listen, Lyndon Johnson, you have gone too far this time. You are a bully with an Air Force, and since you will not call off your Air Force, there are young people who will persecute you back. It is a little thing, but it will hound you into nightmares and endless corridors of nights without sleep, it will hound you. For listen—this is only one of the thousand things they will do. They will print up little pictures of you, Lyndon Johnson, the size of post cards, the size of stamps, and some will glue these pictures to walls and posters and telephone booths and billboards—I do not advise it, I would tell these students not to do it to you, but they will. They will find places to put these pictures. They will want to paste your picture, Lyndon Johnson, on a post card, and send it to you. Some will send it to your advisers. Some will send these pictures to men and women at other schools. These pictures will be sent everywhere. These pictures will be pasted up everywhere, upside down.

Silently, without a word, the photograph of you, Lyndon Johnson, will start appearing everywhere, upside down. Your head will speak out—even to the peasant in Asia—it will say that not all Americans are unaware of your monstrous vanity, overweening piety, and doubtful motive. It will tell them that we trust our President so little, and think so little of him, that we see his picture everywhere upside down.

You, Lyndon Johnson, will see those pictures up everywhere upside down, four inches high and forty feet high; you, Lyndon Baines Johnson, will be coming up for air everywhere upside down. Everywhere, upside down. Everywhere. Everywhere.

And those little pictures will tell the world what we think of you and your war in Vietnam. Everywhere, upside down. Everywhere, everywhere.

30

To William F. Buckley, Jr.

(APRIL 20, 1965; *SELECTED LETTERS OF NORMAN MAILER*, 2014)

Buckley (1925–2008) founded the conservative magazine National Review *in 1955 and was its editor in chief for more than forty years. He and Mailer were good friends and for decades debated the nature and future of American democracy. Joan Didion reviewed Mailer's 1965 novel,* An American Dream, *in the April 20, 1965, issue of* National Review.

Dear Bill,

What a marvelous girl Joan Didion must be. I think that's one conservative I would like to meet. And who would ever have thought that the nicest piece I am to read about myself four weeks after publication should come in the *National Review*. Well, this is the year of literary wonders. What do you think the odds would have been for a parlay of good reviews in *National Review*, *Life*, the *New York Times Sunday Book Review*, Paul Pickrel at *Harper's*, and the *Chicago Tribune*. One hundred fifty million to one, or would we have picked it by light years?

Anyway, I write you this letter in great envy. I think you are going finally to displace me as the most hated man in American life. And of course that position is bearable only if one is number one. To be the second most hated man in the picture will probably prove to be a little like working behind a mule for years, which brings me to your address before the police department's Holy Name Society. I missed all of it at the time; I was in Alaska, and got my first inkling in the *New York Post* that some sort of bomb had gone off. At any rate I was not surprised when I read your speech today to find that it was literate, moderate in relation to your own position, and felicitously phrased. And of course I don't agree with your fundamental premise. On that I think you're all wrong. I'm not the cop-hater I'm reputed to be, and in fact police fascinate me. But this is because I think their natures are very complex, not simple at all, and what I would object to in your speech if we were debating is that you made a one for one correspondence between the need to maintain law and order and the nature of the men who would maintain it. The policeman has I think an extraordinarily tortured psyche. He is perhaps more tortured than the criminal, and so as you can see I can hardly concur with the valuations you put on these matters. At the same time there's no doubt in my mind that the newspapers misquoted you shamefully and the net result of that is to deepen one's sense of an oncoming disaster; for I think humanly it could only drive you further into some of your own most charming surrealisms, such as bombing China's atomic plants. Truly you amaze me, Bill. Did it ever occur to you as a good Christian that it is immoral to destroy somebody else's property?

But listen, I think our public debating days are probably over—for a time at least. As wrestlers we are not both villains, and that excites no proper passions. Still, it may open something interesting—which is that the two of us have a long careful private discussion one night, because I think in all modesty there's much in your thought which is innocent of its own implications, and there's much surplus in mine which could profitably be sliced away by the powers of your logic. I'm going to England this week for a few weeks, but should be back in May, at which time perhaps finally and at last, you and Patsy can come to dinner. I felt awful when I heard about her accident, and told her so last week. Please give her my love. And you, esteemed scalawag—I can't imagine why you would ever wish to quote from this letter, but if the impulse should take you, please clear it with me first. I say this with pain, because I hate to get in the way of your only vice.

31

A Second Letter to William F. Buckley, Jr.

(OCTOBER 18, 1965; *SELECTED LETTERS OF NORMAN MAILER*, 2014)

Mailer refers to Buckley as "Bill-elect" because he was then running for mayor of New York as the Conservative Party candidate. He lost to the Republican candidate, John V. Lindsay.

Dear Bill-elect,

What the hell does emunctory mean? You have here gone too far, sir, even for Buckley. I even heard one Roman turn over distinctly in his grave as the word went by and whisper to his neighbor, "Does that 'emunctory' come from the Greek?" Anyway, you're just an old fraud. You offered to pay a week's wages not to have to hear anyone who talks more predictable nonsense of the subject of foreign policy than myself. Sailor Bill, I come close to loving you here. When the hell did you ever earn a week's wages, you bleeding plutocrat. Of course if you were really indicating you were ready to give up one-fifty-second of your yearly income, then I will go look for such an intellectual and split the swag with him. Maybe Mario Savio [Berkeley Free Speech Movement activist, 1942–96] would like to cut up a five-thousand-dollar pie with me.

At any rate, running for Mayor has made you mellow. I think I'd even contemplate voting for you if you weren't such a hopeless ass on foreign policy, and if I did not like John Lindsay and believe that he is the hope and future of the Republican party.

But you offer me the final word on the subject. Does that mean I could write a few hundred words for your column? If so, I have something tasty on Viet Nam to offer. Something that would be good for everyone's blood.

But indeed it's a relief if we're both becoming so popular. Now one day sometime in the future we'll even be able to go on television and have a calm if crazy conversation in which neither of us need feel that a political catastrophe will occur if the other scores even one small point.

Last, how is Patsy's leg? I hope it's back to everything original. Please give her my love, and let me know about dinner. We still have one to offer you. I expect you'll find it easier after the election, but if you think we can plan anything before, fine, and fine again.

32

A Sharp Searing Love for His Country

(*THE ARMIES OF THE NIGHT*, 1968)

Mailer's report on his participation in the October 21, 1967, antiwar March on the Pentagon might be the place where he most memorably and succinctly details his deep, abiding concern for the preservation of democracy in the United States. His account won the Pulitzer Prize and the National Book Award. In this excerpt, Mailer first refers to the United States as "a mysterious country."

They were on the move again. It was never, however, to become a routine parade. The majority of demonstrators, if one counted the women, had never marched in ranks; there were no leaders sufficiently well-known to command order easily; indeed it was impossible to keep physical contact with a majority of the demonstrators while they were on the bridge, for the bridge was too crowded to pass back and forth. Communication depended on the portable loudspeakers; order on the good will and wit of the speaker employing them. In the center of that March across the bridge, buried in the middle of that half mile, the crush of marchers must have surged back and forth like a wash of waves caught by the change of tides in a channel; there was the promise of chaos everywhere, but order was saved from disorder as the mob, good-humored, then evil, then good-humored again inched its way across the bridge, waiting in place, sitting down, marching again, singing songs, "We Shall Overcome"—blue bruised of misery among the voices, genuine sorrow for happier days on the Left Plantation with the old Civil Rights Negroes, not these new Deep Purple Blacks, still—shouting their slogans, "Hell, no, We Won't Go," "LBJ, how many kids did you kill today?"—it is possible any other group so large, so leaderless, so infused with anxiety for the unknown situation ahead, and so packed upon the bridge would have erupted, but finally it was a pacifist crowd: that was the obvious gamble on which the move across the bridge had been chosen; if not for the underlying composition of these gentle troops, there would have been no way to assemble on Washington's side of the Potomac. The rally would have had to be at the Pentagon itself—which indeed was where many would agree later it should most certainly have been in the first place. In any event, up at the front of this March, in the first line, back of that hollow square of monitors, Mailer and Lowell walked in this barrage of cameras, helicopters, TV cars, monitors, loudspeakers, and wavering buckling twisting line of notables, arms linked (line twisting so much that at times the movement was in file, one arm locked ahead, one behind, then the line would undulate about and the other arm would be ahead) speeding up a few steps, slowing down while a great happiness came back into the day as if finally one stood under some mythical arch in the great vault of history, helicopters bussing about, chop-chop, and the sense of America divided on this day now liberated some undiscovered patriotism in Mailer so that he felt a sharp searing love for his country in this moment and on this day, crossing some divide in his own mind wider than the Potomac, a love so lacerated he felt as if a marriage were being torn and children lost—never does one love so much as then, obviously, then—and an odor of wood smoke, from where you knew not, was also in the air, a smoke of dignity and some calm heroism not unlike the sense of freedom which also comes when a marriage is burst—Mailer knew for the first time why men in the front line of a battle are almost always ready to die: there is a promise of some swift transit—one's soul feels clean; as we have gathered, he was not used much more than any other American politician, litterateur, or racketeer to the sentiment that his soul was not unclean, but here, walking with Lowell and Macdonald, he felt as if he stepped through some crossing in the reaches of space between this moment, the French Revolution, and the Civil War, as if the ghosts of the Union Dead accompanied them now to the Bastille, he was not drunk at all, merely illumined by hunger, the sense of danger to the front, sense of danger to the rear—he was in fact in love with himself for having less fear than he had thought he might have—he knew suddenly then he had less fear now than when he was a young man in some part of himself at least, he had grown; if less innocent, less timid—the cold flame of a perfectly contained exaltation warmed old asthmas of gravel in the heart, and the sense that they were going to face the symbol, the embodiment, no, call it the true and high church of the military-industrial complex, the Pentagon, blind five-sided eye of a subtle oppression which had come to America out of the very air of the century (this evil twentieth century with its curse on the species, its oppressive Faustian lusts, its technological excrement all over the conduits of nature, its entrapment of the innocence of the best—for which young American soldiers hot out of high school and in love with a hot rod and his Marine buddies in his platoon in Vietnam could begin to know the devil of oppression which would steal his soul before he knew he had one), yes, Mailer felt a confirmation of the contests of his own life on this March to the eye of the oppressor, greedy stingy dumb valve of the Wasp heat, chalice and anus of corporation land, smug, enclosed, morally blind Pentagon, destroying the future of its own nation with each day it augmented in strength, and the Novelist induced on the consequence some dim unawakened knowledge of the mysteries of America buried in these liberties to dissent—What a mysterious country it was. The older he became, the more interesting he found her. Awful deadening programmatic inhuman dowager of a nation, corporation, and press—tender mysterious bitch whom no one would ever know, not even her future unfeeling Communist doctors if she died of the disease of her dowager, deadly pompous dowager who had trapped the sweet bitch. (Perhaps this near excess of patriotism in poetic dose came from locking arms with Lowell; it was not Mailer's fortune to cross from the Capital to Virginia every day in the company of a grand poet!) He was, in fact, by now even virtually in love with the helicopters, not because the metaphors of his mind had swollen large enough to embrace even them! No! he loved the helicopters because they were the nearest manifestation of the enemy, and he now loved his enemy for the thundering justification they gave to his legitimate—so he would term it—sentiment

of pride in himself on this proud day, yes, the helicopters, ugliest fly-
ing bird of them all, dragon in the shape of an insect, new vanity of
combat, unutterable conceit, holy hunting pleasure, spills and thrills
of combat on a quick hump and jump from the down-home Vietnam
country club, symbol of tyranny to a city man, for only high officials
and generals and police officers flitted into cities on helicopters this
small in size—Mailer, General Mailer, now had a vision of another
battle, the next big battle, and these helicopters, press, television and
assorted media helicopters hovering overhead with CIA-FBI-all others of the alphabet in helicopters—and into the swarm of the chop-
pers would come a Rebel Chopper in black, or in Kustom-Kar Red,
leave it to the talent of the West Coast to prepare the wild helicopter;
it would be loaded with guns to shoot pellets of paint at the enemy
helicopters, smearing and daubing, dripping them, dropping cans of
paint from overhead to smash on the blades of the chopper like early
air combat in World War I, and Fourth of July rockets to fire past their
Plexiglas canopies. That was the way, Mailer told himself, that was the
way. The media would scream at the violence of those dissenters who
attacked innocent helicopters with paint, and America—if it still had
a humor—would laugh. Until then—insufferable arrogance of these
helicopters swinging and hovering and wheeling overhead, as if to
remind everyone below of their sufferance, their possession, and the
secret of who owned the air—corporation land.

They had one more long wait at the end of the bridge, not twenty
yards from the exit, and sat down, near to safety (from the dangers of
a stampede) but not safe yet for they were still on the bridge. At last
they moved on, continued along a road for a while, passed under a
culvert. On the railing of this culvert, fifteen feet above, stood a handsome young Negro carrying a placard. "NO VIETNAMESE EVER
CALLED ME A NIGGER," and the marchers cheered as they passed
beneath, and Mailer was impressed—not so easy to stand on the edge
of a parapet while thousands marched beneath—confident must be
such a stance against the evil eye. Was a mad genius buried in every
Negro? How fantastic they were at their best—how dim at their
worst.

Now the March was leaving the road, was crossing open fields marked off for their route, and the demand to lock arms became more and more difficult to maintain for the demonstrators in the lead were all in a rush to be first to the Pentagon, now visible in the distance—thin tinge of lead to the silver of the mood. Marchers coming up from behind began to circle forward around the sides of the hollow square which had narrowed to a rectangle going through the culvert, but then widened into a fan as they spread across the field. Some marchers being fatigued, others impatient, the ranks deteriorated at last, and everybody strolled over the grass at his own rate for the last quarter mile. They were now passing fences with high barbed wire—cause to wonder if they were open pens to hold the masses soon to go under arrest—that was Mailer's idea. (Invariably his sound perceptions were as quickly replaced by wild estimates; he should have divined that the government was not going to pen people in full view of others who were free, nor give fields of such photographs to European papers with any faint reminders implicit of when last civilians had been seen behind barbed wire.) Looking at those pens, Mailer's steps passed from grass to concrete. They were in the North Parking Area of the Pentagon. The March was ended. They had come to their goal.

33

THE MARSHAL AND THE NAZI

(*THE ARMIES OF THE NIGHT*, 1968)

Mailer separated from the other marchers and walked across a patch of grass on the Pentagon lawn, where he was stopped by a soldier. He eluded him, but was then caught by two plainclothes officers and arrested for transgressing a police line. Mailer's intense verbal battle with a right-wing demonstrator, re-created here, illumines the polarization of political forces in American life, then and now.

They put him in the rear seat of a Volkswagen camper and he welcomed the opportunity to relax. Soon they would drive him, he guessed, to some nearby place where he would be arraigned, fined, and released. . . .

Now a new man entered the Volkswagen. Mailer took him at first for a Marshal or an official, since he was wearing a dark suit and a white motorcycle helmet, and had a clean-cut stubborn face with short features. But he was carrying something which looked like a rolled-up movie screen over five feet long, and he smiled in the friendliest fashion, sat down next to Mailer, and took off his helmet. Mailer thought he was about to be interrogated and he looked forward to that with this friendly man, no less! (of course the prisoner often looks forward to his interrogation) but then another man carrying a clipboard came up to them, and leaning through the wide double door of the camper, asked questions of them both. When Mailer gave his name, the man with clipboard acted as if he had never heard of him, or at least pretended never to have heard of him, the second possibility seeming possible since word traveled quickly from reporters.

THE MARSHAL AND THE NAZI

"How do you spell it?"

"M.A.I.L.E.R."

"Why were you arrested, Mr. Miller?"

"For transgressing a police line as a protest against the war in Vietnam."

The Clipboard then asked a question of the man sitting next to him. "And why were *you* arrested?"

"As an act of solidarity with oppressed forces fighting for liberty against this country in Southeast Asia."

The Clipboard nodded drily, as if to say, "Yeah, we're all crazy here." Then he asked, pointing to the object which looked like a rolled-up movie screen, "You want that with you?"

"Yessir," said the man next to Mailer. "I'd like to take it along."

The Clipboard gave a short nod, and walked off. Mailer would never see him again. If the History has therefore spent a pointless exchange with him, it is to emphasize that the first few minutes of an arrest such as this are without particular precedent, and so Mailer, like a visitor from Mars, or an adolescent entering polite society, had no idea of what might be important next and what might not. This condition of innocence was not, however, particularly disagreeable since it forced him to watch everything with the attention, let us say, of a man like William Buckley spending his first hour in a Harlem bar—no, come! Things are far safer for Mailer at the Pentagon.

He chatted with his fellow prisoner, Teague, Walter Teague was the name, who had been in the vanguard of the charge Mailer had seen from the parking lot. But before any confused impressions were to be sorted, they were interrupted by the insertion of the next prisoner put into the Volkswagen, a young man with straight blond hair and a Nazi armband on his sleeve. He was installed in the rear, with a table between, but Mailer was not happy, for his eyes and the Nazi's bounced off each other like two heads colliding—the novelist discovered he was now in a hurry for them to get this stage of the booking completed. He was also privately indignant at the U.S. Army (like a private citizen, let us say, who writes a letter to his small-town newspaper) at the incredible stupidity of putting a Nazi in the same Volkswagen camper with Pentagon demonstrators—there were two or three other cars available, at least!—next came the suspicion that this was not an accident, but a provocation in the making. If the Nazi started trouble, and there was a fight, the newspaper accounts would doubtless state Norman Mailer had gotten into an altercation five minutes after his arrest. (Of course, they would not say with whom.) This is all doubtless most paranoid of Mailer, but then he had had nearly twenty years of misreporting about himself, and the seed of paranoia is the arrival of the conviction that the truth about oneself is never told. (Mailer might have done better to pity the American populace—receiving misinformation in systematic form tends to create mass schizophrenia: poor America—Eddie and Debbie are True Love.)

Now they were moved out of the camper and over to an Army truck. There was Teague, and the novelist, and another arrestee—a tall Hungarian who quickly told Mailer how much he liked his books and in much the same breath that he was a Freedom Fighter—there was also a new U.S. Marshal, and the Nazi. The prisoners climbed one by one over the high tailgate, Mailer finding it a touch awkward for he did not wish to dirty his dark blue pinstripe suit, and then they stood in the rear of the truck, a still familiar 2½ ton 6-by of a sort which the novelist hadn't been in for twenty-one years, not since his Army discharge.

Standing in the truck, a few feet apart from each other, all prisoners regarding one another, the Nazi fixed on Mailer. Their eyes locked like magnets coming into line, and for perhaps twenty seconds they stared at each other. Mailer looked into a pair of yellow eyes so compressed with hate that back of his own eyes he could feel the echo of such hatred ringing. The Nazi was taller than Mailer, well-knit, and with neatly formed features and a shock of blond hair, would have been handsome but for the ferocity of his yellow eyes which were sunk deep in their sockets. Those eyes made him look like an eagle.

Yet Mailer had first advantage in this eye-staring contest. Because he had been prepared for it. He had been getting into such confrontations for years, and rarely lost them, even though he sometimes thought they were costing him eyesight. Still, some developed instinct had made him ready an instant before the Nazi. Every bit of intensity he possessed—with the tremors of the March and the Marshal's arm still pent in him—glared forth into the other's eyes: he was nonetheless aghast at what he saw. The American Nazis were all fanatics, yes, poor mad tormented fanatics, their psyches twisted like burning leaves in the fire of their hatreds, yes, indeed! But this man's conviction stood in his eyes as if his soul had been focused to a single point of light. Mailer could feel violence behind violence rocking through his head. If the two of them were ever alone in an alley, one of them might kill the other in a fight—it was not unlike holding an electric wire in the hand. And the worst of it was that he was not even feeling violent himself—whatever violence he possessed had gone to his eyes—by that route had he projected himself on the Nazi.

After the first five seconds of the shock had passed, he realized he might be able to win—the Nazi must have taken too many easy contests, and had been too complacent in the first moment, yes it was like wrestlers throwing themselves on each other: one knuckle of one finger a little better able to be worked on a grip could make the difference—now he could feel the hint of force ebbing in the other's eyes, and could wonder at his own necessity to win. He did not hate the Nazi nearly so much as he was curious about him, yet the thought of losing had been intolerable as if he had been *obliged* not to lose, as if the duty of his life at this particular moment must have been to look into that Nazi's eye, and say with his own, "You claim you have a philosophical system which comprehends all—you know nothing! My eyes encompass yours. My philosophy contains yours. You have met the wrong man!" and the Nazi looked away, and was hysterical with fury on the instant.

"You Jew bastard," he shouted. "Dirty Jew with kinky hair."

They didn't speak that way. It was too corny. Yet he could only answer, "You filthy Kraut."

"Dirty Jew."

"Kraut pig."

A part of his mind could actually be amused at this choice—he didn't even hate Germans any more. Indeed Germans fascinated him now. Why they like his books more than Americans did. Yet here he could think of nothing better to return than "Kraut pig."

"I'm not a Kraut," said the Nazi, "I'm a Norwegian." And then as if the pride of his birth had tricked him into communication with an infidel, thus into sacrilege, the Nazi added quickly, "Jew bastard red," then cocked his fists. "Come here, you coward," he said to Mailer, "I'll kill you."

"Throw the first punch, baby," said Mailer, "you'll get it all."

They were both absolutely right. They had a perfect sense of the other. Mailer was certainly not brave enough to advance on the Nazi—it would be like springing an avalanche on himself. But he also knew that if the Nazi jumped him, one blond youth was very likely to get massacred. In retrospect, it would appear not uncomic—two philosophical monomaniacs with the same flaw—they could not help it, they were counterpunchers.

"Jew coward! Red bastard!"

"Go fuck yourself, Nazi baby."

But now a tall U.S. Marshal who had the body and insane look of a very good rangy defensive end in professional football—that same hard high-muscle build, same coiled spring wrath, same livid conviction that everything opposing the team must be wrecked, sod, turf, grass, uniforms, helmets, bodies, yes even bite the football if it will help—now leaped into the truck and jumped between them. "Shut up," he said, "or I'll wreck both of you." He had a long craggy face somewhere in the physiognomical land between Steve McQueen and Robert Mitchum, but he would never have made Hollywood, for his skin was pocked with the big boiling craters of a red lunar acne, and his eyes in Cinemascope would have blazed an audience off their seat for such gray-green flame could only have issued from a blowtorch. Under his white Marshal's helmet, he was one impressive piece of gathered wrath.

Speaking to the Marshal at this point would have been dangerous. The Marshal's emotions had obviously been marinating for a week in the very special bile waters American Patriotism reserves for its need. His feelings were now caustic as a whip—too gentle the smile!— he was in agonies of frustration because the honor of his profession kept him from battering every prisoner's head to a Communist pulp. Mailer looked him over covertly to see what he could try if the

Marshal went to work on him. All reports: negative. He would not stand a chance with this Marshal—there seemed no place to hit him where he'd be vulnerable; stone larynx, leather testicles, ice cubes for eyes. And he had his Marshal's club in his hand as well. Brother! Bring back the Nazi!

Whether the Marshal had been once in the Marine Corps, in Vietnam, or if half his family were now in Vietnam, or if he just hated the sheer Jew York presumption of that slovenly, drug-ridden weak contaminating America-hating army of termites outside this fortress' walls, he was certainly any upstanding demonstrator's nightmare. Because he was full of American rectitude and was fearless, and savage, savage as the exhaust left in the wake of a motorcycle club, gasoline and cheap perfume were one end of his spectrum, yeah, this Marshal loved action, but he was also in that no man's land between the old frontier and the new ranch home—as they, yes *they*—the enemies of the Marshal—tried to pass bills to limit the purchase of hunting rifles, so did *they* try to kill America, inch by inch, all the forces of evil, disorder, mess and chaos in the world, and *cowardice!* And city ways, and slick shit, and despoliation of national resources, all the subtle invisible creeping paralyses of Communism which were changing America from a land where blood was red to a land where water was foul—yes in this Marshal's mind—no lesser explanation could suffice for the Knight of God light in the flame of his eye—the evil WAS WITHOUT, America was threatened by a foreign disease, and the Marshal was threatened to the core of his sanity by any one of the first fifty of Mailer's ideas which would insist that the evil was within, that the best in America was being destroyed by what in itself seemed next best, yes American heroism corrupted by American know-how—no wonder murder stood out in his face as he looked at the novelist—for the Marshal to lose his sanity was no passing psychiatric affair: think rather of a rifleman on a tower in Texas and a score of his dead on the street.

But now the Nazi began to play out the deepest of ceremonies. The truck standing still, another Marshal at the other end of the van (the one indeed who had arrested Mailer) and Teague and the Hungarian to different sides, everyone had their eyes on the Norwegian.

He now glared again at Mailer, but then whipped away his eyes before a second contest could begin, and said, "All right, Jew, come over here if you want a fight."

The Marshal took the Nazi and threw him against the side-wall of the truck. As he bounced off, the Marshal gave him a rap below the collarbone with the butt of his club. "I told you to shut up. Now, just shut up." His rage was intense. The Nazi looked back at him sullenly, leaned on the butt of the club almost defiantly as if the Marshal didn't know what foolish danger he was in to treat the Nazi so, the Nazi had a proud curved hint of a smile, as if he were recording the features of this Marshal forever in the history of his mind, the Nazi's eyes seemed to say to the Marshal, "You are really on my side although you do not admit it—you would like to eat me now because in the future you know you will yet kiss my boots!" And the Marshal traveling a high edge of temper began to slam the Nazi against the wall of the truck with moderate force, but rhythmically, as if he would pacify them both by this act, bang, and bang, step by step, the imaginary dialogue of the Marshal to the Nazi now sounding in Mailer's ear somewhat like this, "Listen, Nazi, you're nothing but a rat fart who makes my job harder, and gives the scum around me room to breathe, 'cause they look at you and feel righteous. You just keep me diverted from the real danger."

And the Nazi looked back with a full sullen pouting defiance as if from deep in himself he was all unconsciously saying to the Marshal, "You know I am beautiful, and you are frightened of me. I have a cause, and I am ready to die for it, and you are just ready to die for a uniform. Join me where the real war is. Already the strongest and wildest men in America wear our symbol on their motorcycle helmets."

And the Marshal, glaring back at the Nazi, butt of his club transfixing him against the wall of the van, gave a contemptuous look, as if to drop him with the final unspoken word. "Next to strong wild men, you're nothing but a bitch."

Then the truck began to move, and the Marshal calmer now, stood silently between Mailer and the Nazi; and the Nazi, also quiet now, stood in place looking neither at the Marshal nor Mailer. Some small storm of hysteria seemed to have worked itself out of the van.

34

A Love Affair with America

(INTERVIEW WITH ERIC JAMES SCHROEDER, *VIETNAM, WE'VE ALL BEEN THERE,* 1992)

In February 1966, Mailer turned in his draft card in New York City during a protest rally against the Vietnam War.

Vietnam was just exercising the hell out of me all those years. It's such a peculiar position to be in—to be hating a war so much that you're truly opposed to your own country, that you live in this odd relation to your own country. It's your country and yet you know that you may be in jail in a year or two because of this war and your opposition to it. I remember there was one period when a bunch of us swore allegiance to those who tore up their draft cards. In other words, if any of them went to jail, we'd go with them; there were over a hundred of us writers who did this one night at the Town Hall [New York City performance hall]—we all stood up and took the pledge. And that was a funny moment because it was an open-ended action—maybe in a year or two one's life could be changed completely if one went to jail. We didn't know, but our hope was that the size of our group would inhibit the government from doing anything, and it probably did. But we were, technically, guilty of encouraging sedition. The threat of jail was very real. And as you know there were a lot of timid people in that gang who had no taste for jail. That was the oddest phenomenon; there's been no period of my life quite like it.

But the one thing to be said for it was that it gave us a great sense of purpose; we were fighting against something that we felt right about fighting. . . . I've always had this sort of half-assed love affair with America. If you grow up in Brooklyn and you're Jewish (which means, in effect, that you're ethnic), then you're out of it—you're out of it, but you're still a part of it. For anyone who's ethnic in America, however, it's also possible not to have a love affair with America. It's something like the love affair a man has when he's married to a woman who's richer than himself or vastly more beautiful; it's not a marriage of equality, it's not a comfortable marriage. But it should be a very important marriage. I think most ethnics in America do end up with that peculiarly enraged but passionate commitment to America. I know that when I'm in foreign countries I feel so American that it's comic to me.

35

ROBERT KENNEDY'S MAGIC

(MESSAGE READ TO WILLIAM WALTON, MAY 18, 1968)

William E. Walton (1909–94) was a journalist and confidante of President Kennedy. This message was delivered by telephone three weeks before Senator Robert Kennedy's assassination in response to a request from Walton.

I met Senator [Eugene] McCarthy once and liked him, and think he is a fine man who would make a good president. But I think Bobby Kennedy would make a great president, for he has grown more in the last ten years than any man in America's political life. As a consequence, I think America might grow more with him than any other candidate, and American life might thereby become more adventurous and more responsible. That is a magical paradox, but the candidacy of Robert F. Kennedy is not void of that magic, and without magic American life may yet prove to be nothing but a preparation for living in the endless automated corridors of a super-technological society.

36

THE REPORTER OBSERVES THE WASPS

(MIAMI AND THE SIEGE OF CHICAGO, 1968)

Perhaps Mailer's most discerning portrait of American conservatives, this excerpt from his account of the 1968 national political conventions was made possible by the accident of Mailer being mistaken for a security guard.

That evening at the Fontainebleau, on the night before the convention was to begin, the Republicans had their Grand Gala, no Press admitted, and the reporter by a piece of luck was nearly the first to get in. The affair was well-policed, in fact strict in its security, for some of the most important Republican notables would be there, but strolling through the large crowd in the lobby the reporter discovered himself by accident in the immediate wake of Governor Reagan's passage along a channel of security officers through the mob to the doors of the Gala. It was assumed by the people who gave way to the Governor that the reporter must be one of the plainclothesmen assigned to His Excellency's rear, and with a frown here, judicious tightening of his mouth there, look of concern for the Governor's welfare squeezed onto his map, offering a security officer's look superior to the absence of any ticket, he went right in through the ticket-takers, having found time in that passage to observe Governor Reagan and his Lady, who were formally dressed to the hilt of the occasion, now smiling, now shaking hands, eager, tense, bird-like, genial, not quite habituated to eminence, seeking to make brisk but not rude progress through the crowd, and obviously uneasy in the crowd (like most political figures) since a night in June in Los Angeles. It was an expected observation, but Mr. and Mrs. Reagan looked very much like an actor and actress playing Governor and Wife. Still Reagan held himself sort of uneasily about the middle, as if his solar plexus were fragile, and a clout would heave him like a fish on the floor.

Once inside the ballroom, however, the reporter discovered that the Governor had been among the first guests to enter. His own position was therefore not comfortable. Since there were no other guests among whom to mix (nothing but two hundred and forty empty tables with settings for two thousand people, all still to come in) and no cover to conceal him but small potted trees with oranges attached by green wire, since Security might be furious to the point of cop-mania catching him thus early, there was no choice but to take up a stand twenty feet from the door, his legs at parade rest, his arms clasped behind, while he scrutinized the entrance of everybody who came in. Any security officer studying him might therefore be forced to conclude that he belonged to *other* Security. Suffice it, he was not approached in his position near the entrance, and for the next thirty minutes looked at some thousand Republicans coming through the gate, the other thousand entering out of view by an adjacent door.

It was not a crowd totally representative of the power of the Republican Party. Some poor delegates may have been there as guests, and a few other delegates might have chosen to give their annual contribution of $1,000 for husband and wife here ($500 a plate) rather than to some other evening of fund raising for the party, indeed an air of sobriety and quiet dress was on many of the Republicans who entered. There were women who looked like librarians and school-teachers, there were middle-aged men who looked like they might be out for their one night of the year. The Eastern Establishment was of course present in degree, and powers from the South, West, Midwest, but it was not a gang one could hold up in comparative glitter to an opening at the Met. No, rather, it was modesty which hung over these well-bred subscribers to the Gala.

Still, exceptions noted, they were obviously in large part composed of a thousand of the wealthiest Republicans in the land, the corporate and social power of America was here in legions of interconnection he could not even begin to trace. Of necessity, a measure of his own ignorance came over him, for among those thousands, except for candidate, politicians and faces in the news, there were not ten people he recognized. Yet here they were, the economic power of America (so far as economic power was still private, not public), the family power (so far as position in society was still a passion to average and ambitious Americans), the military power (to the extent that important sword-rattlers and/or patriots were among the company, as well as cadres of corporations not unmarried to the Pentagon), yes, even the spiritual power of America (just so far as Puritanism, Calvinism, conservatism and golf still gave the Wasp an American faith more intense than the faith of cosmopolitans, one-worlders, trade-unionists, Black militants, New Leftists, acid-heads, tribunes of the gay, families of Mafia, political machinists, fixers, swingers, Democratic lobbyists, members of the Grange, and government workers, not to include the *Weltanschauung* of every partisan in every minority group). No, so far as there was an American faith, a belief, a mystique that America was more than the sum of its constituencies, its trillions of dollars and billions of acres, its constellation of factories, empyrean of communications, mountain transcendent of finance, and heroic of sport, transports of medicine, hygiene, and church, so long as belief persisted that America, finally more than all this, was the world's ultimate reserve of rectitude, final garden of the Lord, so far as this mystique could survive in every American family of Christian substance, so then were the people entering this Gala willy-nilly the leaders of this faith, never articulated by any of them except in the most absurd and taste-curdling jargons of patriotism mixed with religion, but the faith existed in those crossroads between the psyche and the heart where love, hate, the cognition of grace, the all but lost sense of the root, and adoration of America congregate for some.

Their own value was in this faith, the workings of their seed from one generation into the next, their link to the sense of what might be life-force was in the faith. Yes, primitive life was there, and ancestral life, health concealed in their own flesh from towns occupied and once well-settled, from farms which prospered, and frontiers they had—through ancestors—dared to pass. They believed in America as they believed in God—they could not really ever expect that America might collapse and God yet survive, no, they had even gone so far as to think that America was the savior of the world, food and medicine by one hand, sword in the other, highest of high faith in a nation which would bow the knee before no problem since God's own strength was in the die. It was a faith which had flared so high in San Francisco in 1964 that staid old Republicans had come near to frothing while they danced in the aisle, there to nominate Barry, there to nominate Barry. But their hero had gone down to a catastrophe of defeat, blind in politics, impolite in tactics, a sorehead, a fool, a disaster. And if his policies had prevailed to some degree, to the degree of escalating the war in Vietnam, so had that policy depressed some part of America's optimism to the bottom of the decade, for the country had learned an almost unendurable lesson—its history in Asia was next to done, and there was not any real desire to hold armies on that land; worse, the country had begun to wear away inside, and the specter of Vietnam in every American city would haunt the suburb, the terror of a dollar cut loose from every standard of economic anchor was in the news, and some of the best of the youth were mad demented dogs with teeth in the flesh of the deepest Republican faith.

They were a chastened collocation these days. The high fire of hard Republican faith was more modest now, the vision of America had diminished. The claims on Empire had met limits. But it was nonetheless uncommon, yes bizarre, for the reporter to stand like an agent of their security as these leaders of the last American faith came through to the Gala, for, repeat: they were in the main not impressive, no, not by the hard eye of New York. Most of them were ill-proportioned in some part of their physique. Half must have been, of course, men and women over fifty and their bodies reflected the pull of their character. The dowager's hump was common, and many a man had a flaccid paunch, but the collective tension was rather in the shoulders, in the girdling of the shoulders against anticipated lashings on the back, in the thrust forward of the neck, in the maintenance of the muscles of the mouth forever locked in readiness to bite the tough meat of resistance, in a posture forward from the hip since the small of the back was dependably stiff, loins and mind cut wary from each other by some abyss between navel and hip.

More than half of the men wore eyeglasses, young with old—the reporter made his count, close as a professional basketball game, and gave up by the time his score was up to Glasses 87, No Glasses 83. You could not picture a Gala Republican who was not clean-shaven by eight a.m. Coming to power, they could only conceive of trying to clean up every situation in sight. And so many of the women seemed victims of the higher hygiene. Even a large part of the young seemed to have faces whose cheeks had been injected with Novocain.

Yet he felt himself unaccountably filled with a mild sorrow. He did not detest these people, he did not feel so superior as to pity them, it was rather he felt a sad sorrowful respect. In their immaculate cleanliness, in the somewhat anti-septic odors of their astringent toilet water and perfume, in the abnegation of their walks, in the heavy sturdy moves so many demonstrated of bodies in life's harness, there was the muted tragedy of the Wasp—they were not on earth to enjoy or even perhaps to love so very much, they were here to serve, and serve they had in public functions and public charities (while recipients of their charity might vomit in rage and laugh in scorn), served on opera committees, and served in long hours of duty at the piano, served as the sentinel in concert halls and the pews on the aisle in church, at the desk in schools, had served for culture, served for finance, served for salvation, served for America—and so much of America did not wish them to serve any longer, and so many of them doubted themselves, doubted that the force of their faith could illumine their path in these new modern horror-hard times. On and on, they came through the door, the clean, the well-bred, the extraordinarily prosperous, and for the most astonishing part, the almost entirely proper. Yes, in San Francisco in '64 they had been able to be insane for a little while, but now they were subdued, now they were modest, now they were looking for a leader to bring America back to them, their lost America, Jesus-land.

37

Richard M. Nixon, GOP Convention, 1968

(MIAMI AND THE SIEGE OF CHICAGO, 1968)

Mailer pondered Richard Nixon's roots, personality, body language, political skills, and palpable hypocrisy more thoughtfully than that of any other American politician, seeking always the reasons for his enduring appeal, and hoping, until his disastrous fall, that Nixon would shed his unctuous hypocrisy and become an American hero. In the 1980s, Donald Trump became a pen pal of Nixon's. John Dean, Nixon's White House counsel, when later reading their correspondence, said he could see his old boss and Trump picking up "the waves of each other's personality." He went on to say, "These are two authoritarian personalities who would have a natural affinity for each other."

Nixon had come in earlier that day. A modestly large crowd, perhaps six hundred at the entrance to the Miami Hilton. . . . The crowd had been enthusiastic without real hurly-burly or hint of pandemonium. More in a state of respectful enthusiasm, and the hot patriotic cupidity to get near the man who is probably going to be the next American President. The office, not the man, is moving them. And Nixon passes through them with the odd stick-like motions which are so much a characteristic of his presence. He is like an actor with good voice and hordes of potential, but the despair of his dramatic coach (again it is High School). "Dick, you just got to learn how to move." There is something almost touching in the way he does it, as if sensitive flesh winces at the way he must expose his lack of heart for being warm and really winning in crowds, and yet he is all heart to perform his task, as if the total unstinting exercise of the will must finally deliver every last grace, yes, he is like a missionary handing out

Bibles among the Urdu. Christ, they are filthy fellows, but deserving
of the *touch*. No, it is not so much that he is a bad actor (for Nixon in
a street crowd is *radiant* with emotion to reach across the prison pen
of his own artificial moves and deadly reputation and show that he
is sincere) it is rather that he grew up in the worst set of schools for
actors in the world—white gloves and church usher, debating team,
Young Republicanism, captive of Ike's forensic style—as an actor,
Nixon thinks his work is to signify. So if he wants to show someone
that he likes them, he must smile; if he wishes to show disapproval of
Communism, he frowns; America must be strong, out goes his chest.
Prisoner of old habit or unwitting of a new kind of move, he has not
come remotely near any modern moves, he would not be ready to
see that the young love [Senator Eugene] McCarthy because he plays
forever against his line. "If I'm nominated, I can't see how I'd possibly
fail to win," says McCarthy in a gloomy modest mild little voice, then
his eyes twinkle at the myriad of consequences to follow: raps in the
newspaper about his arrogance, the sheer delicious zaniness of any
man making any claim about his candidacy—yes, many people love
McCarthy because his wan wit is telling them, "We straddle ultimates:
spitballs and eternals."

Nixon has never learned this. He is in for the straight sell. No
wonder he foundered on "America can't stand pat."

But the reporter is obsessed with him. He has never written anything nice about Nixon. Over the years he has saved some of his
sharpest comments for him, he has disliked him intimately ever since
his Checkers speech in 1952—the kind of man who was ready to
plough sentimentality in such a bog was the kind of man who would
press any button to manipulate the masses—and there was large fear
in those days of buttons which might ignite atomic wars. Nixon's
presence on television had inspired emotions close to nausea. There
had been a gap between the man who spoke and the man who lived
behind the speaker which offered every clue of schizophrenia in the
American public if they failed to recognize the void within the presentation. Worse. There was unity only in the way the complacency
of the voice matched the complacency of the ideas. It was as if Richard Nixon were proving that a man who had never spent an instant

inquiring whether family, state, church, and flag were ever wrong could go on in secure steps, denuded of risk, from office to office until he was President.

In 1962 the reporter had given a small celebration for the collapse of Nixon after his defeat in the election for Governor of California. To the Press: "Well, gentlemen," the defeated man had said, "you won't have Nixon to kick any more." It had seemed the absolute end of a career. Self-pity in public was as irreversible as suicide. In 1964, Nixon had stood about in the wings while Barry [Goldwater] was nominated. Now, in 1968, he was on the edge of becoming the nominee. It was obvious something was wrong with the reporter's picture. In his previous conception of Richard Nixon's character there had been no room for a comeback. Either the man had changed or one had failed to recognize some part of his character from the beginning. So there was interest, even impatience to hear him speak.

The room filled slowly. By the time Nixon began, it was apparent that 500 seats had been an excessive estimate. Perhaps half of them were filled, certainly no more than two-thirds. It was nonetheless a large press conference. Nixon came in wearing a quiet blue-gray suit, white shirt, black and blue close-figured tie, black shoes, and no handkerchief for the breast pocket. He stepped up on the dais diffidently, not certain whether applause would be coming or not. There was none. He stood there, looked quietly and warily at the audience, and then said that he was ready for questions.

This would be his sole press conference before the nomination. He was of course famous for his lack of sparkling good relation with the Press, he had in fact kept his publicity to a functional minimum these past few months. The work of collecting delegates had been done over the last four years, particularly over the last two. Their allegiance had been confirmed the last six months in his primary victories. He had no longer anything much to gain from good interviews, not at least until his nomination was secured; he had everything to lose from a bad interview. A delegate who was slipping could slide further because of an ill-chosen remark.

To the extent that the Press was not Republican, and certainly more than half, privately, were not, he would have few friends and

more than a few determined enemies. Even among the Republicans
he could expect a better share of the Press to go to Rockefeller. Even
worse, for the mood of this conference, he did not, in comparison
with other political candidates, have many reporters who were his
personal friends. He was not reputed to smoke or drink so he did not
have drinking buddies as Johnson once had, and Goldwater, and Bill
Miller, and Humphrey; no brothel legends attached to him, and no
outsize admiration to accompany them; no, the Press was a necessary
tool to him, a tool he had been obliged to employ for more than
twenty years but he could not pretend to be comfortable in his use
of the tool, and the tool (since it was composed of men) resented its
employment. . . .

Nonetheless his posture on the stage, hands to his side or clasped
before him, gave him the attentive guarded look of an old ballplayer—
like Rabbit Maranville, let us say, or even an old con up before the
Parole Board. There was something in his carefully shaven face—the
dark jowls already showing the first overtones of thin gloomy blue
at this early hour—some worry which gave promise of never leaving him, some hint of inner debate about his value before eternity
which spoke of precisely the sort of improvement that comes upon
a man when he shifts in appearance from looking like an undertaker's assistant to looking like an old con seriously determined to go
respectable. The Old Nixon, which is to say the young Nixon, used
to look, on clasping his hands in front of him, like a church usher
(of the variety who would twist a boy's ear after removing him from
church). The older Nixon before the Press now—the *new* Nixon—
had finally acquired some of the dignity of the old athlete and the old
con—he had taken punishment, that was on his face now, he knew
the detailed schedule of pain in a real loss, there was an attentiveness
in his eyes which gave offer of some knowledge of the abyss, even
the kind of gentleness which ex-drunkards attain after years in AA. As
he answered questions, fielding them with the sure modest moves of
an old shortstop who hits few homers but supports the team on his
fielding (what sorrow in the faces of such middle-aged shortstops!),
so now his modesty was not without real dignity. Where in Eisenhower days his attempts at modesty had been as offensive as a rich

boy's arrogance, for he had been so transparently contemptuous of the ability of his audience to *witness* him, now the modesty was the product of a man who, at worst, had grown from a bad actor to a surprisingly good actor, or from an unpleasant self-made man—outrageously rewarded with luck—to a man who had risen and fallen and been able to rise again, and so conceivably had learned something about patience and the compassion of others.

When the reporter was younger, he might have said, "Nixon did not rise again; they raised him; if a new Nixon did not exist, they would have had to invent him." But the reporter was older now—presumably he knew more about the limits of the ruling class for inventing what they needed; he had learned how little talent or patience they had. Yes, at a certain point they might have decided, some of them at any rate, to dress Richard Nixon for the part again, but no one but Nixon had been able to get himself up from the political deathbed to which his failure in California had consigned him. He was here, then, answering questions in a voice which was probably closer to his own than it had ever been.

And some of the answers were not so bad. Much was Old Nixon, extraordinarily adroit at working both sides of a question so that both halves of his audience might be afterward convinced he was one of them. ("While homosexuality is a perversion punishable by law, and an intolerable offense to a law-abiding community, it is life-giving to many of those who are in need of it," he might have said if ever he had addressed a combined meeting of the Policemen's Benevolent Association and the Mattachine Society.) So he worked into the problem of Vietnam by starting at A and also by starting at Z which he called a "two-pronged approach." He was for a negotiated settlement, he was for maintaining military strength because that would be the only way to "reach negotiated settlement of the war on an honorable basis." Later he was to talk of negotiations with "the next superpower, Communist China." He spoke patiently, with clarity, gently, not badly but for an unfortunate half-smile pasted to his face. The question would come, and he would back-hand it with his glove or trap it; like all politicians he had a considered answer for every question, but he gave structure to his answers, even a certain relish for their dialectical complexity. Where once he had pretended to think in sentimentalities and slogans, now he held the question up, worked over it, deployed it, amplified it, corrected its tendency, offered an aside (usually an attempt to be humorous), revealed its contradiction, and then declared a statement. With it all, a sensitivity almost palpable to the reservations of the Press about his character, his motive, and his good intention. He still had no natural touch with them, his half-smile while he listened was unhappy, for it had nowhere to go but into a full smile and his full smile was as false as false teeth, a pure exercise of will. You could all but see the signal pass from his brain to his jaw. "SMILE," said the signal, and so he flashed teeth in a painful kind of joyous grimace which spoke of some shrinkage in the liver, or the gut, which he would have to repair afterward by other medicine than good-fellowship. (By winning the Presidency, perhaps.) He had always had the ability to violate his own nature absolutely if that happened to be necessary to his will—there had never been anyone in American life so resolutely phony as Richard Nixon. Nor anyone so transcendentally successful by such means—small wonder half the electorate had regarded him for years as equal to a disease. But he was less phony now, *that was the miracle*, he had moved from a position of total ambition and total alienation from his own person (at the time of Checkers, the dog speech) to a place now where he was halfway conciliated with his own self. As he spoke, he kept going in and out of focus, true one instant, phony the next, then quietly correcting the false step.

Question from the Press: *You emphasized the change in the country and abroad. Has this led you to change your thinking in any shape or form specifically?*

Answer: *It certainly has.* (But he was too eager. Old Nixon was always ready to please with good straight American boyhood enthusiasm. So he tacked back, his voice throttled down.) *As the facts change, any intelligent man* (firm but self-deprecatory, he is including the Press with himself) *does change his approaches to the problems.* (Now sharp awareness of the next Press attitude.) *It does not mean that he is an opportunist.* (Now modestly, reasonably.) *It means only that he is a pragmatist, a realist, applying principles to the new situations.* (Now he will

deploy some of the resources of his answer.) *For example . . . in prepar-*
ing the acceptance speech I hope to give next Thursday, I was reading over my
acceptance speech in 1960, and I thought then it was, frankly, quite a good
speech. But I realize how irrelevant much of what I said in 1960 in foreign
affairs was to the problems of today. (The admission was startling. The
Old Nixon was never wrong. Now, he exploited the shift in a move
to his political left, pure New Nixon.) *Then the Communist world was a*
monolithic world. Today it is a split world, schizophrenic, with . . . great diver-
sity . . . in Eastern Europe (a wholesome admission for anyone who had
labored in John Foster Dulles' world.) *. . . after an era of confrontation . . .*
we now enter an era of negotiations with the Soviet Union.

While he was never in trouble with the questions, growing surer
and surer of himself as he went on, the tension still persisted between
his actual presence as a man not altogether alien to the abyss of a real
problem, and the political practitioner of his youth, that snake-oil
salesman who was never back of any idea he sold, but always off to
the side where he might observe its effect on the sucker. The New
Nixon groped and searched for the common touch he had once
been able to slip into the old folks with the ease of an incubus on
a spinster. Now he tried to use slang, put quotes around it with a
touching, almost pathetic, reminder of Nice-Nellyism, the inhibition
of the good clean church upbringing of his youth insisting on exhibiting itself, as if he were saying with a YMCA slick snicker, "After we
break into slang, there's always the danger of the party getting *rough*."
It was that fatal prissiness which must have driven him years ago
into all the militaristic muscle-bending witch-hunting foam-rubber
virilities of the young Senator and the young Vice President. So, now
he talked self-consciously of how the members of his staff, counting
delegates, were "playing what we call 'the strong game.'" SMILE said
his brain. FLASH went the teeth. But his voice seemed to give away
that, whatever they called it, they probably didn't call it "the strong
game," or if they did, *he* didn't. So he framed little phrases, like "a leg
up." Or "my intuition, my 'gut feelings,' so to speak." Deferential air
followed by SMILE-FLASH. Was it possible that one of the secrets
of Old Nixon was that his psyche had been trapped in rock-forma-
tion, nay, geological strata of Sunday school inhibitions? Was it even

possible that he was a good man, not a bad man, a good man who had been trapped by an early milieu whose habits had left him with such innocence about three-quarters of world's experience that he had become an absolute monster of opportunism about the quarter he comprehended all too well? Listening to Nixon now, studying his new modesty, it was impossible to tell whether he was a serious man on the path of returning to his own true seriousness, out to unite the nation again as he promised with every remark: "Reconciliation of the races is a primary objective of the United States," or whether the young devil had reconstituted himself into a more consummate devil, Old Scratch as a modern Abe Lincoln of modesty.

38

RONALD REAGAN, GOP CONVENTION, 1968

(MIAMI AND THE SIEGE OF CHICAGO, 1968)

It was rare when Mailer failed to refer to classic American films and actors when evaluating American politicians. In this excerpt, he notes Ronald Reagan's longtime status as a good-natured loser in a number of Hollywood romantic films (he made more than fifty) in this profile of the then-governor of California.

Let us ... look at Reagan. He had come forward immediately after the first ballot was in, and made a move that the nomination be unanimous. Reagan was smiling when he came up for his plea, he looked curiously more happy than he had looked at any point in the convention, as if he were remembering Barry Goldwater's renunciation of the nomination in 1960, and the profitable results which had ensued, or perhaps he was just pleased because the actor in his soul had issued orders that this was the role to play. For years in the movies he had played the good guy and been proud of it. If he didn't get the girl, it was because he was too good a guy to be overwhelmingly attractive. That was all right. He would grit his teeth and get the girl the next time out. Since this was conceivably the inner sex drama of half of respectable America, he was wildly popular with Republicans. For a party which prided itself on its common sense, they were curiously, even outrageously, sentimental.

Now as Reagan made his plea for unity, he spoke with mildness, a lack of charisma, even a simplicity, which was reminiscent of a good middle-aged stock actor's simplicity—well, you know, fellows, the man I'm playing is an intellectual, and of course I have the kind of mind which even gets confused by a finesse in bridge.

They cheered him wildly, and he looked happy, as if something had gone his way. There was much occasion to recollect him on Thursday when Agnew for Vice President was announced; as the story of this selection developed, the reporter was to think of a view of Reagan he had had on Tuesday afternoon after the reception Nixon had given for the delegates in the American Scene.

On Tuesday the reporter had found Reagan at the Di Lido in downtown Miami Beach where the Alabama and Louisiana delegation were housed. In with Louisiana in a caucus, the Governor came out later to give a quick press conference, pleading ignorance of this situation. Listening to him, it was hard to believe he was fifty-seven, two years older than Nixon, for he had a boy's face, no gray in his head—he was reputed to dye his hair—and his make-up (about which one could hear many a whisper) was too excellent, if applied, to be detected.

Still, unlike Nixon, Reagan was altogether at ease with the Press. They had been good to him, they would be good again—he had the confidence of the elected governor of a big state, precisely what Nixon had always lacked; besides, Reagan had long ago incorporated the confidence of an actor who knows he is popular with interviewers. In fact, he had a public manner which was so natural that his discrepancies appeared only slightly surrealistic: at the age of fifty-seven, he had the presence of a man of thirty, the deferential enthusiasm, the bright but dependably unoriginal mind of a sales manager promoted for his ability over men older than himself. He also had the neatness, and slim economy of move, of a man not massive enough to be President, in the way one might hesitate, let us say, ever to consider a gentleman like Mr. Johnny Carson of television—whatever his fine intelligence—as Chief Executive of a Heavyweight Empire. It was that way with Reagan. He was somehow too light, a lightweight six feet one inch tall—whatever could he do but stick-and-move? Well, he could try to make Generals happy in order to show how heavy he really might be, which gave no heart to consideration of this politics. Besides, darkening shades of the surreal, he had a second personality

which was younger than the first, very young, boyish, maybe thirteen or fourteen, freckles, cowlick, I-tripped-on-my-sneaker-lace aw
shucks variety of confusion. For back on Tuesday afternoon they had
been firing questions at him on the order of how well he was doing
at prying delegates loose from Nixon, and he could only say over and
over, "I don't know. I just don't know. I've been moving around so
quickly talking to so many delegations in caucus that I haven't had
time to read a paper."

"Well, what do the delegations say, Governor?"

"Well, I don't know. They listen to me very pleasantly and politely,
and then I leave and they discuss what I've said. But I can't tell you if
we're gaining. I think we are, but I don't know, I don't know. I hon-
estly don't know, gentlemen," and he broke out into a grin, "I just
don't know," exactly like a thirteen year old, as if indeed gentlemen
he *really* didn't know, and the Press and the delegates listening laughed
with him as if there were no harm in Ronald Reagan, not unless the
lightning struck.

39

EUGENE MCCARTHY I

(MIAMI AND THE SIEGE OF CHICAGO, 1968)

*An admirer of Senator Eugene McCarthy (contender for the Democratic nom-
ination for president) for his opposition to the Vietnam War, Mailer was also
attracted to his Irish love of language and his saturnine wit. In 1996, he and
McCarthy briefly considered making a quixotic run for president (McCarthy)
and vice president (Mailer) on the Democratic ticket.*

The crowd of 5,000 at Midway [Airport in Chicago] waiting for
Gene McCarthy were remarkably homogeneous, young for the
most part, too young to vote, a disproportionate number of babies in
mother's arms—sly hint of middle-class Left mentality here at work!
(The middle-class Left would never learn that workingmen in greasy
dungarees make a point of voting against the mother who carries
the babe—the righteous face of any such mother reminds them of
schoolteachers they used to hate!) Yes, the rally taking place in a special reserved area of the parking lot at Midway gave glimpses of faces
remarkably homogenous for a political rally. One could pass from
heavy-set young men with a full chop of beard and a fifty-pound
pack on their back to young adolescent poetesses, pale as Ophelia,
prim as Florence Nightingale, from college boys in sweaters with
hints of Hippie allegiance, to Madison Avenue types in side-burns,
straw hats, and a species of pill-taking panache; through decent,
mildly fanatic ranks of middle-class professionals—suggestion of viti-
ated blood in their complexion—to that part of theater and show biz
which dependably would take up cause with the cleaner cadres of the
Left. One of their ranks, a pretty brunette in a red dress, was leading

a set of foot-tapping songs while the crowd waited for the Senator's plane, the style of the lyrics out on that soft shoulder between liberalism and wit, and so reminiscent of the sort of songs Adolph Green and Betty Comden had been composing and Tom Lehrer singing for years. "The special fascination of . . . we think he's just sensational . . . *Gene!!!*" two notes sounding on "Gee-yene," so humorous in its vein, for the lyrics implied one was team with a limited gang of humans who derived from Noel Coward, Ogden Nash, and juke hill-billy— "Gee-yene! Gee-yene!"

Song went on: "The GOP will cry in its beer, for here is a man who will change the scene. Gee-yene! Gee-yene!" Depression came over the reporter. Try as he would, he could not make himself happy with McCarthy supporters. Their common denominator seemed to be found in some blank area of the soul, a species of disinfected idealism which gave one the impression when among them of living in a lobotomized ward of Upper Utopia. George Wallace, pay heed!

Of course, the reporter had been partisan to Bobby Kennedy, excited by precisely his admixture of idealism plus willingness to traffic with demons, ogres, and overloads of corruption. This had characterized the political style of the Kennedys more than once. The Kennedys had seemed magical because they were a little better than they should have been, and so gave promise of making America a little better than it ought to be. The reporter respected McCarthy, he respected him enormously for trying the vengeance of Lyndon Johnson, his heart had been given a bit of life by the success of the New Hampshire primary campaign. If there had then been little to make him glad in the abrupt and unhappy timing of Bobby Kennedy's immediate entrance into the race for nomination, he had, nonetheless, remained Kennedy's man— he saw the battle between the two as tragic; he had hardly enjoyed the Kennedy-McCarthy debate on television before the California primary; he had not taken pleasure in rooting for Kennedy and being thereby forced to condemn McCarthy's deadness of manner, blankness of affect, and suggestion of weakness in each deep pouch beneath each eye. The pouches spoke of clichés—eyes sitting in staffing brassieres of flesh, such stuff. He knew that McCarthy partisans would find equal fault somewhere in Kennedy.

40

Eugene McCarthy II

(MIAMI AND THE SIEGE OF CHICAGO, 1968)

This second excerpt depicting Senator McCarthy is a brilliant thumbnail portrait of the candidate in action. It also reveals the admiration for the poetry of Robert Lowell that he shared with Mailer. Lowell was a strong supporter of McCarthy's candidacy and spoke at several of McCarthy's campaign events.

Years ago, in 1960, the reporter had had two glimpses of Eugene McCarthy. At the Democratic National Convention in Los Angeles that nominated John F. Kennedy, McCarthy made a speech for another candidate. It was the best nominating speech the reporter had ever heard. He had written about it with the metaphor of a bullfight:

> He held the crowd like a matador gathering their emotion, discharging it, creating new emotion on the wave of the last, driving his passes tighter and tighter as he readied for the kill. "Do not reject this man who made us all proud to be called Democrats, do not leave this prophet without honor in his own party." McCarthy went on, his muleta furled for the naturales. "There was only one man who said let's talk sense to the American people. He said the promise of America is the promise of greatness. This was his call to greatness.... Do not forget this man.... Ladies and gentlemen, I present to you not the favorite son of one state, but the favorite son of the fifty states, the favorite son of every country he has visited, the favorite son of every country which has not seen him but is secretly thrilled by his name." Bedlam. The kill. "Ladies and gentlemen, I present to

you Adlai Stevenson of Illinois." Ears and tail. Hooves and bull.
A roar went up like the roar one heard the day Bobby Thomp-
son hit his home run at the Polo Grounds and the Giants won
the pennant from the Dodgers in the third playoff of the 1951
season. The demonstration cascaded on to the floor, the gallery
came to its feet, the sports arena sounded like the inside of a
marching drum.

Perhaps three months later, just after this piece on that convention had appeared, and election time was near, he had met Senator
McCarthy at another cocktail party on Central Park West to raise
money for the campaign of Mark Lane, then running for state assem-
blyman in New York. The reporter had made a speech himself that
day. Having decided, on the excitements of the Kennedy candidacy
and other excitements (much marijuana for one) to run for Mayor
of New York the following year, he gave his maiden address at that
party, a curious, certainly a unique political speech, private, personal,
tortured in metaphor, sublimely indifferent to issues, platform or any
recognizable paraphernalia of the political process, and delivered in
much too rapid a voice to the assembled bewilderment of his audience, a collective (and by the end very numb) stiff clavicle of Jewish
Central Park West matrons. The featured speaker, Senator McCarthy,
was to follow, and climbing up on the makeshift dais as he stepped
down, the Senator gave him a big genial wide-as-the-open-plains
Midwestern grin.

"Better learn how to breathe, boy," he whispered out of the corner of his mouth, and proceeded to entertain the audience for the
next few minutes with a mixture of urbanity, professional elegance,
and political savvy. That was eight years ago.

But now, near to eight years later, the hour was different, the
audience at this cocktail party in Cambridge with their interminable
questions and advice, their over-familiarity yet excessive reverence,
their desire to touch McCarthy, prod him, *galvanize* him, seemed to
do no more than drive him deeper into the insulations of his fatigue,
his very disenchantment—so his pores seemed to speak—with the
democratic process. . . . And now the threat of assassination over all,

that too, that his death might come like the turn of a card, and could a man be ready? The gloomy, empty, tomb-like reverberations of the last shot shaking rough waves doubtless through his own dreams, for his eyes, sensitive, friendly, and remote as the yellow eyes of an upper primate in a cage, spoke out of the weary, sagging face, above the sagging pouches, seeming to say, "Yes, try to rescue me—but as you see, it's not quite possible." And the reporter, looking to perform the errand of rescue, went in to talk about the speech of 1960 in Los Angeles, and how it was the second best political speech he had ever heard.

"Oh," said McCarthy, "tell me, what was the best?"

And another questioner jostled the circle about McCarthy to ask another question, the Secret Service man in the gray suit at McCarthy's elbow stiffening at the impact. But McCarthy held the questioner at a distance by saying, "No, I'd like to listen for a while." It had obviously become his pleasure to listen to others. So the reporter told a story about Vito Marcantonio in Yankee Stadium in 1948, and the Senator listened carefully, almost sadly, as if remembering other hours of oratory.

On the way to the door, in the press of guests and local party workers up to shake his hand before he was gone, a tall bearded fellow, massive chin, broad brow for broad horn-rimmed glasses spoke out in a resonant voice, marred only by the complacency of certain nasal intrigues. "Senator, I'm a graduate student in English, and I like your politics very much, but I must tell you, I think your poetry stinks."

McCarthy took it like a fighter being slapped by the referee across the forearms. "You see what it is, running for President," said the laughter in his eyes. If he worshipped at a shrine, it was near the saint of good humor. "Give my regards to Robert Lowell," said the reporter. "Say to him that I read 'The Drunken Fisherman' just the other day."

McCarthy looked like the victim in the snow when the St. Bernard comes up with the rum. His eyes came alight at the name of the poem. "I will catch Christ with a greased worm," might have been the line he remembered. He gave a little wave and was out the door.

Yet the reporter was depressed after the meeting. McCarthy did not look or feel like a President, not that tall tired man with his bright subtle eyes which could sharpen the razor's edge of a nuance, no he seemed like the dean of the finest English department in the land. There wasn't that sense of a man with vast ambition and sufficient character to make it luminous, so there was not that charisma which leaves no argument about the nature of the attempt.

41

MAYOR DALEY, CLANSMAN

(MIAMI AND THE SIEGE OF CHICAGO, 1968)

Richard J. Daley, mayor of Chicago from 1955 to 1976, was one of the last big city political bosses. On August 28, 1968, during the Democratic Convention, it was at his order that policemen brutally attacked massed antiwar demonstrators as well as reporters and bystanders on Michigan Avenue as they chanted, "The whole world is watching." The violence was later described by a national investigative commission on violence as "a police riot." Mailer's portrait of the mayor culminates in a damning assessment of President Johnson's role behind the scene prior to the convention.

On March 31 [1968], on a night when the latest Gallup Poll showed President Lyndon B. Johnson to be in favor with only 35 percent of the American public (while only 23 percent approved his handling of the war), he announced on national television that he would not seek nor "accept the nomination of my party as your President." On April 2, there was talk that [Vice President] Humphrey would run— McCarthy had taken the Wisconsin primary with 57 percent of the vote to Johnson's 35 percent (and it was estimated that if Johnson had not resigned, the vote would have been more like 64 percent to 28 percent).

On April 4, Martin Luther King, Jr. was assassinated by a white man, and violence, fire and looting broke out in Memphis, Harlem, Brooklyn, Washington, D.C., Chicago, Detroit, Boston and Newark over the next week. Mayor Daley gave his famous "shoot to kill" instruction to the Chicago police, and National Guard and U.S. troops were sent to some of these cities.

On April 23 Columbia students barricaded the office of a Dean. By another day the campus was disrupted, then closed, and was never to be comfortably open again for the rest of the semester. On May 10, as if indicative of a spontaneous world-wide movement, the students of the Sorbonne battled the Paris police on barricades and in the streets. On the same day, Maryland was quietly pledging its delegates to Humphrey.

On June 3, Andy Warhol was shot. On June 4, after winning the California primary 45 percent to 42 percent for McCarthy, and 12 percent for Humphrey, RFK was shot in the head and died the next day. The cannibalistic war of the McCarthy and Kennedy peace forces was at an end. McCarthy had been all but finished in Indiana, Nebraska, Iowa, and South Dakota; Kennedy had been badly mauled by his defeat in Oregon. Meanwhile Humphrey had been picking up delegates in states like Missouri, which did not have primaries, and the delegates in states which did, like Pennsylvania, after it had given 90 percent of its vote to McCarthy.

So went the month. Cleveland with its first Negro Mayor still had a riot. Spock, Goodman, Ferber and Coffin were sentenced to two years in jail [for interfering with the draft]. Kentucky with 46 delegates gave 41 to Humphrey, and the McCarthy supporters walked out. There were stories every other day of Humphrey's desire to have Teddy Kennedy for Vice President, and much comment in columns on the eagerness of the Democrats to move the convention from Chicago. Chicago had a telephone strike and the likelihood of a taxi strike and a bus strike. Chicago was to be unwilling host to a Yippie (Youth International Party) convention the week the Democrats would be there. Chicago had the massive bull temper of Mayor Daley for the Democratic Party to contend with—much work went on behind the scenes to move the convention to Miami where the telephone and television lines were in, and Daley would be out. But Daley was not about to let the convention leave his city. Daley promised he would enforce the peace and allow no outrageous demonstrations, Daley hinted that his wrath—if the convention were moved—might burn away whole corners of certain people's support. Since Hubert Humphrey was the one who could most qualify for certain people, he was in no hurry to offend the Mayor. Lyndon Johnson, when beseeched by interested parties to encourage Daley to agree to the move, was rumored to have said, "Miami Beach is not an American city."

The TV networks applied massive pressure to shift the convention. In Chicago, because of the strictures of the strike, their cameras would be limited to the hotels and to the Amphitheatre—they would not be able to take their portable generators out to the street and run lines to their color cameras. That would not be permitted. They were restricted to movie cameras, which would make them half a day late in reporting action or interviews in the streets (half a day late for television is equal to being a week late). How they must have focused their pressure on Daley and Johnson. It is to the Mayor's curious credit that he was strong enough to withstand them. It should have been proof interior that Daley was no other-directed twentieth-century politician. Any such man would have known the powers of retaliation which resided in the mass media. One did not make an enemy of a television network for nothing; they could repay injury with no more than a chronic slur in the announcer's voice every time your deadly name was mentioned over the next twelve months, or next twelve years. Daley, however, was not a national politician, but a clansman— he could get 73 percent of the vote in any constituency made up of people whose ancestors were at home with rude instruments in Polish forests, Ukrainian marshes, Irish bogs—they knew how to defend the home: so did he. No interlopers for any network of Jew-Wasp media men were going to dominate the streets of his parochial city, nor none of their crypto-accomplices with long hair, sexual liberty, drug license and unbridled mouths. It was as if the primitive powers of the Mayor's lungs, long accustomed to breathing all variety of blessings and curses (from the wind of ancestors, constituents, and screaming beasts in the stockyards where he had once labored for a decade or more) could take everything into his chest, mighty barrel of a chest in Richard J. Daley, 200 pounds, 5 feet 8 inches tall. These blessings and curses, once prominently and in public breathed in, could be processed, pulverized, and washed into the choleric blood, defiance in the very pap and hemoglobin of it—"I'll swallow up their spit and shove it through," the Mayor could always bellow to his electorate. So Daley was ready to take on the electronic wrath of the semi-conductors of the world, his voter-nourished blood full of beef and curses against the transistorized communicatory cabals of the media. And back of him—no evidence will ever be produced to prove such a thought—must have been Lyndon Johnson, great wounded secret shaman of the Democratic Party. If Teddy Roosevelt had once wrecked William Howard Taft and the Republican Party by running as a Bull Moose, so Lyndon Johnson was now a warlock of a Bull Moose, conceiving through all the months of June, July and August how he could proceed to create a cursed convention, a platform, a candidate, and a party which would be his own as much as the nightmarish vision of a phantom ship is the soul of a fever; he would seek to rend his party, crack it in two—that party to which his own allegiance in near to forty years could hardly be questioned—because the party had been willing to let him go. In revenge he would create a candidate who need never run, for his campaign would be completed by the nomination. Conceive what he would have thought of a candidate who could attract more votes than himself.

42

HIPPIES, YIPPIES, AND SCHIZOPHRENIA

(MIAMI AND THE SIEGE OF CHICAGO, 1968)

The Yippies' involvement in the antiwar activities at the 1968 Democratic Convention in Chicago was led by Abbie Hoffman and Jerry Rubin, both of whom had joined Mailer in the 1967 March on the Pentagon. Both Hoffman and Rubin were arrested in Chicago, which led to the notorious trial of the Chicago Seven for conspiracy and crossing state lines to incite a riot. After appeal, all seven were exonerated.

The Hippies founded their temple in that junction where LSD crosses that throb of an electric guitar in full volume in the ear, solar plexus, belly, and loins. A tribal unity had passed through the youth of America (and half the nations of the world), a far-out vision of orgiastic revels stripped of violence or even the differentiation of sex. In the oceanic stew of a non-violent, tribal ball on drugs, nipples, arms, phalluses, mouths, wombs, armpits, short-hairs, navels, breasts and cheeks, incense of odor, flower and funk went humping into Break-through Freak-out Road together, and children on acid saw Valhalla, Nepenthe, and the Taj Mahal. Some went out forever, some went screaming down the alleys of the mad where cockroaches drive like Volkswagens on the oilcloth of the moon, gluttons found vertigo in centrifuges of consciousness, vomitoriums of ingestion; others found love, some manifest of love in light, in shards of Nirvana, sparks of satori—they came back to the world a twentieth-century tribe wearing celebration bells and filthy garments. Used-up livers gave their complexions a sickly pale, and hair grew on their faces like weeds. Yet they had seen some incontestable vision of the good—the universe was not absurd to them; like pilgrims they looked at society with the eyes of children: society was absurd. Every emperor who went down the path was naked, and they handed flowers to policemen.

It could hardly last. The slum in which they chose to live—for they were refugees in the main from the middle class—fretted against them, fretted against their filth, their easy casual cohabiting, their selflessness (which is always the greatest insult to the ghetto, for selflessness is a luxury to the poor, it beckons to the spineless, the undifferentiated, the inept, the derelict, the drowning—a poor man is nothing without the fierce thorns of his ego). So the Hippies collided with the slums, and were beaten and robbed, fleeced and lashed and buried and imprisoned, and here and there murdered, and here and there successful, for there were scattered liaisons with bikers and Panthers and Puerto Ricans on the East Coast and Mexicans on the west. There came a point when, like most tribes, they divided. Some of the weakest and some of the least attached went back to the suburbs or moved up into commerce or communications; others sought gentler homes where the sun was kind and the flowers plentiful; others hardened, and like all pilgrims with their own vision of a promised land, began to learn how to work for it, and finally, how to fight for it. So the Yippies came out of the Hippies, ex-Hippies, diggers, bikers, drop-outs from college, hipsters up from the South. They made a community of sorts, for their principles were simple—everybody, obviously, must be allowed to do (no way around the next three words) his own thing, provided he hurt no one doing it—they were yet to learn that society is built on many people hurting many people, it is just who does the hurting which is forever in dispute. They did not necessarily understand how much their simple presence hurt many good citizens in the secret velvet of the heart—the Hippies and probably the Yippies did not quite recognize the depth of that schizophrenia on which society is built. We call it hypocrisy, but it is schizophrenia, a modest ranch-house life with Draconian military adventures; a land of equal opportunity where a white culture sits upon a black; a horizontal community of Christian love and a vertical society of churches—the cross was well designed! A land of family, a land of illicit heat; a politics of principle, a politics of property; nation of mental hygiene with movies and TV reminiscent of a mental pigpen; patriots with a detestation of obscenity who pollute their rivers; citizens with a detestation of government control who cannot bear any situation not controlled. The list must be endless, the comic profits are finally small—the society was able to stagger on like a 400-pound policeman walking uphill because living in such an unappreciated and obese state it did not at least have to explode into schizophrenia—life went on. Boys could patiently go to church at home and wait their turn to burn villages in Vietnam. What the Yippies did not recognize is that their demand for all-accelerated entrance into twentieth-century Utopia (where modern mass man would have all the opportunities before him at once and could create and despoil with equal conscience—up against the wall mother-fucker, let me kiss your feet), whether a vision to be desired or abhorred, was nonetheless equal to straight madness for the Average Good American, since his liberated expression might not be an outpouring of love, but the burning of his neighbor's barn. Or, since we are in Chicago, smashing good neighbor's skull with a brick from his own back yard. Yippies, even McCarthyites, represented nothing less by their presence than the destruction of every saving hypocrisy with consequent collision for oneself—if it is not easy to live every day holding up the wall of your own sanity.

43

GOOD COPS, BAD COPS

(MIAMI AND THE SIEGE OF CHICAGO, 1968)

Mailer's anatomy of the psychology of the police is especially relevant after the murder of George Floyd by Minneapolis policeman Derek Chauvin in May 2020.

It is that minority—cop and crook—which seeks issue for violence who now attract our attention. The criminal attempts to reduce tension within himself by expressing in the direct language of action whatever is most violent and outrageous outraged in his depths; to the extent he is not a powerful man, his violence is merely antisocial, like self-exposure, embezzlement, or passing bad checks. The cop tries to solve his violence by blanketing it with a uniform. That is virtually a commonplace, but it explains why cops will put up with poor salary, public dislike, uncomfortable working conditions and a general sense of bad conscience. They know they are lucky; they know they are getting away with a successful solution to the criminality they can taste in their blood. This taste is practically in the forefront of a cop's brain; he is in a stink of perspiration whenever he goes into action; he can tolerate little in the way of insult, and virtually no contradiction; he lies with a simplicity and quick confidence which will stifle the breath of any upright citizen who encounters it innocently for the first time. The difference between a good cop and a bad cop is that the good cop will at least do no more than give his own salted version of events—the bad cop will make up his version. That is why the police arrested the pedestrians at the Haymarket Inn at the Conrad Hilton: the guiltier the situation in which a policeman finds himself, the more he will attack the victim of his guilt.

There are—it is another commonplace—decent policemen. A few are works of art. And some police, violent when they are young, mellow into modestly corrupt, humorous and decently efficient officials. Every public figure with power, every city official, high politician or prominent government worker knows in his unspoken sentiments that the police are an essentially criminal force restrained by their guilt, their covert awareness that they are imposters, and by a sprinkling of career men whose education, rectitude, athletic ability, and religious dedication make them work for a balance between justice and authority. These men, who frighten the average cop as a priest frightens a choirboy, are the thin restraining edge of civilization for a police force. That, and the average corrupt cop's sense that he is not wanted that much by anyone.

What staggered the delegates [to the Democratic National Convention] who witnessed the attack—more accurate to call it a massacre, since it was sudden, unprovoked and total—on Michigan Avenue, was that it opened the specter of what it might mean for the police to take over society. They might comport themselves in such a case not as a force of law and order, not even as a force of repression upon civil disorder, but as a true criminal force, chaotic, improvisational, undisciplined, and finally—sufficiently aroused—uncontrollable.

Society was held together by bonds no more powerful proportionately than spider's silk: no one knew this better than the men who administered a society. So images of the massacre opened a nightmare. The more there was disorder in the future, the more there would be need for larger numbers of police and more the need to indulge them. But if the Army became the punitive force of society, then the Pentagon would become the only meaningful authority in the land.

44

A NATIONAL DISORDER

(MIAMI AND THE SIEGE OF CHICAGO, 1968)

The complex, tattered relations between Blacks and whites in the United States, which is at the heart of Mailer's fears for the devolution of democracy into chaos, is described in this excerpt, which also explores Mailer's fears about how his life as a writer might be endangered by taking a prominent role in the Chicago antiwar demonstrations.

He had an enormous amount of work before him if he was going to describe this convention, and only two weeks in which to do it if his article was to appear before election. A bad beating might lose him days, or a week; each day of writing would be irreplaceable to him. Besides, a variety of militant choices would now be present for years. One simply could not accept the dangerous alternative every time; he would never do any other work. And then with another fear, conservative was this fear, he looked into his reluctance to lose even the America he had had, that insane warmongering technology land with its smog, its superhighways, its experts and its profound dishonesty. Yet it had allowed him to write—it had even not deprived him entirely of honors, certainly not an income. He had lived well enough to have six children, a house on the water, a good apartment, good meals, good booze, he had even come to enjoy wine. A revolutionary with a taste for wine has come already half the distance from Marx to Burke [Edmund, conservative writer and parliamentarian, 1729–97]; he belonged in England where one's radicalism might never be tested; no, truth, he was still enough of a novelist to have the roots of future work in every vein and stratum he encountered, and a profound part

of him (exactly that enormous literary bottom of the mature novelist's property!) detested the thought of seeing his American society—
evil, absurd, touching, pathetic, sickening, comic, full of novelistic
marrow—disappear now in the nihilistic maw of a national disorder.
The Yippies might yet disrupt the land—or worse, since they would
not really have the power to do that, might serve as a pretext to bring
in totalitarian phalanxes of law and order. Of course that was why he
was getting tired of Negro rights and Black Power—every black riot
was washing him loose with the rest, pushing him to the point where
he might have to throw his vote in with revolution—what a tedious
perspective of prisons and law courts and worse; or stand by and
watch as the best Americans white and black would be picked off,
expended, busted, burned and finally lost. No, exile would be better.
Yet he loathed the thought of living anywhere but America—he was
too American by now: he did not wish to walk down foreign streets
with imperfect nostalgia of dirty grease on groovy hamburgers, not
when he didn't even eat them here. And then there might not be any
foreign lands, not for long. The plague he had written about for years
seemed to be coming in—he would understand its social phenomena
more quickly than the rest. Or would, if he did not lose his detachment and have to purchase cheap hope. Drinking across the street
from Grant Park, the possibility of succumbing to fears larger than
himself appeared. If not more than a spot on the horizon, still possible
to him. No more than a spot on the horizon had seemed [Senator
Hubert] Humphrey's candidacy when first it was bruited. Was that
why delegates were marching now with candles? So that they would
not succumb to fears larger than themselves?

It was as if the historical temperature of America went up every
month. At different heats, the oils of separate psyches were loos-
ened—different good Americans began to fry. Of course their first
impulse was to hope the temperature would be quickly reduced. Perhaps they could go back to the larder again. But if it continued, then
the particular solution that had provided him with a modicum at
least of worldly happiness—the fine balance he might have achieved
between the satisfaction of idealism and the satisfaction of need (call
it greed) would be disrupted altogether, and then his life could not go

on as it had. In the size of his fear, he was discovering how large a loss that would be. He liked his life. He wanted it to go on, which meant he wanted America to go on—not as it was going, not Vietnam—but what price was he really willing to pay? Was he willing to give up the pleasures of making his movies, writing his books? They were pleasures finally he did not want to lose.

Yet if he indulged his fear, found all the ways to avoid the oncoming ugly encounters, then his life was equally spoiled, and on the poorer side. He was simply not accustomed to living with a conscience as impure as the one with which he watched from the nineteenth floor. Or had it really been impure. Where was his true engagement? To be forty-five years old, and have lost a sense of where his loyalties belonged—to the revolution or to the stability of the country (at some painful price it could be expected) was to bring upon himself the anguish of the European intellectual in the Thirties. And the most powerful irony for himself is that he had lived for a dozen empty hopeless years after the Second World War with the bitterness, rage, and potential militancy of a real revolutionary, he had had some influence perhaps upon this generation of Yippies now in the street, but no revolution had arisen in the years when he was ready—the timing of his soul was apocalyptically maladroit.

These are large thoughts for a reporter to have. Reporters live happily removed from themselves. They have eyes to see, ears to hear, and fingers for the notes in their report. It was as if the drink he took in now moved him millimeter by millimeter out from one hat into another. He would be driven yet to participate or keep the shame in his liver—the last place to store such emotion! Liver disease is the warehousing of daily shame—they will trace the chemistry yet!

45

Bobby Kennedy Remembered

(MIAMI AND THE SIEGE OF CHICAGO, 1968)

Mailer supported Senator Robert F. Kennedy for the 1968 Democratic presidential nomination and, after his June 1968 assassination, was asked by the Kennedy family to stand watch next to his coffin in St. Patrick's Cathedral, along with New York City newspaperman Jimmy Breslin, Mailer's running mate when he sought the nomination for mayor of New York the following year.

He looked more like a boy on the day of his death, a nice boy, nicer than the kid with the sharp rocky glint in his eye, who had gone to work for [Senator] Joe McCarthy in his early twenties, and had then known everything that there was to know about getting ahead in politics. He had grown modest as he grew older and his wit had grown with him—he had become a funny man ... wry, simple for one instant, shy and off to the side in the next, but with a sort of marvelous boy's wisdom, as if he knew the world was very bad and knew the intimate style of how it was bad, as only boys can sometime know (for they feel it in their parents and their schoolteachers and their friends). Yet he had confidence he was going to fix it.... Since his brother's death a subtle sadness had come to live in the tone of his confidence, as though he were confident he would win—if he did not lose. That could also happen, and that could happen quickly. He had come into that world where people live with the recognition of tragedy, and so are often afraid of happiness, for they know that one is never in so much danger as when victorious/and or happy—that is when the devils seems to have their hour, and hawks seize something living from the gambol of the field.

The reporter met Bobby Kennedy just once. It was on an afternoon in May [1968] in New York just after his victory in the Indiana
[presidential] primary and it had not been a famous meeting, even
though it began well. The Senator came in from a conference (for the
reporter was being granted an audience) and said quickly with a grin,
"Mr. Mailer, you're a mean man with a word." He had answered, "On
the contrary, Senator, I like to think of myself as a gracious writer."

"Oh," said Senator Kennedy, with a wave of his hand, "that too,
that too!"

So it had gone well enough, and the reporter had been taken
with Kennedy's appearance. He was slimmer even than one would
have thought, not strong, not weak, somewhere between a blade of
grass and a blade of steel, fine, finely drawn, finely honed, a fine flush
of color in his cheeks, two very white front teeth, prominent as the
two front teeth of a rabbit, so his mouth had no hint of the cruelty
or calculation of a politician who weighs counties, cities, and states,
but was rather a mouth ready to nip at anything that attracted its
contempt or endangered its ideas. Then there were his eyes. They
were most unusual. His brother Teddy Kennedy spoke of those "who
followed him, honored him, lived in his mild and magnificent eye,"
and that was fair description for he had very large blue eyes, the iris
wide in diameter, near to twice the width of the average eye, and the
blue was a milky blue like a marble so that his eyes, while prominent,
did not show the separate steps and slopes of light some bright eyes
show, but rather were gentle, indeed beautiful—one was tempted to
speak of velvety eyes—their surface seemed made of velvet as if one
could touch them, and the surface would not be repelled.

He was as attractive as a movie star. Not attractive like his brother
had been, for Jack Kennedy had looked like the sort of leading man
who would steal the girl from Ronald Reagan every time, no, Bobby
Kennedy had looked more like a phenomenon of a movie star—he
could have filled some magic empty space between Mickey Rooney
and James Dean, they would have cast him sooner or later in some
remake of *Mr. Smith Goes to Washington*, and everyone would have
said, "Impossible casting! He's too young." And he was too young.
Too young for Senator, too young for President, it felt strange in his

presence thinking of him as President, as if the country would be giddy, like the whirl of one's stomach in the drop of an elevator or jokes about an adolescent falling in love, it was incredible to think of him as President, and yet marvelous, as if only a marvelous country would dare have him.

That was the best of the meeting—meeting him! The reporter spent the rest of his valuable thirty minutes arguing with the Senator about Senator McCarthy. He begged him to arrange some sort of truce or liaison, but made a large mistake from the outset. He went on in a fatuous voice, sensing error too late to pull back, about how effective two Irish Catholics would be on the same ticket for if there were conservative Irishmen who could vote against one of them, where was the Irish Catholic in America who could vote against two? . . .

Kennedy said, "I wonder why you don't support Senator [Eugene] McCarthy. He seems more like your kind of man, Mr. Mailer," and in answer, oddly moved, he had said in a husky voice, "No, I'm supporting you. I know it wasn't easy for you to go in." And even began to mutter a few remarks about how he understood that powerful politicians would not have trusted Kennedy if he had moved too quickly, for his holding was large, and men with large holdings were not supportable if they leaped too soon. "I know that," he said looking into the Senator's mild and magnificent eye, and Kennedy nodded, and in return a little later Kennedy sighed, and exhaled his breath, looked sad for an instant, and said, "Who knows? Who knows? Perhaps I should have gone in earlier." A few minutes later they said goodbye, not unpleasantly. That was the last he saw of him.

The closest he was to come again was to stand in vigil for fifteen minutes as a member of the honor guard about his coffin in St. Patrick's. Lines filed by. People had waited in line for hours, five hours, six hours, more, inching forward through the day and through the police lines on the street in order to take one last look at the closed coffin.

The poorest of the working-class of New York had turned out, poor Negro men and women, Puerto Ricans, Irish washerwomen, old Jewish ladies who looked like they ran grubby little newsstands, children, adolescents, families, men with hands thick and lined and horny as oyster shells, calluses like barnacles, came filing by to bob a look at that coffin covered by a flag. Some women walked by praying, and knelt and touched the coffin with their fingertips as they passed, and after a time the flag would slip from the pressure of their fingers and an usher detailed for the purpose would readjust it. The straightest line between two points is the truth of an event, no matter how long it takes or far it winds, and if it had taken these poor people six hours of waiting in line to reach that coffin, then the truth was in the hours. A river of working-class people came down to march past Kennedy's coffin, and this endless line of people had really loved him like no political figure in years has been loved.

46

PAT NIXON: PORTRAIT OF A FIRST LADY

(ST. GEORGE AND THE GODFATHER, 1972)

Pat Nixon (1912–93) married Richard Nixon in 1940. They had two daughters, Tricia and Julie. Mailer's admiration for her poise and grit is obvious in this excerpt from his account of the 1972 national political conventions.

Pat Nixon arrives with her daughters at the gate of the Fontaine-bleau. . . . There is a flood of cheers when she comes up in her black Cadillac—much like the on-off hysteria you hear when the team hits the field, and all the signs wave. Now, the signs painted by the YVPers all begin to wave, these Young Voters for the President who in the eyes of the liberal Press will yet look as ears of goldenrod to hay fever sufferers. Somebody has provided all YVPers with the paint, no dark secret, Republican money can be spent for Republican posters and paint, but the kids have done the work themselves and the signs say "We stand for Pat"; "We Love Julie"; "Trish You're a dish"; "Miami loves the 1st family"—there is just a hint of the slovenly in the uncertain use of capital letters. "Welcome back, Pat"; "Agnew for peace"; "Vote for a WINNER"; "Nixon gives a damn"—here is one—"Nixon is For Love." Now kids are chanting "Four more years," "Hey, hey, whateya say, Nixon, Nixon, all the way." They are not the most attractive faces he has seen. Hundreds of young faces and not one is a beauty, neither by natural good looks nor by the fine-tuning of features through vitality or wit—the children in this crowd remind him of other crowds he knows well, and does not like. Of course!—they are the faces of the wad!—all those blobs of faces who line up outside TV theaters and wait for hours that they may get in to see the show live, yes, the show will be more alive than their faces. The genius of Nixon! Has he selected this gaggle of mildly stunted minds from photograph files? Or had they been handed applications as they left the theaters after the live shows? Aquarius [using the third person, Mailer refers to himself as Aquarius] remembers the look of the television set in his room at the Fontainebleau. It was up on a small pickled-white dais and looked like some kind of altar for a medico-religious event. Nixon may have drawn the deep significance from such a sight twenty years ago—how valuable must be the insights he could pass on to McLuhan, well, Aquarius was frothing again and so came near to missing the value of Pat Nixon's entrance ... to the hotel in a pink dress, then her immersion later into the reception crowd with a royal-blue dress, long-sleeved, straight-skirted, a light soft material vulnerable to crowds, she was able to demonstrate that particular leathery hard-riding sense of grace she possessed which spoke of stamina first, for she could knee and elbow her own defense through a crowd and somehow never involve the dress, that was one of the straight-out tools of her trade and she knew how to employ it—that material was not going to get snagged on some dolt's ragged elbow or *ripped* any more than a seaman would get his feet caught in a rope he was coiling in a storm.

So, for instance, had she managed her passage through the lobby for the reception, pointing her head at an angle up to the glare of the Media lights poised like flaming swords over her way, the ears inured to the sound of another brass combo (with one black trumpeter, trombone, banjo, other trumpet, and drums), still she moves a little to it, just a flash, as though to demonstrate that dancing is one of the hundred and sixty-eight light occupations she can muster.... There are liver spots to perceive on her hands, and her teeth must be capped, she has obviously pinched and pushed and tightened her presentation of herself all her life, but she had ridden the beast of such discipline, she looks better now than when she entered politics. No, she has emerged as a pro, such a pro indeed with such a pride in having mastered every side of her occupation that one did not ask oneself if she liked shaking hands. Possibly the question did not exist for her, since it was a matter of indifference whether she liked it or no—she was not on earth to like things but to do them! ...

If Pat Nixon had been a writer, she would have gravitated to the commonest words that everyone used or the most functional words— she would have wanted to reach the largest audiences with ideas they could comprehend on first reading—that was how she shook hands. Like a *Reader's Digest* editor attacked a paragraph. She loved to work with the wad. Give her the plainest dullest face, no spark, no flair, just the urgency to get what it wants—her autograph, her handshake. She gave them out equally, like the bills and smiles of a bank teller. There are faces to greet, currency to handle, stay on top of the job!

In his own mayoralty campaign, Aquarius ended up by shaking hands wherever he could, had in fact to his surprise ended up liking that act more than anything else in politics, at least once he comprehended that the only way to do it was to offer as much of himself as was present with every greeting. The phenomenon was that energy came back, and the hand did not get tired. It was as if in shaking a thousand hands, six hundred may have returned a little more energy than they took, as if the generosity of a mass of people might be larger than their greed, a belief which was as it should be if one wanted to become a politician, for it gave, on balance, some confidence at the thought of working for others.

But Pat Nixon had obviously come from folds of human endeavor which believed the reward for service was not to be found in the act but afterward. Naturally she gave energy and she took energy, impossible not to, and was somewhat wilted if with a glow when she was done, but it was the muscles of her arm which worked, and the muscles in her smile, her soul was the foreman of the act, and so did not reside in her muscles, but off to the side and vigilant as she worked the machine. She no longer saw faces, no, she was a heavy worker on an assembly line, and bodies came her way, there were touches and taps, a gloved rhythm to keep—she moved in some parallel perhaps to the burden of a slim tight-mouthed Negress with heavy family worries on a heavy assembly line for whom the pay was good and so she was in it until death or double overtime. So, too, would Pat Nixon have no inner guilt before trade unionists or blacks—she had worked as hard as any of them in her own way, she moved as well. Afterward, her fixed expression stayed in memory for she had the features of a woman athlete or the heroine of some insurmountable disease which she has succeeded in surmounting.

A man getting an autograph from her asks, "How do you stay so young?"

She smiles carefully. "With hard work," she says.

47

Lunch with Kissinger

(ST. GEORGE AND THE GODFATHER, 1972)

Henry Kissinger (b. 1923), Nixon's secretary of state, a hard-knuckle prac-
titioner of realpolitik, was nevertheless courtly and approachable, and Mailer
had harbored a small hope that they might find a patch of common ground for
dialogue ever since Kissinger had invited him to speak at one of his Harvard
seminars. Kissinger also made a favorable comment in print about Mailer's
1991 CIA novel, Harlot's Ghost, *a kindness which drew from Mailer an*
appreciative note and the observation that this approval put them in the swim
together. As the following excerpt shows, they relished each other's company,
even though nothing separated their political views but an abyss.

A young Secret Service man ... conducted him across the North
Lawn. A receptionist apologized politely for the delay. Ushered
through a door into a hallway, he was met by Kissinger who gave
the greatest of broad smiles, pumped his hand, and said in a deep and
gutty German accent, "Today must be my day for masochism since I
dare to be interviewed by you."

Almost immediately, they were in his office, large and full of light.
"We have a momentous decision to make instantly," said Kissinger.
"It is: where shall we eat? I can offer you respectable food if you
wish the interview here, not exciting but respectable, and we won't
be interrupted. Or we can go to a restaurant just around the corner
where the food will be very good and we will be interrupted a little
although not very much."

Similar in height and build, it was probable they would not wish
to miss a good lunch. So in much less time than it took him to

enter, he left the White House (that most placid of mansions!) with Kissinger, hardly noticing the same Secret Service man who unobtrusively—it was the word!—had stopped the traffic on Pennsylvania Avenue while they crossed. If not for just such a rare American pomp, he could have had the impression that he knew Kissinger over the years. For as they walked along, chatting with no pain, it was much as if the learned doctor had been an editor of some good and distinguished quarterly, and they were promenading to lunch in order to talk over a piece.

In fact, that was the first topic—his piece. "We must, from the beginning," said Kissinger, "establish ground rules. We may make them whatever you wish, but we have to keep them. I can speak frankly with you, or not so frankly. But if I am frank, then you have to allow me the right to see what you put into my mouth. It is not because of vanity, or because of anything you may say about me, you may say anything you wish about me, in fact"—with the slyest grin—"you will probably hurt my position more if you say good things than bad, but I have, when all is said, a position I must be responsible to. Now if you don't wish to agree to such a procedure, we can do the interview at arm's length, which of course I'm used to and you need show me nothing. Either method is agreeable, provided we establish the rules."

They had by now reached Sans Souci, and Kissinger's advance to his table was not without ceremony. Since he was hardly back twenty-four hours from Paris and some talks with the North Vietnamese, the headwaiter teased him over the pains of quitting Parisian cuisine. Passing by the table of Larry O'Brien there were jokes about Watergate.

"That was good luck, Henry, to get away just before it hit the fan," said O'Brien.

"Ah, what a pity," said Kissinger. "You could have had me for the villain of the sixth floor."

And a friend intercepted him before he could take his seat. "Henry, what truth to the rumor that McGovern is picking you for Vice President?"

Kissinger chuckled. "Twenty-two thousand people in the State Department will be very happy." He was animated with the pleasure these greetings had given him. While not a handsome man, he was obviously more attractive to women now than when he had been young, for he enjoyed what he received, and he was a sensuous man with a small mouth and plump lips, a Hapsburg mouth; it was not hard to see his resemblance to many a portrait of many an Austrian archduke and prince. Since he gave also every sign of the vanity and vulnerability and ruddy substance of a middle-aged man with a tendency to corpulence—the temptation to eat too much had to be his private war!—his weaknesses would probably be as amenable to women as his powers, and that German voice, deep, fortified with an accent which promised emoluments, savories, even meat gravies of culture at the tip of one's tongue, what European wealth! produced an impression altogether more agreeable than his photographs. So one mystery was answered—Kissinger's reputation as a ladies' man. And a difficulty was commenced—Aquarius' when work might have been simplified if he liked the Doctor less. A hint of some sinister mentality would have been a recognizable aid.

Yet even the demand for ground rules was reasonable. The meal ordered, Kissinger returned to the subject—he repeated: he would obviously expect the rules to be clarified before he could go further. Nor was there much impulse to resist him with argument. Secretly, he respected Kissinger for giving the interview—there was indeed not a great deal the Doctor could gain, and the perils were plentiful, including the central risk that Kissinger would have to trust him to keep his side of the bargain. Since his position not only as Assistant to the President on National Security Affairs but as court favorite must excite the ten thousand furies of bureaucracy—"this man who can't speak English that they keep hidden in the White House" being a not uncommon remark—the medium of this interview was not without its underlying message: Kissinger, in some part of himself at least, must be willing to function as a cultural ambassador across the space of mind between the constellations of the White House and the island galaxies of New York intellectual life. So Aquarius made his own speech. Like a virgin descending the steps of sexual congress, he said that he had never done this before, but since he was not unsympathetic to Kissinger's labors, and had no wish to jeopardize his position, which he would agree was delicate . . . so forth. They set up some ground rules.

"Now what should we talk about?" asked Kissinger.

Well, they might talk about the huge contradiction between the President's actions in Russia and China as opposed to Vietnam. "You know, if not for the bombing I might have to think about voting for Nixon. Certainly no Democrat would have been able to look for peace with Russia and China. The Republicans would never have let him. So Nixon's achievement is, on the one hand, immense, and on the other ghastly." Kissinger nodded, not without a hint of weariness to show his familiarity with the argument.

"If I reply to you by emphasizing the difference in our styles of negotiation in each country, it is not to pretend that these negotiations preempt moral questions, but rather that I'm not so certain we can engage such questions properly if they're altogether stripped of context. For instance, it would be impossible to discuss the kind of progress we made with China and Russia unless I were to give you the flavor of those negotiations, for they were absolutely characteristic and altogether different. For instance, I was not unfamiliar with Russian matters, but my ignorance about China was immense on the first secret visit, and I had no idea of how they would receive me"—a hint of the loneliness of his solitary position now passes across the table at Sans Souci—"nor even what we necessarily would be able to talk about. In the beginning I made the mistake of assuming that they negotiate like the Russians, and they don't. Not at all. With the Russians you always know where you stand. If, for example, you are hammering out a joint statement, you can be certain that if you ask them to remove a comma in one place, depend on it they will ask you for a comma in return. Whereas the character of men like Chou must emerge to a great degree from experiences like the Long March, and so I discovered—and not immediately—that you always had to deal with them on the real substance of the question. I remember when the President visited China, and I was working with Chou on the joint statement we would issue describing our areas of agreement and difference, I asked if a certain point the Chinese had brought up could be dropped because the wording would be difficult for us in America.

In return I would give up a point to them. Chou said 'Explain to me why this point causes you difficulty, and if your explanation makes sense I will cede it to you. If it doesn't convince me, however, then nothing can make me give it up. But I don't need or want your point. You can only give your points back to your President, you cannot give them to us.' So he shamed me," Kissinger finished.

"And the Vietnamese?"

"They could hardly be more different. The problem is to convince them we really want peace."

"Don't you think a million tons of bombs a year makes it hard for them to believe?"

"No. I know this has to sound unendurably callous to you, but the North Vietnamese are inconceivably tough people, and they've never known peace in their lives. So to them the war is part of the given. They are able to live with it almost as a condition of nature. But when it comes to negotiation, they refuse to trust us on the most absurd little points. Let them feel if they will that we are not to be relied on in the larger scheme of things, that is—not my point of view, but an argument can obviously be advanced—it is just that they refuse to trust us on the pettiest points where it would not even be to our interest to cheat them. So they are not easy to comprehend. On the one hand they have a fortitude you cannot help but admire; on the other, they are near to little lawyers who are terrified of the larger processes of the law—and so cling to the most picayune items. That is one difficulty in dealing with the North Vietnamese. The other is their compulsion to the legalistic which bears no relation to reality, nor to the possibility of reality. In effect they expect us to win their war for them for they want us to write up into the peace agreement their literal investiture of the government of South Vietnam. And that obviously we can't do. There's nothing we want more than for the war to end, but they must take their chances too. They have to win their own war."

"When they began their offensive in April, why then didn't the President just let them drive ahead and solve the problem for you? Why, just at that point, did he choose to escalate the bombing?"

Kissinger did not reply. The difficulty in continuing the discussion was that they would now be obliged to talk about the character of Richard Nixon rather than the nature of the North Vietnamese: given Kissinger's position, that was hardly possible: so the character of the interview changed. If it was easy for Aquarius to have the idea that Nixon and Kissinger were more in accord on Russia and China than on Vietnam, there was no evidence for it. Kissinger took pains to express his respect. "The President is a very complex man," he said, "perhaps more complex than anyone I've known, and different from the public view of him. He has great political courage for instance."

"Yes. It was no ordinary gamble to go to China."

"And he made moves in Russia which would take too long to explain now, but believe me he showed extraordinary decisiveness."

"Still, don't you think it's a vice that he has a personality which is of no use to the country?"

"Nixon is wary of exhibiting anything personal in himself. You have to consider the possibility it's for very good cause considering the way he has been treated by the Media."

"Still his wariness creates contempt."

"And a spirit of debunking which I don't find very happy. It was like that in the Weimar Republic. Just the kind of wholesale debunking that may yet lead to totalitarianism." Kissinger shrugs. "I wonder if people recognize how much Nixon may be a bulwark against that totalitarianism."

"Can he be?"

"I'm not certain I know what you mean."

"As people grow up, don't they form their characters to some extent on the idea a President gives of his person to the public. Nixon may give too little."

"Is it your point of view then that in the presidency one needs to have a man it is worth being like?"

"Yes. Nixon offers nothing authentic of himself."

"You would argue that he is not primarily a moral leader. I do not wish to agree. But perhaps you go along with me that he has political genius," Kissinger said.

"Absolutely."

It was indeed Aquarius' opinion. Still, that was a thought he could return to. Their lunch broke up with the passing of their table by [columnist] Art Buchwald who announced to Kissinger that [Russian Ambassador Anatoly] Dobrinin was coming to his house one night soon to play chess, and schedules permitting, he thought, granting Dobrinin's status as a chess player, that they should make a date to team up against the Ambassador. Kissinger agreed.

On the way back to the White House, they talked companionably of the hazards of working life, of jet-lag and fatigue. "How much sleep do you get?" asked Aquarius.

"I am happy if I can average five hours."

"Is it enough?"

"I always thought my mind would develop in a high position. But, fatigue becomes a factor. The mind is always working so hard that you learn little. Instead, you tend to work with what you learned in previous years."

They said good-bye in the white office in the White House with its blue sofas, its Oriental rugs, and its painting by [Jules] Olitsky, a large canvas in blue-purple, a wash of dark transparencies with a collection of pigment near the center as if to speak of revery and focus. "I've only come to like modern art in the last few years," Kissinger remarked.

Aquarius was to think again of focus. Because Kissinger opened to him a painful question on the value of the act of witness: lunch had been agreeable. Yet how could one pretend that Kissinger was a man whose nature could be assessed by such a meeting: in this sense, he was not knowable—one did not get messages from his presence of good or evil, rather of intelligence, and the warm courtesy of Establishment, yes, Kissinger was the essence of Establishment, his charm and his presence even depending perhaps on just such emoluments of position as the happiness he obtained in the best restaurants. If there was a final social need for Establishment, then Kissinger was a man born to be part of it and so automatically installed in the moral schizophrenia of Establishment, a part of the culture of moral concealment, and yet never was the problem so perfect, for the schizophrenia had become Aquarius' own. Kissinger was a man he liked, and in effect was ready to protect—he would even provide him with his own comments back to read. So Aquarius wondered if he had come into that world of the unendurably complex where one gave parts of one's allegiance to men who worked in the evil gears and bowels and blood left by the moral schizophrenia of Establishment, but still worked there, as one saw it, for good more than ill. It was a question to beat upon every focus of the brain.

48

NIXON'S FALL

(*THE NEW YORKER*, MAY 20, 1974)

Mailer's statement is part of a New Yorker *magazine symposium of political writers responding to the release of transcripts of the tapes of President Nixon's White House conversations, as ordered by the US Supreme Court in a landmark decision.*

Nixon's crime is his inability to rise above admiration for the corporation. Throughout the transcripts, he is acting like the good, tough, even-minded, cool-tempered, and tastefully foul-mouthed president of a huge corporation—an automobile man, let us say, who has just discovered that his good assistants have somehow, God knows how, allowed more than a trace of tin to get into the molybdenum. Now they have the choice of calling back one hundred thousand cars with faulty bearings or letting a few pile up at the traffic lights. He has no more and no less sense of values than any big corporation president in the land. Who, after all, polluted America in the first place? Now we're having an Aztec ceremony to clean up the mess. We won't be happy until we cut Richard Nixon's heart out and hold it high on the summit of the presidential pyramid while an ooh goes up from the crowd. But his crime, moral insensitivity, is the one with which he began, prospered, lost, despaired, and finally succeeded in the passion of Richard Nixon. Good old American moral inanition. Was Lyndon Johnson less disgusting in Vietnam, or Jack Kennedy less cynical in some of the conversations he had—doubtless had—about the little workings of the C.I.A.? Poor Nixon. He makes the peace with Russia and China by pitching the political equivalent of a shutout on his own right-wing Murderers' Row (which no Democrat ever had the nerve to do). Then he slips on the dugout steps. One could pity him if not for having been shamed by his presence as the Uriah Heep of the Indo-Chinese war—all those years when one had to listen to Nixon speak of the enemy as he spoke of the carnage and bombardment. For that, Nixon will never be forgiven, but these are schizophrenic years—the separate parts of ourself hardly communicate—and so one is even tempted to admire the final release of these unreleasable transcripts. What a boon to historians, what a blow to ambiguity. How much easier it might have been for Nixon to resign and cry foul for the rest of his life, thereby to muddy the last washes of Watergate. Instead, he takes the gamble, he rages "against the dying of the light." Yet as he takes this last desperate step, he nonetheless repeats the theme of his life—he cannot take the step with all of himself in the same place. Expletive deleted. He lacks the simple New York smart to keep the obscenities in. All his life he has been trying to tell us he is a man, a real man, and we keep replying he ain't. A real man knows how to swear. Now he finally has the stuff to show it. Better, he flings himself on the final court of public opinion. Yet we still do not know if he even swears well. He could have had the bars of America laughing with his prejudices, saying, Hey the guy is no good and he can prove it, but he's one funny guy, he'll make you laugh. Instead, out Richard squirts deodorant at the smell in the room, and we all feel the pall. I'm beginning to think he is doomed. The stubbornest man in America, and doomed. With all his congealed and unadmitted boldness, with all his transcendent hypocrisy (the gas of his false pieties enters the very spirit of anti-matter), still he has always been, in the final crisis, the fool of small-town caution. So, in the grand boiling of the pots of American opinion, our National Yard bird goes into the broth without his feathers, and all salts withheld. We will be a great nation on the day we come to see that his ability to poach in his own juice is the American disease of us all. For the flavor of his moral invention, as he cooks himself, is saccharin, preservative, and gobs of super-burger. Bile in the stomach, canker on the tongue, and woe in the pit. What if his horror is the same as ours when we say at 3 a.m. *we are not so bad as they think we are,* and writhe in the thought that God may not agree? Let someone say, at any rate, that if ever a human was obliged to drink the cup of his own excretions, then the last or next-to-last of the classic American Presidents has been that man. What a curiosity is our Democracy, what a mystery. No novelist unwinds a narrative that well.

49

A Visit with Jimmy Carter in Plains, Georgia

(*NEW YORK TIMES*, SEPTEMBER 26, 1976)

The following excerpt from Mailer's report on his 1976 visit with Jimmy Carter captures his somewhat comic attempt to engage the then Democratic presidential candidate in a discussion of the philosophic ideas of Sören Kierkegaard (1813–55), among other matters.

When his private interview with Jimmy Carter took place, it proved to be the oddest professional hour Norman Mailer ever spent with a politician—it must have seemed twice as odd to Carter. In retrospect, it quickly proved mortifying (no lesser word will do), since to his embarrassment, Mailer did too much of the talking. Perhaps he had hoped to prime Carter to the point where they could have a conversation, but the subject he chose to bring up was religion, and that was ill-chosen. A man running for President could comment about Christ, he could comment a little, but he could hardly afford to be too enthusiastic. Religion had become as indecent a topic to many a contemporary American as sex must have been in the nineteenth century. If half the middle-class people in the Victorian period held almost no conscious thoughts about sex, the same could now be said of religion, except it might be even more costly to talk about than sex, because religious conversations invariably sound insane when recounted to men or women who never feel such sentiments. Since it was a safe assumption that half of America lived at present in the nineteenth century and half in the twentieth, a journalist who had any respect for the candidate he was talking to would not ask an opinion on sex or religion. Still, Mailer persisted. He was excited about Carter's theological convictions. He wanted to hear more of them. He had read the transcript of Bill Moyers' one-hour TV interview with Carter ... and had been impressed with a few of Carter's remarks, particularly his reply to Moyers' question "What drives you?"

After a long silence Carter had said, "I don't know ... exactly how to express it.... I feel I have one life to live. I feel that God wants me to do the best I can with it. And that's quite often my major prayer. Let me live my life so that it will be meaningful." A little later he would add, "When I have a sense of peace and self-assurance ... that what I'm doing is the right thing, I assume, maybe in an unwarranted way, that that's doing God's will." ...

These were hardly historic remarks, and yet on reflection they were certainly remarkable. There was a maw of practicality that engulfed Presidents and presidential candidates alike. They lived in all those supermarkets of the mind where facts are stacked like cans; whether good men or bad, they were hardly likely to be part of that quintessential elevation of mind that can allow a man to say, "Let me live my life so that it will be meaningful." It was in the nature of politicians to look for *programs* to be meaningful, not the psychic substance of their lives. Reading the Moyers interview shortly before leaving for Plains must therefore have excited a last-minute excess of curiosity about Carter, and that was last-minute to be certain. Through all of the political spring when candidates came and went, Mailer had not gone near the primary campaigns. Working on a novel, he had made the whole decision not to get close to any of it. One didn't try to write seriously about two things at once. Besides, it was hard to tell much about Carter. Mailer thought the media had an inbuilt deflection that kept them from perceiving what was truly interesting in any new phenomenon. Since he rarely watched television any longer, he did not even know what Carter's voice was like, and photographs proved subtly anonymous. Still, he kept reading about Carter. In answer to the people who would ask, "What do you think of *him*?" Mailer would be quick to reply, "I suspect he's a political genius." It was all he knew about Carter, but he knew that much.

He also had to admit he enjoyed Carter's reaction to meeting Nixon and Agnew, McGovern and Henry Jackson, Hubert Humphrey,

George Wallace, Ronald Reagan, Nelson Rockefeller, Ed Muskie. Carter confessed he had not been impressed sufficiently to think these men were better qualified to run the country than himself. Mailer understood such arrogance. He had, after all, felt enough of the same on meeting famous politicians to also think himself equipped for office, and had been brash enough to run for Mayor of New York in a Democratic primary: Mailer had always assumed he would be sensational as a political candidate; he learned, however, that campaign work ran eighteen hours a day, seven days a week, and after a while it was not yourself who was the candidate but 50 percent of yourself. Before it was over, his belly was drooping—one's gut is the first to revolt against giving the same speech eight times a day. He came in fourth in a field of five, and was left with a respect for successful politicians. They were at least entitled to the same regard one would offer a professional athlete for his stamina. Later, brooding on the size of a conceit that had let him hope he could steal an election from veteran Democrats, Mailer would summarize his experience with the wise remark, "a freshman doesn't get elected president of the fraternity."

But Carter had. Carter must be a political genius. Nonetheless, Mailer felt a surprising lack of curiosity. Genius in politics did not interest him that much. He thought politics was a dance where you need not do more than move from right to left and left to right while evading the full focus of the media. The skill was in the timing. You tried to move to the left at that moment when you would lose the least on the right; to the right, when the damage would be smallest on the left. You had to know how to steer in and out of other news stories. It was a difficult skill, but hardly possessed of that upper esthetic which would insist skill be illumined by a higher principle—whether elegance, courage, compassion, taste, or the eminence of wit. Politics called for some of the same skills you needed in inventing a new plastic. Politics called to that promiscuous material in the personality which could flow into many a form. Sometimes Mailer suspected that the flesh of the true politician would yet prove nonbiodegradable and fail to molder in the gravel.

Still, there was no question in his mind that he would vote for Carter. In 1976 he was ready to vote for many a Democrat. It was not that Mailer could not ever necessarily vote for a Republican, but after eight years of Nixon and Ford, he thought the country could use a Democratic administration again. It was not that Ford was unendurable. Like a moderately dull marriage, Ford was endlessly endurable—one could even get fond of him in a sour way. Jerry Ford, after all, provided the clue to how America had moved in fifty years from George Babbitt to Jerry Ford. He even offered the peculiar security of having been shaped by forces larger than himself. Maybe that was why Ford's face suggested he would do the best he could with each problem as he perceived it: "Don't worry about me," said his face, "I'm not the least bit dialectical."

Of course, the President was only a handmaiden to the corporate spirit. The real question was whether the White House could afford another four years of the corporate spirit, that immeasurably self-satisfied public spirit whose natural impulse was to cheat on the environment and enrich the rich. It was certainly time for the Democrats. He would probably vote for any Democrat who got the nomination. Nonetheless, it was irritating to have so incomplete an idea of Carter, to be so empty of any thesis as to whether he might be deemed ruthless, a computer, or saintly. . . .

Jimmy Carter's home was on a side street, and you approached it through a barricade the Secret Service had erected. It was possible this was as unobtrusive a small-town street as the Secret Service had ever converted into an electronic compound with walkie-talkies, sentries, and lines-of-sight. The house was in a grove of trees, and the ground was hard-put to keep its grass, what with pine needles, pecan leaves, and the clay of the soil itself, which gave off a sandy-rose hue in the shade.

The rambling suburban ranch house in those trees spoke of California ancestry for its architecture, and a cost of construction between $50,000 and $100,000, depending on how recently it was built. The inside of the house was neither lavish nor underfurnished, not sumptuous or mean—a house that spoke of comfort more than taste; the colors laid next to one another were in no way brilliant, yet neither did their palette of soft shades depress the eye, for they were cool in the Georgia summer. Carter's study was large and dark with books and there were busts of Kennedy and Lincoln, and his eight-year-old daughter Amy's comic book (starring Blondie) was on the floor. It was the only spot of red in all the room. Over his desk was a fluorescent light. . . .

Now, sitting across the desk from Carter, he was struck by a quiet difference in Carter this Sunday afternoon. Maybe it was the result of church, or maybe the peril implicit for a politician in any interview—since one maladroit phrase can ruin a hundred good ones—but Carter seemed less generous than he had expected. Of course, Mailer soon knew to his horror that he was close to making a fool of himself, if indeed he had not done it already, because with his first question taking five minutes to pose, and then ten, he had already given a speech rather than a question. What anguish this caused, that he—known as criminally egomaniacal by common reputation, and therefore for years as careful as a reformed criminal to counteract the public expectation of him—was haranguing a future President of the United States. He had a quick recollection of the days when he ran for Mayor and some fool or other, often an overly educated European newspaperman, would ask questions that consisted of nothing but long-suppressed monologues. To make matters worse, Carter was hardly being responsive in his answer—how could he be? Mailer's exposition dwelt in the bowels of that limitless schism in Protestantism—between the fundamental simplicities of good moral life as exemplified a few hours ago in Bible class and the insuperable complexities of moral examination opened by Kierkegaard, whose work, Mailer now told Carter with enthusiasm, looked to demonstrate that we cannot know the moral role we enact. We can feel saintly and yet be evil in the eyes of God, feel we are evil (on the other hand) and yet be more saintly than we expect; equally, we may do good even as we are feeling good, or be bad exactly when we expect we are bad. Man is alienated from his capacity to decide his moral worth. Maybe, Mailer suggested, he had sailed on such a quick theological course because Carter had quoted Kierkegaard on the second page of his autobiography. "Every man is an exception," Kierkegaard had written.

But it was obvious by the smile on Carter's face—a well of encouragement to elicit the point of this extended question—that

Carter was not necessarily one of America's leading authorities on Kierkegaard. How foolish of Mailer to expect it of him—as if Norman in his turn had never quoted an author he had not lived with thoroughly.

Having failed with the solemnity of this exposition, but his voice nonetheless going on, beginning to wonder what his question might be—did he really have one, did he really enter this dialogue with the clean journalistic belief that ultimate questions were to be answered by presidential candidates?—he now began to shift about for some political phrasing he could offer Carter as a way out of these extensive hypotheses. The sexual revolution, Mailer said hopefully, the sexual revolution might be a case in point. And he now gave the lecture he had prepared the night before—that the family, the very nuclear family whose security Carter would look to restore, was seen as the enemy by a large fraction of Americans. "For instance," said Mailer, clutching at inspiration, "there are a lot of people in New York who don't trust you. The joke making the rounds among some of my friends is 'How can you put confidence in a man who's been faithful to the same woman for thirty years?'"

Carter's smile showed real amusement, as if he knew something others might not necessarily know. Of course, whether he was smiling to the left or right of this issue was another matter. Curiously encouraged by the ambiguous fiber of the smile, Mailer went on toward asking his first question. He had presented the joke, he suggested, to show the gulf of moral differences that awaited a Carter presidency—for instance, to talk of the drug problem just a moment, statistics re-examined showed that addicts deprived of heroin, or methadone, did not commit more crimes to get scarce heroin but instead took speed or barbiturates or pot, or even went to bourbon. The implication of this, Mailer said, is that there's a chasm in the soul that might have to be filled, a need precisely not to be oneself but rather to give oneself over to the Other, to give oneself to some presence outside oneself; the real answer to drug addiction might not be in social programs but in coming to grips with the possibility that Satanism was loose in the twentieth century. One question he would like to ask in line with this was whether Carter thought much about the hegemony of Satan, or did he—yes, this unasked question was now being silently answered by Carter's eyes, yes, Carter's concern was not with Satan but with Christ. On and on went Mailer with considerable fever, looking, for instance, to propose that one difference between Carter's religious point of view as he, Mailer, presumed to comprehend it, and his own might be that he had a notion of God as not clearly omnipotent but rather as a powerful God at war with other opposed visions in the universe—a ridiculous picture of God to present to Carter, Mailer told the candidate, except that going back to the Moyers interview, where Carter had certainly said that he felt he might be doing God's will when he felt a sense of peace and self-assurance—did it ever bother Carter, keeping Kierkegaard's Principle of Uncertainty in mind, if he, Mailer, could, heh, steal a title from Heisenberg—did it ever bother him that God might be in anguish or rage at what He had not accomplished across the heavens? . . .

Well, answered Carter soberly, thoughtfully, he was not certain that he could reply to everything that had been raised since their points of view were not the same in many respects. He was not, for instance, as devout and as prayerful as the press had perhaps made him out to be. Religion was something he certainly did and would live with but he didn't spend as much time as people might expect exploring into the depths of these questions; perhaps—he suggested politely—he ought to be more concerned, but in truth, he did not think his personal beliefs were to be carried out by the government; there were limits to what government could do, yet in those limits, he thought much more could be done than was now being done. For example, he would recognize that there is little that government could do directly to restore the family. Welfare payments might, for example, be revised in such a way that fathers would not be directly encouraged to desert their families, as they were most ironically now encouraged to do, but he would admit that this, of course, was to the side of the question. He supposed, Carter said, that the answer, as he saw it, was in turning government around so that it would be more of a model. There was yearning in this country for the restoration of something precious. "There's been a loss of pride in this country that I find catastrophic." The deterioration of family values was linked,

Carter thought, to that loss of pride. It would be his hope that if he could get the actual workings of the government turned around, so that government was at once more efficient and more sensitive, then perhaps it could begin to serve as more of a model to counteract the fundamental distrust of people in relation to government, that is, their feeling they won't find justice. "The real answer is to get those of us who are running the government going right." You see, Carter went on to say, he was not looking to restore the family by telling people how to live; he did not wish to be President in order to judge them. "I don't care," he said in his quiet decent voice, as if the next words, while not wholly comfortable, had nonetheless to be said, "I don't care if people say," and he actually said the famous four-letter word that the *Times* has not printed in the 125 years of its publishing life.

He got it out without a backing-up of phlegm or a hitch in his rhythm (it was, after all, not the easiest word to say to a stranger), but it was said from duty, from the quiet decent demands of duty, as if he, too, had to present his credentials to that part of the twentieth century personified by his interviewer.

No, Carter went on, his function was not to be a religious leader but to bring the human factor back into economics. The same economic formula, he suggested, would work or not work depending on the morale of the people who were doing the work.

Mailer nodded. He believed as much himself. But he was still dissatisfied with his lack of contact on questions more fundamental to himself. Like a child who returns to the profitless point (out of obscure but certain sense of need), Mailer looked to return their conversation to Kierkegaardian ambiguities and so spoke of marijuana, for it was on marijuana, he told Carter, that he had had the first religious experience he had ever known; indeed, marijuana might even pose the paradox of arriving at mystical states for too little. One began to feel the vulnerability of God about the time one recognized a little more clearly in the unwinding of the centers of one's consciousness that one was consuming one's karma, possibly stripping—for no more than the pleasure of the experience—some of the resources of one's future lives. He asked Carter then if he had any belief in reincarnation, in the reincarnation of karma as our purgatory here on earth?

And Carter said no, Carter said he believed we had our one life and our judgment. And then with that gentle seductiveness all good politicians have, Carter mentioned that his understanding was not wholly alien to drugs, his sons had experimented with marijuana a few years ago, and had later done some work in the rehabilitation of addicts. He felt as if their experiences had helped them in such work. . . .

Mailer was finally beginning to feel the essential frustration of trying to talk about religion with Carter on equal terms. Carter had more troops, which is to say he had more habits. If you go to church every Sunday for most of your life, then you end with certain habits. You live in a dependable school of perception. In the case of Baptists, it might be living with the idea that if you were good enough and plucky and lucky and not hating your neighbor for too little, Christ was quietly with you. Certainly, if you had the feeling He was with you at all, He was with you in church on Sunday. So you could form the habit over the years of thinking about Him in a comfortable way. . . .

They had come to the end of their hour. The author was feeling a dull relief that he would have, at least, another hour tomorrow. How fortunate that that had been scheduled in advance. He started to apologize in some roundabout form for how the first hour had gone, and Carter replied with his gracious smile: it was all right, he said, they had needed the first hour to loosen up, to become acquainted. Mailer left with the twice dull sense that he liked Carter more than Carter had any reason to like him.

50

TO MARY BANCROFT

(OCTOBER 18, 1976; *SELECTED LETTERS OF NORMAN MAILER*, 2014)

Author and intelligence analyst Mary Bancroft (1903–97) corresponded with a number of writers and politicians, including Harry S. Truman, Joan Didion, Henry Miller, and Robert Kennedy. Her memoir, Autobiography of a Spy, *was published in 1983. She had a low opinion of Jimmy Carter. Mailer described her as "tough" and "grand."*

Dear Mary,

Either you're a very good writer or I'm just an old club fighter who gets mad when you miss because I enjoy the letters where you tell me I am dumb as much as the letters where you tell me I am not. Anyway, I find it hard to burn with your passion about Carter, for I have only to think of Ford or, God save my ass, Reagan, and wonder how a self-respecting conservative like you can get it up one more time to put the dipper in the bile pot. Yes, I think Carter is ambiguous as hell and yes he could be the devil and yes he could sure have taken me in and yes the Democrats will take us to war before the Republicans and yes it could be the biggest mistake I've ever made, but all I could tell you is I've learned over the years to get simpler and simpler. I decided it's finally no accident if I walk away liking somebody or not liking them. Rather, everything that's happened to me in my purchase on fifty-three years is in the judgment. And I walked away from Carter and I really liked him, he stayed with me in a good glow. Not many people do that to me. Since that part is incontestable for me, I have to recognize that if he is the devil, then so am I, and it was that good glow of fellowship devils feel when they encounter one another in high and secret places. But as for Ford, Reagan, Dole and the rest of that pirate ship—Mary, they're puke. They're hideous. Don't you know what they've done to this country? Johnson was a tragic monstrosity and he got us into Vietnam ten times as much as Kennedy—I'll grant you that. But what Nixon did in not getting us out for four long years is unspeakable, and what Ford and Reagan do in terms of the economy that is run by the guys who roll around in the golf cart, oh the corruption, oh the ooze, oh I miss you. Oh god I miss you. Mary, why do I never visit? Now that I know you will beat me to death with a blivet when I come through the door (two pounds of shit in a one-pound bag), I promise to come along soon.

51

To President Jimmy Carter

(MARCH 2, 1977, UNPUBLISHED)

Mailer's letter to President Carter is another affirmation of his unshakable conviction that ferreting out and publishing the buried facts about momentous events in the nation's life is critical to the psychic health of the country. If Mailer were alive now, he'd be an avid supporter of and commentator on the hearings of the House Select Committee to Investigate the January 6th Attack on the United States Capitol.

Dear President Carter,

One is tempted to speculate on the recent troubles of the House Select Committee on Assassinations. Would it be, one can wonder, in the interest of high officials in the CIA and the FBI to cooperate with such a committee when such questions as Oswald's links to the CIA or the FBI's alleged malfeasance in the investigation of the slaying of Martin Luther King could be patiently, even authoritatively explored while new evidence further damning the FBI and CIA could also be discovered? (Indeed, who in these organizations would be certain there was no such damning evidence?) Under these circumstances, how could the CIA and the FBI live with the Select Committee on Assassinations? How could they not be ready to apply pressure and sabotage against its workings?

It is, however, in the interest of the American public to have the Committee in existence. The Select Committee on Assassinations may be imperfect, impractical, and a demon for poor publicity. For all we know, it may be riddled with undercover men. But it is the only investigating body we have in the House of Representatives with the obligation to subpoena recalcitrant witnesses on these matters and the duty to listen to witnesses who have studied the flaws in the Warren Commission report for years. By its existence, therefore, the Committee represents a threat to anybody who would hope to maintain public apathy about the assassinations.

Such public apathy exists for good reason. So long as we believe that it is impossible to learn the truths of Dallas or the truths of the murders of Martin Luther King and of Bobby Kennedy, then such deaths are too depressing to contemplate. Yet we pay an incalculable price for living with these unsolved crimes. A clear idea of the character of the events of the recent past is essential to a democracy: without knowledge of what actually happened in an event, how can one debate its meaning? If we do not know whether Jack Kennedy was killed by the demented act of an isolated man, or whether by the concerted acts of a group of conspirators who employed Oswald as the set-up; if we do not know whether the murder of Oswald by Jack Ruby was an attempt to spare the First Lady all the discomfort of appearing at a trial, or an order that came to Jack Ruby out of the chain of communication that ran between the CIA and the Mafia, then we do not know which history we can act upon.

Now we have a new administration seeking to take America out of the historical despondency of the last decade. How promising if this new administration and Congress will recognize that the assassinations of the sixties are not old scars to be covered but unseen bruises that still deaden the confidence of America. For the shadow of the assassinations keeps us thinking we do not have a history that can bear exposure. That is a deadening suspicion. Basic [to] good feeling about our country is our ability to believe that our representatives are brave enough to undertake thoroughgoing investigations of the role of government itself, no matter where that may lead: Such a need will obviously not be satisfied by stopping the work of the House Select Committee on Assassinations and we, the undersigned, send this letter to President Carter and to the House of Representatives in the hope it will serve the idea that the continued life of the Select Committee and the voting of an appropriation adequate to its needs are matters of significance to the psychic well-being of this Republic.

52

NIXON'S CURTAIN CALL

(*PIECES AND PONTIFICATIONS*, 1982)

This piece, excerpted from a 1977 Esquire *essay on the pernicious effects of television, "Of a Small and Modest Malignancy, Wicked and Bristling with Dots," is Mailer's valedictory reflection on Richard Nixon. It is notable for its tone of forbearance, if not forgiveness.*

In his partial comprehension of television, in his researches into the mystery of that hum in its void, he had always centered his hypotheses around the familiar certainty that Richard Nixon owned the human personality closest to the persona of the television set. Mailer had even built his distrust of TV and Nixon on their similarity to one another, their incorporation of baleful disregard for the finer possibilities of human attention.

Yet, when he replayed in his mind, that is on the curved walls of the mansion, Nixon's first appearance before David Frost, where the ex-President spoke of Watergate, Mailer was cheered by that ninety minutes. In later years, his detestation of TV close to complete, ninety minutes had become an immense dose of video, and left Mailer feeling like a canceroid (that is, like someone who could not justify why he should not bear the disease). Yet Nixon's ninety minutes were of another order; on the scale of video, they were alchemy itself: the American with the least charismatic personality of the twentieth century, the American most ready to be emitted from the tube and infiltrated into your pores had become for a few minutes a personality capable of moving multitudes, and had done it by the refractory art of the actor.

He had always believed Richard Nixon was the most untalented actor he had ever witnessed, and Mailer had often brooded on the first meeting decades ago of Richard and Pat Nixon in an amateur theatrical company, and wondered whether Nixon, if he had been somewhat better in those early years as an actor, would have become in later life a politician more like Ronald Reagan. Instead, his acting career had been given over to the practice of law, and Nixon had become one of the few politicians who was a consummately abominable actor on the American scene. His lack of conviction vibrated through the diodes, triodes, and later the transistors of every American set; the message he gave was profoundly depressing. Even as a district attorney who speaks in too-righteous tones to a jury will depress us on questions of law and order and their relation to justice (since the fact that a D.A. can prosper on such hypocritical terms has either to speak ill of the jury or of a system that encourages us to believe that phony voices carry the real tones of avenging authority) so Nixon's inability to act had always, by reflection, intimated that something in the American public must be atrocious if millions were ready to accept his transparent lack of sincerity, his push-button smile, and his simple lack of ability to offer even that resonance of the throat which is a ham actor's emotion.

Yet in the interview with Frost that Mailer witnessed, a miracle was visible—Richard Nixon had become not merely a good actor but a great actor, great by the measure of actors like Bogart, and Fonda, and old Spencer Tracy, great—good God!—like Edward G. Robinson, like Edward G. Robinson playing Richard Nixon full of woe at what had come to him from Watergate, and after thirty or forty minutes of watching Nixon, it did not matter what the truth might be, any more than one would find fault with a great stage actor for bringing life and splendor and passion and the monumental echoes of tragic woe to lines that were not his own and that he could say in his sleep or while shaving, he had practiced them so well, yes, Nixon struck America with a miracle—a talentless actor had become a splendid actor—yes, Nixon now went to the root of good acting, where before he had lived in the center of bad acting. In his political years, Nixon used to comport himself as if acting were a

set of semaphores and you frowned if you wished to look stern, and
glanced heavenward to demonstrate that your motives were benign;
now, face to face with Frost, he was an actor from the guts out, which
is that he got his words out through every effort to control himself.
The great actor does not play a drunk by staggering; rather, he plays
a man whose stomach is raw and whose head is whirling, but a man
who nonetheless believes he is sober and so will make every effort
to convince others he is sober. The power of his drunkenness comes
over the audience by his attempts to conceal it from us. That was
Nixon's power on this night. What a mighty emotion he was seeking to hold like a man. It did not matter after a while that a part of
one's brain could still remember many an intricacy of Watergate that
Nixon was debauching once again; that was like saying of Olivier
in *Marathon Man* that he might be playing an ex-Nazi, but actually
was still Olivier and born British, what indeed did the truth of Nixon's guilt have to do with the higher truth that a talentless man had
become a powerful actor? A fact such as this was kin to a miracle and
warmed the heart. So as Richard came forth with those beautiful and
unforgettable lines, beautiful, that is, and unforgettable, as examples of
the actor's, not the playwright's, art, as he said: "... it was springtime.
The tulips had just come out ... it was one of those gorgeous days
when, you know, no clouds were on the mountain. And"—his voice
went husky here from the effort not to be husky—"I was pretty
emotionally wrought-up, and I remember that I could just hardly
bring myself to tell Ehrlichman that he had to go. I said, 'I hoped,
I almost prayed I wouldn't wake up this morning.' Well, it was an
emotional moment. I think there were tears in our eyes, both of us.
He said, 'Don't say that.' We went back in. Then he said goodbye to
Haldeman and Ehrlichman, and took their resignation. . . . It was late,
but I did it." No actor alive, not Ralph Richardson, Jack Nicholson,
or John Gielgud could have given a better reading than he gave on
the next line. "I cut off one arm," Nixon said manfully, and in partial
control of great pain, "and then cut off the other arm." He nodded.
"... You could sum it all up," he said to Frost, "the way one of your
British Prime Ministers summed it up, Gladstone, when he said that
'the first requirement for a Prime Minister is to be a good butcher.'

Well, I think . . . I did some of the big things rather well. But I . . . have to admit, I wasn't a good butcher."

It would come out later that Nixon's version of these events was not necessarily accurate; first Ehrlichman, then Haldeman, would dispute what he had said. He was not cutting off his own arms so quickly, it seemed, as he was cutting off their legs. Yet with what a difference did he lie! In the past, a deadening actor and a lifeless politician, Nixon had lied with every dull light in his eye; now, his eye was bright, he had learned to act; his lies partook of art.

53

A TALK WITH CLINT EASTWOOD

(*PARADE*, OCTOBER 23, 1983)

The most remarkable thing about this profile-interview is that Mailer is utterly serious in his suggestion to Eastwood, a registered Libertarian, that he consider running for president.

"My dad was Scots-English; my mother's Dutch Irish, strange combination. All the pirates and people who were kicked out of everyplace else."

—Clint Eastwood

Norman Mailer: I've seen an awful lot of Presidential candidates, and you're one of the few people who could go far that way.

Clint Eastwood: (laughs)

M: I'm not kidding. There's one guy in 500 who's got a Presidential face and usually nothing else.

E: If I've got the Presidential face, I'm lacking in a lot of other areas.

M: Well, all lack it.

E: I don't feel I could get up and say a lot of things that I know I couldn't perform on. Yet I'd have to do that to win. The ones that are honest about what they can or can't do don't have a chance.

By any physical terms Eastwood was a brave man. Once, after a plane crashed at sea, he saved his life by swimming three miles to shore. He did a number of his own stunts in movies and learned to rock climb for *The Eiger Sanction*. The film was embarrassing, a prodigiously multi-colored plot equal to ice cream on turnips, but Eastwood's rock climbing was good. He rode a horse well. He did car racing. He even looked, on the basis of *Every Which Way But Loose* and *Any Which Way You Can*, as if he might make some kind of boxer. He had a quick left jab with good weight behind it. He could certainly draw a gun. If it came to great box office movie stars competing in a decathlon, Eastwood would hold his own.

He was also capable of fine acting. With a few exceptions, he invariably understood his role and did a good deal with the smallest moves. Critics had been attacking him for years over how little he did onscreen, but Eastwood may have known something they did not. The plot of a film works, after all, for the star. The more emotion that a story will stir in an audience, the more will the audience read such feeling into the star's motionless face. Sometimes the facial action of the movie star might offer no more movement than a riverbank, yet there is nothing passive about such work. A riverbank must brace itself to support the rush around a bend.

> I always was a different kind of person, even when I started acting. I guess I finally got to a point where I had enough nerve to do nothing. My first film with Sergio Leone had a script with tons of dialogue, tremendously expository, and I just cut it all down. Leone thought I was crazy. Italians are used to much more vocalizing, and I was playing this guy who didn't say much of anything. I cut it all down. Leone didn't speak any English so he didn't know what the hell I was doing, but he got so he liked it after a while.

There is a moment in *Play Misty for Me* when Eastwood's character, an easygoing disc jockey, realizes that he has gotten himself into an affair with a hopelessly psychotic woman. As the camera moves in, his stare is as still as the eyes of a trapped animal. He is one actor who can put his soul into his eyes.

The real question might have little to do, however, with how much of an actor he could be. What separated Eastwood from other box-office stars was that his films (especially since he had begun to

direct them) had come to speak more and more of his own vision of
life in America. One was encountering a homegrown philosophy, a
hardworking everyday subtle American philosophy in film.

Burt Reynolds also gives us a private vision of the taste of life in
America, but it is not so much a philosophy as a premise. Eat high on
the hog, Reynolds suggests. The best way to get through life is drunk.
Since it's possible that half the male population of America under 40
also believes this, Reynolds is endlessly reliable.

Eastwood is saying more. If you discount his two worst films in these
last 10 years, *Firefox* and *The Eiger Sanction*, if you bypass *Dirty Harry*,
Magnum Force, and *The Enforcer* as movies made to manipulate audiences
and satisfy producers, you are also left with *High Plains Drifter*, *The Outlaw
Josey Wales*, *Every Which Way But Loose*, *Bronco Billy*, and *Honkytonk Man*.

A protagonist in each of these five films stands near to his creator,
Eastwood has made five cinematic relatives. They are spread over more
than 100 years, from the Civil War to the present, and the action is in
different places west of the Mississippi, from Missouri to California.
They are Okies and outlaws, truckers, rodeo entertainers, and country
and western singers, but they come out of the odd, wild, hard, dry, sad,
sour redneck wisdom of small town life in the Southwest. All of Eastwood's knowledge is in them, a sardonic, unsentimental set of values
that is equal to art for it would grapple with the roots of life itself.
"When things get bad," says the outlaw Josey Wales, "and it looks like
you're not going to make it, then you got to get mean, I mean plain
plumb dog mean, because if you lose your head then, you neither live
nor win. That's just the way it is."

One has to think of the Depression years of Eastwood's childhood when his father was looking for work and taking the family
up and down the San Joaquin and Sacramento Valleys, out there with
a respectable family in a mix of Okies also wandering up and down
California searching for work. Those Okies are in Eastwood's films,
as must be the gritty knowledge he gained over the seven years he
worked on *Rawhide*. How many bit players and cowboy stunt men
passing through *Rawhide*'s weekly episodes were also a part of that
migrating country culture that was yet going to present itself to us
by way of CBS and pickup trucks and western music? "You've got to

outlast yourself" was the only way to talk of overcoming fatigue. The words happen to be Eastwood's, but the language was shared with his characters, brothers in the same family, ready to share a family humor: It is that a proper orangutan will not miss a good opportunity to defecate on the front seat of a police cruiser, as indeed it did in *Every Which Way But Loose*. Smalltown humor, but in *Honkytonk Man,* his last film before the one he's shooting now, it became art.

M: How did you feel about *Honkytonk Man* before it came out?

E: I thought it was good, as good as I could do it. I did it in five weeks, five weeks of shooting, and I felt good about it. I felt it might find a small audience somewhere that might enjoy it. I wasn't looking for a big film. I just figured sometimes you have to do some things that you want to do and be selfish about it.

Honkytonk Man starts in the Oklahoma dust bowl of the Thirties and follows a drunk, all-but-destroyed country singer named Red Stovall on his car trip east to Nashville. He has been given an invitation to audition at the Grand Ole Opry, and it is the most important event of his life. Red Stovall has very little left: ravaged good looks, a guitar, and a small voice reduced to a whisper by his consumptive cough. He's a sour, cantankerous, mean-spirited country singer who smokes too much, drinks too much, and has brought little happiness to man or woman, a sorry hero but still a hero. He will die before he will deviate from his measure of things. So he drives over the bumpy stones of his used-up lungs to get to the audition.

On stage at the Grand Ole Opry, out front before the producers, there in the middle of singing his best, he coughs. Worse. He is so stifled with phlegm that he must stagger off the stage. The picture is about to end in disaster. Still, he is given a reprieve. A man who makes records is also at the audition. He has liked Red's voice and comes forward with a proposal. Red, given the treachery of his throat, can hardly perform before an audience, but maybe he can do a record session. They can lay the track between the coughs. So he is able to sing on the last day of his life and makes one record before he dies. His whispery voice, close to extinction, clings to the heart of the film.

So I lost my woman and you lost your man
Who knows who's right and who's wrong?
But I've still got my guitar and I've got a plan,
Throw your arms 'round this honkytonk man.

It is as if every economy Eastwood has picked up in acting and directing found its way into the film. Something of the steely compassion that is back of all the best country singing is in the movie, and the harsh, yearning belly of rural America is also there, used to making out with next to nothing but hard concerns and the spark of a dream that will never give up.

Honkytonk Man was the finest movie made about country plains life since *The Last Picture Show,* and it stood up to that comparison because of what Eastwood did with the role. A subtle man was brought to life with minimal strokes, a complex protagonist full of memories of old cunning deeds and weary sham. It was one of the saddest movies seen in a long time, yet, on reflection, terrific. One felt a tenderness for America, while looking at it. . . .

Eastwood once said, "I was never a discovery of the press," and the remark is crucial. He had been discovered by the box office. He could forgo favorable reviews but not good box office. Now, after the jolting failure of *Honkytonk Man,* there was pressure from all sides to do another film about Dirty Harry Callahan. Of the five movies bringing in Eastwood's greatest profits, three had been about Dirty Harry Callahan, an outlaw cop who did things on his own. Callahan broke villains in two with his Magnum. Audiences cheered.

Eastwood had tired of making profitable movies about Dirty Harry Callahan. After filming three in the years between 1971 and 1976, he had shot none since. But now he accepted. He would act in and direct *Sudden Impact.*

I wasn't intending to do any more of these characters. I never particularly wanted to. I thought I'd done all I can with it, and I might have, I don't know. But everybody kept asking about it.

One cannot say how much will be retained in the finished film, but the script of *Sudden Impact* shows three men fatally shot in the groin by a woman. It is in retaliation for being raped by them. Dirty Harry knocks off eight sleazos himself. There are also six flashbacks to the rape. It is a Dirty Harry Film. But for the new emphasis on women's rights (which moves Callahan to allow the girl to go free at the end), there are no new elements. The script gives us 40 killings, rapes, fights, and other condiments. It is as full of ingredients as the first *Dirty Harry*.

That film bears summary. It is not just the amount of violent action, on average something new every three minutes, but the choice of items. There is something for everyone in *Dirty Harry*. Right off, a girl swimming in a bikini is shot in a pool. We see the blood on her back. Soon after, a naked black is gunned down. He had to shoot the fellow, Callahan explains, because the man was chasing a girl up an alley while brandishing a butcher knife and an erection.

We hear of a 13-year-old girl buried alive. As proof of her existence, a detective holds up a bloodstained molar that has arrived in the mail. It was sent to her parents. Later, we will see the child removed from a manhole, nude, covered with dirt, dead, but chastely photographed.

A man ready to jump from a high ledge is informed by Dirty Harry that he will leave a mess on the pavement if he jumps. This so horrifies the prospective suicide that he threatens to throw up. Dirty Harry requests him not to vomit on the firemen below. He replies by trying to pull Harry with him. Now with the aid of another detective's binoculars, we look across into an apartment window. A naked girl opens her door to welcome a couple. They begin to make love. The sniper has them in his sights but is interrupted and guns down a cop instead. Then he shoots out a 30-foot neon sign reading JESUS SAVES in flame-red letters.

We find the killer. His name is Scorpio, and he gets Dirty Harry—almost—Callahan has lost his guns, is down and is having his face kicked in, but comes up with a last weapon, a long-bladed knife taped to his ankle. He throws it into the killer's thigh to the hilt. The killer screams, staggers off. Harry picks up his Magnum, begins to track the man, finds him later, fires, hits him in the shin. Scorpio's leg is now broken. Harry steps on it to make him confess.

In between these episodes are quiet vistas of Callahan walking the street or going down long halls. Full time is taken for such shots. Despite its violence, the beat of the film is laconic. The movie is almost as open in its space as a western. Maybe that is why the violence works. For the movie, when seen, is considerably less than this description of it. The violence is not so much unendurable as frequent and successful like a cruise with many ports of call. Dirty Harry looks as clean and well turned out as any young Senator with a promising future. In scenes where we see him striding the street, he could be walking from one campaign stop to another. Eastwood knows the buried buttons in his audience as well as any filmmaker around. Is it out of measure to call him the most important smalltown artist in America? One of the buried secrets to smalltown life is about is knowing how to press other people's buttons—that is, the ones concealed from themselves. . . .

M: Does the question of moral responsibility weigh on you?

E: How do you mean?

M: You can have arguments whether Dirty Harry reforms more criminals than he stimulates.

E: I never feel any moral problems with these pictures. I felt they're fantasy.

M: Come on. In *Sudden Impact*, three men are shot in the groin by a woman. It's possible that some man or woman out there who never thought of doing that before, may now.

E: I don't think my movies are that stimulating. People in the audience just sit there and say,

"I admire the independence. I'd like to have the nerve to tell the boss off or have that control over my life." In the society we live in, everything is kind of controlled for us. We just grow up and everything's kind of done. A lot of people are drawn to an original like *Dirty Harry*. The general public interpreted it on that level, a man concerned with a victim he'd never met. . . . And I think a lot of people believe that there isn't anybody who's willing to expend that kind of effort if they were in that situation.

M: There may not be.

E: There may not be. Right. That may be the fantasy—that there might be someone interested in my problem if I was ever in that spot. That preys on people's minds these days with crime in America, in the world. Jesus, is there somebody there, is there anybody there?

M: Do you think this is one reason why blacks like your movies so much?

E: Well, maybe the blacks feel like he is an outsider like they felt they've been.

I let it go. He was making a film, and I did not know that I had the right to argue with a fellow artist when he was at work.... Besides, I was not sure how I felt. Violence in films might have no more impact on future deeds than violence in dreams. Who could separate the safety valve from the trigger spring?

I let it go. I liked Clint Eastwood. Kin to him, I trusted my instincts. What if several hundred bodies were strewn across the 30 films he had made? It did not matter. In his movie gunfights, those bodies flew around like bowling pins. The violence happened so quickly that an audience was more likely to feel the kinetic satisfactions of a good strike in a bowling alley than savor the blood. Besides, nobody of virtue was ever killed by Eastwood. Perhaps he was right. Perhaps it was fantasy. How else account for the confident sense of duty in his person, his character, and his deeds?

What an American was Clint Eastwood! Maybe there was no one more American than he. What an interesting artist. He portrayed psychopaths who acted with all the silence, certainty, and gravity of saints. Or would it be closer to say that he played saints who killed like psychopaths? Not all questions have quick answers. Sometimes, it is worth more to dwell with the enigma. In the interim, he is living proof of the maxim that the best way to get through life is cool.

54

MARRIED TO AMERICA

(DREAMS AND NIGHTMARES: MAILER'S AMERICA, 2000)

In this excerpt, Mailer elaborates a simile he first used in The Armies of the Night, *where he said that his love for his wife and his love of America were "damnably parallel."*

I see my relationship to America as analogous to a marriage. You know, I love this country. I hate it. I get angry at it. I feel close to it. I'm charmed by it. I'm repelled by it. It's a marriage that's gone on, for at least the fifty years of my writing life. And in the course of that what's happened? The marriage has gotten worse. It's not what it used to be. In the time of Kennedy, one could feel that, with all his faults, with all his limitations, he was a real man with a real set of desires to make a good and exciting and interesting change in history. Then we went through various ups and downs. We had a giant who came after him who was immensely corrupt, a blind giant, an almost tragic figure, Lyndon Johnson. Then you had a political genius following him, Richard Nixon, a man with an unpleasant personality, who succeeded in getting the largest electoral vote of any President. Any man who can do that, I'd argue, is a political genius. And then you had Jimmy Carter, who was a very decent man but did not have a large political imagination. And then you get this fellow who's shallow as spit on a rock, Ronald Reagan, and he charms America. America loves him.

This country is my spiritual wife, if you will, and I've lost respect for it, just like losing respect in a marriage. If you're married for 40–50 years and you start to lose respect for your mate, it's sad. There's a similar unhappiness in my relation to my country. It has not become as great and as noble as I wanted it to become. So these are depressing years. As you get older, you have other things in your life besides your country. I have my work. I have my children. I have a lot of things. I don't consider myself a miserably unhappy man. I don't consider myself profoundly depressed, but if there's anything that does depress me, it's picking up a paper and seeing what's going on in this country every day. We're very far away from the New Frontier now. The New Frontier now is money and more money and more money. We've lost a lot of values en route.

55

JESSE JACKSON FOR PRESIDENT

(NEW YORK TIMES, APRIL 18, 1988)

As a native New Yorker, Mailer was well aware of how relations in the city between Blacks and Jews, warm and mutually supportive (as only members of parallel diasporas can be) before World War II, became defensive and angry, partially because of the hateful speeches railing against Jews delivered by Louis Farrakhan and other leaders of the Nation of Islam. Mailer hoped that Democratic presidential candidate Jesse Jackson's Rainbow Coalition might ameliorate these strains. Jackson was an unsuccessful presidential candidate in 1984 and 1988.

In the spring of 1977 when Ed Koch was beginning his first successful campaign for Mayor, I gave him a small fund-raising party. Ed always took nice cognizance of that. He showed up at my wedding; he invited my wife and me to dinner a couple of times at Gracie Mansion. I liked him. I still do. It is just that now I cannot forgive him.

Koch's statement that any Jew who would vote for Jesse Jackson is "crazy" may have succeeded in blasting the last rickety catwalk of communication between Jews and blacks in this city. That is unforgivable. I write these words as one of the crazies who will support Jesse Jackson for President. It is not only that Jackson is the sole candidate who can wage both an effective battle against drugs and give black people the conviction that this country can belong to them as well, but, paradoxically, I believe he will yet be good for the Jews in the best and highest sense, even if the Jews, with some justice, will never be able to trust him completely.

Let me hope to explain this last remark. Since World War II, I have lived like every other Jew, with the fundamental ill of the Holocaust. Hitler succeeded in wiping out more than a third of the Jewish population of the world, and upon the rest of us he left a fearful curse: The legacy of Naziism, now in its fifth decade, is still there to poison one's finer moral substance.

What made us great as a people is that we, of all ethnic groups, were the most concerned with the world's problems. If we had come out of centuries of ghetto life with profound psychic scars, there was, nonetheless, a noble spirit alive in enough of us to permit the feeling that we were the first children of the Enlightenment. We understood, as no other people, how the concerns of the world were our concerns. The welfare of all the people of the world came before our own welfare.

Hitler succeeded in smashing such generosity of spirit. After the Holocaust, a natural terror descended on world Jewry. If somewhere between two-thirds and three-quarters of all the Jews living in Europe—half the Jews on earth at the time—could be destroyed in a few years, then we were the most endangered of the human species. Survival took on a new order of magnitude for us.

Now we are relatively wealthy, powerful and accepted. Yet, we are still oppressed. Perhaps more than ever. It takes no insight to recognize that oppression of the spirit is the meanest poverty of them all. We have descended from parlous defense of the Jews as being able to bleed to Ed Koch's inaccurate assumption—I hope it is inaccurate—that we are by now, by and large, conditioned reflexes—that is, machines, buttons, for a politician to push. If any-Jew-who-votes-for-Jackson-is-crazy proves to be a useful political button, then I say we Jews have become machines and can no longer look at serious matters by their true merits, or face up to fundamental problems.

56

BLACK POWER, POLITICAL PARTIES, AND PRISON CAMPS

(*HOW THE WIMP WON THE WAR*, 1992)

It was Mailer's long-standing conviction that the fruits of slavery—segrega-tion, lynchings, Jim Crow laws, profound economic disparities, and myriad other related evils—threaten the continuance of American democracy more than any other phenomenon. He wrote about the destructive miseries of racism in several of his works, including this essay on the 1990–91 Gulf War.

The Black Power movement of the sixties, intended to give blacks a more powerful sense of identity, had, in the absence of real improve-ment, succeeded in merely moving whites and blacks even further away from each other. Encapsulated among themselves (in direct rela-tion to how poor they were), the blacks were now divided between a bare majority who worked and a socially unassimilable minority that did not. Legions of black youth were marooned in hopelessness, rage at how the rich grew obscenely richer during the eighties, and self-pity. If there was a fair possibility that black people were more sensitive than white people, then the corollary was that they suffered poverty more. Sensual people who are poor can drown in self-pity as they dream of how much real pleasure they could have if they had money. It is a point of view that will draw you to the luminous inner life of drugs. Afterward the luminosity is used up, the habit keeps one chasing the high through crime, for crime is not only quick money but the heady rewards of risk, at least when risk is successful. Prison, the unsuccessful consequence, comes to be seen as a species of higher education. It is a way of life for young blacks that does not gear into the working black community, and it has nothing to do with the working white community. The Democratic Party has a hole in its flank from the spearhead of this problem, and the Republican Party had a hole in its head. Republican thoughts on the subject had run out long ago.

Mailer decided that America—no matter how much of it might still be generous, unexpected and full of surprises—was nonetheless sliding into the first stages of fascism. The left, classically speaking, might be the best defense against fascism, but what was the left now able to contest? No part of it seemed able to work cooperatively with any other part, nor was it signally ready to work with the Democratic Party for any set of claims but its own. The Democratic Party was bereft of vision and real indignation, and, given the essential austerity of the Christian ethic, the Republican Party was never really comfortable with the idea that Americans like themselves ought to be that rich. Their unspoken solution became the righteous prescription: if those drug bastards don't work, throw them in jail.

Of course, the jails were another disaster system. The best of them were overcrowded, and there were no budgets for new prisons. If avalanches of new prisoners came along, the only place for them would be camps, guarded by the military.

This was merely a scenario, no more than one doomsday scenario as long as the economy held. Money could still soothe some crucial margin of every American's exacerbated feelings. Let the river of money go dry, however, and what would hold the country together? There might be revolts in the ghetto, curfews in the inner cities, and martial law. . . .

It did not matter whom you blamed. It was multiple choice, and all of the answers might be correct. The fact was that America was mired in grievances, miseries, miscalculations, slave history, and obsessions.

57

WARREN BEATTY: ONE ON ONE

(*VANITY FAIR*, NOVEMBER 1991)

Having failed to elicit even a smidgin of interest in running for president from Clint Eastwood, Mailer tried the idea out on Warren Beatty, with whom he was friendly. Behind both overtures was Mailer's awareness of the potent effects of JFK's movie-star looks on the voting public, and also the success of Ronald Reagan.

We are in the summer of 1991 and Warren Beatty and Norman Mailer are getting along well. Beatty is fifty-four and, depending on mood, looks ten to fifteen years younger. Mailer is sixty-eight and gets out of armchairs a little more carefully these days. However, they share a disposition: they both feel old enough to form new friendships slowly. Over a few nights of conversation, they have been exploring the unfamiliar condition of discovering an equal with whom it is possible that a new and agreeable relation can be formed.... All the same, they come to trust each other to a degree. For media figures, that is a phenomenon equal to Arab leaders negotiating with each other at face value.

The key is Warren's charm. Ignore his attainments: the two classics, *Shampoo* and *Bonnie and Clyde*; his exceptionally successful box office on *Heaven Can Wait*; his monumental attempt at a great film in *Reds*; the total of thirty-five Academy Award nominations for the four films and his several recognitions as producer, director, actor, and screenwriter; his aesthetically satisfying modern house, which he designed himself; and then there is his formidable good looks—who could defeat him in an election to determine the handsomest male star in America over the last three decades? Beatty's ace, however, is still his charm, yes, that tricky term. It slides around definition. . . . He never does or says what you expect—on the other hand, he is never wholly out of the zone of expectation. So he is friendly but elusive, as vain as molybdenum steel in the tensile strength of his ego, yet as modest and haunted as an unsuccessful actor at the prospect of failure.

On the morning of the day in 1980 when Norman Mailer would be getting married for the sixth time, he sat up in bed, put his feet on the floor, and said to the bride-to-be, née Barbara Davis, now Norris Church, "You know, all I ever wanted out of life was to be free and alone in Paris."

She had been a Wilhelmina model, a big, beautiful redheaded country girl from Arkansas with funds of common sense, so she knew it was not unnatural for a man who has been married many times to be miserable on an occasion like this.

"Look," she said gently, "suppose you were free and alone in Paris. You'd meet a girl and fall in love and live with her. You know how you are, honey. She would get pregnant and you would marry her. Then you wouldn't be free and alone in Paris anymore."

His mood lifted. She was right. His sixth wife would be wise, and it was his fate to get married. They had been together now for sixteen years and he could still say they loved each other, but there were times when the friction of marriage would prevail and her cautious mind, so much at odds with his dialectical extravagances, would proceed to infuriate him. . . .

So Norman Mailer and Norris Church had a war in early June 1991 about the upcoming evenings he would spend on the Coast with Warren Beatty. As he made the mistake of admitting to his spouse, he was going to talk to the movie star about running for president.

"That is the stupidest idea I ever heard," she said. "Warren Beatty for president? You will make a fool of yourself."

"If Ronald Reagan could lead us down the garden path for eight years, let's at least put a couple of talented actors into a contest. Warren Beatty for the Democrats, Clint Eastwood for the Republicans."

"Go right ahead," she said. "Everybody is waiting for you to do something stupid."

He did not come out on top of such debates. They ended, at best, in draws. Actually, for all he knew, Clint Eastwood was a Democrat. Besides, it could hardly matter. The thought of either man receiving a nomination was so improbable that a presidential contest between the two barely qualified as a metaphor.

Nonetheless, he had been thinking about just such a contest for years. Somewhere back in the early eighties, he had interviewed Clint Eastwood and been impressed with the star's character. One would trust him even when one did not agree with him. In the course of the interview Mailer did ask Eastwood if he had presidential ambitions, and the actor, while conceivably pleased by the question, replied, of course, in the negative. A few months after the cover story appeared, however, Ronald Reagan agreed to an interview for the same magazine (*Parade*—40 million readers), and Reagan was soon pictured on the same cover pumping iron. Mailer would never rid himself of the suspicion that Ronnie read little else but *Parade* and was a hint worried by Clint. Such a fear would not seem absurd to Ronald Reagan. Who better than him knew how little it took within to fill the role? And Eastwood was a man you could cast for president in a serious movie. For that matter, he later ran for mayor of Carmel and was elected.

Mailer took up the theme occasionally on the lecture circuit. All through the eighties, when asked who he would like to see as candidates, he would reply, "Warren Beatty for the Democrats; Clint Eastwood for the Republicans," and an unmistakable current of happiness was in the audience's mirth. While they knew it was impossible, and assumed that Mailer was looking to entertain them, they were stimulated by the thought.

Ronald Reagan had shown the way. . . . He was, after all, the leading man in America's number-one soap opera. Ponder it. The perils and fortunes of the American nation have become a collective narrative to absorb us more and more, and we are always seeking a leader to make the drama more compelling, and thereby give us a little more interest in life. Ronald Reagan was one captain of the ship of state who liked to sleep while his crew was gorging on the ship's stores, but Ronnie was always awake when the media lights came up to the bridge. Picayune may have been his larger dimensions, but all too many Americans loved him because he gave them what they needed on that malignant little screen where the family gathered. Hope was the subtext, and Ronnie, with the sly instincts of a B-movie actor, knew all about sentimentality, country, flag, dogs, Mother, children, loyalty to the cause, cavalry, and gather-the-wagons-round. . . . You were better off if you attached those concepts to no logic and no ascertainable facts. The game went on for eight years: nobody could say just when the machine went tilt. The nation, however, now had a malady without a name.

Norman Mailer, who rarely called on his modesty machine, had come up with no less than a name for this malaise. It was lividity.

W.B.: An actor whom I won't name said to me last year—quite an important man, not someone that I'm very close to, so you can't guess who it is—he said to me, "Alcohol really saved my life . . . the eight, ten years I was drunk."

N.M.: Alcohol saves a lot of people's lives; that's why it's so hard to give up. A lot of people drink to get close to some kind of mood again. We need a drink when we're a thousand leagues beyond a mood, when we can't get into any kind of mood at all. Then, even if we drink and begin to feel tragic, that's better than not being in any mood at all.

li-vid-i-ty, n. the state or quality of being livid.
liv-id, adj. 1. discolored by a bruise; 2. grayish-blue; lead-colored; as livid with rage.

Yes, lividity could serve as the name for a malady whose first symptom was to linger in a mood that produced the incapacity to get into a better mood; multitudinous were the social and economic processes that went into it. Lividity was everywhere—in one's fingertips at an outdoor cocktail party when the drinks came in plastic glasses. Lividity was in the downturn of one's mood every time one looked at a faceless high-rise office building, which offered nothing to the man on the street but a sense of abstract power, someone else's power.

Lividity oozed out of the offices filled with computers and fluorescent lights. Lividity was in the homogenization of every American city until, in most cases, you could not tell which major American city you were in any longer. Lividity was strip-mining the topography of nature with superhighways that screened you from the land through which you passed and informed you how many miles it was to the next stop, at a fast-food factory. Lividity was shopping malls. Lividity was a part of everything unhappy that had happened to America since the Second World War: television, the ravages of jet lag, the hollow in your gut left by antibiotics, the dead Latinate formulations used in political correctness, and the indefinable depression that came from paying too much for a product that was not as good as it used to be....

It was evident that if the situation was as dire as Mailer feared, its roots went too deep for any politician. No one could contend with it unless the dispositions of history were ready to move in a new direction. When that time came, a new man might be more useful than a familiar face, for only a new man could begin to express some of the new ideas that were necessary. Mailer had begun to think of Warren Beatty. He hardly knew him, but, with reservations, he respected him. Beatty had been active in presidential campaigns since 1968, when he worked for Bobby Kennedy: he had been part of McGovern's campaign staff in '72, on a serious and near-to-equal footing with Gary Hart and Frank Mankiewicz. As *Shampoo*, in 1975, and *Heaven Can Wait*, in 1978, brought in startlingly large returns at the box office, the reflection of such success became one more factor in encouraging other people to talk about Beatty running for public office. After 1974, when Reagan chose not to serve again as governor of California, a private poll showed that Beatty was the leading candidate among Democrats for the seat in Sacramento. It was Mailer's opinion that if Beatty entered the Democratic presidential primaries in 1992 the media would take care of his credibility automatically. "Is Warren Beatty a bona fide candidate?" would be the leads in feature stories, and the act of asking the question would, by the illogical laws of media logic, move the answer to the affirmative.

N.M.: If I came out here to ask you to run for president, I also suspect that you have lived with the thought and given it up. You wouldn't mind being anointed, but you don't want to go through the horror of campaigning.

W.B.: The horror? That's nothing but fun. Going out and shaking the hands—that's fun. Shaking the hands—that's really what's fun. That's politics. But governing is something else. There's nothing glamourous about the government. There's something very libidinous about politics. But government is a compromise in which everyone loses something and gets angry at you without seeing the result can be for the common good. What you need to talk about is how much preparation it takes. If you want to be president, you have to know, basically how to manage the economy, how to manage defense, how to—

N.M.: I don't agree. I think you have to know which of your experts is making sense at any given moment. It doesn't come from knowledge but from something deeper. No one knew government better than Lyndon Johnson. What he didn't understand was history. He took Communism seriously because he never spent a moment of his life thinking about it. If he had, he would have come to certain conclusions, such as: Maybe Communism can't work in advanced countries. It's not a real threat.

W.B.: Forget history. All Johnson needed was to wait for an elevator in the Metropole Hotel in Moscow.

N.M.: One of the fascinating things in the U.S. is the way this country believed that if we stopped fighting Reds for just one moment the Communists were going to succeed. We never believed in capitalism all these years. I think that's one of the reasons we've violated it so.

W.B.: Yes, both countries secretly feared the grass was greener on the other side. Now, without the Russians to fight, we have to find out how to make capitalism work, really work, for everyone. I think it can, you know.

N.M.: All right, you for president: my feeling is, yes, if you can take on the question of your national reputation.

W.B.: That's not the problem.

N.M.: The hell it's not! If they slaughtered Gary Hart, what would they do to you?

W.B.: I am the only guy who hasn't cheated on his wife. No, that's not the problem.

N.M.: If Gary Hart had possessed a different frame of mind, he could have said, "I've lived in marriage, I've loved my wife, I've cheated on her, yes, it happened. Marriage is the most difficult single human relationship of them all, the most sacramental, and the most difficult. And I fell from grace."

Many people would have said to themselves, "Yes, yes, it's true for me as well." He could have done it in such a way that he would have seemed more human than the other candidates. Of course, he would have been more human if he could have done it. Concerning you, however, people say, "That son of a bitch has been screwing beautiful women for the past thirty years, and never bit the bullet, never went into the pits, never fought those trench wars in marriage." That would be your obstacle. Envy. They envy you.

W.B.: Well, let's put that to the side.

N.M.: (Laughing) Thanks a lot! Discreet isn't dishonest. I haven't been hypocritical about it.

W.B.: Well, look, I'm not ashamed of my love life. I don't have anything to hide.

N.M.: OK. OK for now.

W.B.: One thing I have learned, because I've spent a lot of time in politics for twenty-three years, is that, while it would be nice for the Democratic Party to stand for something, we are doing patch-work nonsense, junior-Republican silliness. The Democrats are a hopeless case until some major new notion takes flight, and it could be that major new notions cannot take flight with anyone who has been trained in a conventional way. New notions won't come from careerists who've been getting elected by pandering to what they've been told is public opinion. More likely, solutions will come from a citizen willing to confront public opinion and enlighten it. Someone who risks losing. We're surrounded by careerist politicians who don't want to put their careers on the line to do what has to be done.

What's always struck me about the identity of this kind of politician is that he's like an actor who has committed to a long-term contract in a daytime soap opera. He has to keep that identity in order to keep his audience. So he plays the same part, year in, year out, and it's not even himself. Ronald Reagan was certainly not trained conventionally, but there was a major new notion involved, new in our time anyway: right-wing conservatism. Liberalism had spent itself.

N.M.: Reagan didn't have any new idea; he just said that the Free Market Is an Unmitigated Good. Anything that gets in the way is an Unmitigated Evil.

W.B.: What's the new idea for Democrats?

N.M.: That our purpose here on earth is to take care of those who are weaker than us.

W.B.: That's a new idea? Pretty hard to sell that now.

N.M.: Ripping off the economy, which is what the Republicans have been doing for ten years, is not what it's all about, either. Why, it isn't even capitalism.

W.B.: I said it's pretty hard to sell that now. I don't say you can't reach people with it next year. Or in five years. Someday we'll be able to. Because in order to take care of myself, I'm going to have to take care of you. That you can sell. You can say: I have to make peace with you; I have to love you; I have to take care of you; I have to take care of your mother. You have to take care of my mother. But a candidate is not going to get very far telling the country how high its cholesterol is . . .

N.M.: Why not say, "I'm looking for one fundamental law to change this country deeply and profoundly, to give us a cleaner and healthier and more exciting capitalism—which is that all companies and corporations are to be taxed in direct proportion to how much they spend on advertising and promotion"? That gives the economy a chance to clean itself out through its own means—which is, you make better products rather than promoting inferior ones. Look, political campaigns have become meaningless. Remember years ago when it was very important to millions of Democrats whether Adlai Stevenson could beat Dwight D. Eisenhower? People were emotionally involved. We need a candidate who can get Americans to care that he is running. He doesn't have to win, but he has to start something going that will shake the foundations of the present political system, which isn't even that hard to do anymore. Everybody is sick of what we have now. If the Soviet Union went quickly, then the odd, corporate oppression we live in could also change quickly.

W.B.: We may have hastened the end of Communism by upping our military spending, but there may be another shoe to drop on what we've done to capitalism. If we're going to save it, the ideas will have to come from the outside of our political structures. If you're seriously proposing that as some sort of avenue for me, I'm not doing it. But I can say that I believe that there's a huge franchise waiting to be taken over. That franchise is well known, and can be taken over from the outside and refurbished. The Democratic Party practically doesn't exist with its own set of principles now, so an insurgency could probably be more effective now than ever before.

N.M.: Anyone who could do it would, first of all, have to be able to talk to people on the basis of their feelings. The premise underlying my notions is that people are not drawn to any of the politicians around now because politicians use the old, dead vocabulary and all the good words have not only been used up, as they already were in Hemingway's day, but we're inhaling the ashes. . . .

W.B.: We need someone who can come along and truly speak to the people. If a person were to attack all those hypocrisies out there with short words and, as you say, real emotion, yes, I do believe they would change the vocabulary, they would change the dialogue—and they would, of course, lose the election. Their candor would be co-opted by the existing franchises, and things wouldn't be moved far. But they'd be moved some. The bottom line would be to the good.

So, just find someone who wants to put a year or two of their life into doing that.

N.M.: I think you have to go with the idea that lightning's going to strike and something's going to happen.

W.B.: You mean, win the election? Well, I don't agree with you. Most people who run for president think there will be ancillary benefits. The idea of actually winning is terrifying to them.

N.M.: Why are they doing it, then?

W.B.: To raise the level of political dialogue, to invigorate the franchise, to come to the aid of the party, to please their children. . . . There can be a multitude of reasons. But I've known very few people who ran for president who thought that they were going to win.

N.M.: Let me ask you a question from another quadrant. I'm entertaining a fantasy: If the Republicans have a major scandal or get into economic trouble, at a certain point some of their guys may say, "Listen, we did it before, let's do it again. Let's get another actor to run for office. Clint Eastwood for president." At that point, would you reconsider?

W.B.: Done! (Hearty laughter) I do think the kind of politics you and I are interested in could really be reduced to saying, "Look, the haves have to take care of the have-nots." Love Thy Neighbor is not a horrendously complicated thought. If someone is able to demonstrate the fun of that, the joy of that, that would be creative. That would be good. I don't think it's going to be accomplished through guilt. I think we'll have to feel the joy of creating something together and reaping the benefits of it together. . . .

In the main, I feel a little cynical. I know I'm experienced; I know that politics is an enjoyable profession for me, just as it is for you. It does bring the libido into play; there's nothing that I enjoy more than shaking hands with a bunch of people; there's nothing that has kept me up all day and all night like that. That's my idea of a good time. And I think that you have some of the same feelings or you wouldn't have done it yourself. I feel a little like the good people are waiting for an opening. . . . As you say, the weakness here might be a political scandal, or a depression. The opening might be the collapse of the banks.

I don't like any of the weaknesses. They're terrible. So I want to rest here on the ground and kind of use it as a timeout. And the timeout may go on for a while. But when the huddle is formed, I won't be able to keep from running back to it. And neither will you.

N.M.: You'll probably be penalized for delay of game.

There is a long moment in which the actor stares at the writer.

W.B.: Oh, all right, all right, OK, all right. Let's go. I'll select my vice president, my chief of staff, and my Cabinet in advance so the voters will know what they're getting into. The Democratic Party will be appalled and convulsed but will reemerge as the majority party. You've articulated the theme well. LOVE, NOT LIVIDITY. That's good. I like that.

I will now need your full participation. What the hell, you can go back to writing in a few years. Oh, uh, forgive me, but is there anything in your past I should know about? And while you're thinking about that, could you write out a check for $1,000 to Warren Beatty?

58

TO HILLARY CLINTON

(JUNE 26, 1992; *SELECTED LETTERS OF NORMAN MAILER*, 2014)

Mailer's recommendation in this letter—that Bill Clinton announce that Black-white relations and healing "the wound of racism" be adopted as the overriding task of his administration—was not taken, although President Clinton did address the issue in various ways.

Dear Hillary,

Let this serve as an expanded sketch of our conversation on Tuesday night. If Bill's economic program produces positive results in the polls, my suggestions here may seem like too much of a gamble; if matters, however, haven't improved notably by convention time, then I repeat: He has to give a speech that is going to knock everybody's socks off. To do that, I believe the speech has to have one powerful simple overriding theme.

That battle once won, every issue and program that Bill has thought and talked about through the primaries will become most important again—government *is* detail—but a major convention speech is hats-in-the-air time. The electorate listening and viewing here on this one occasion, will consist of a large portion, conceivably more than half of the total who have never seen Bill on radio or TV; if they have, they never really watched or listened. This is obviously the moment in which a candidate who wishes to be great can not only seize people's emotions but electrify them with an idea, a cause, a rich and hopeful sentiment that is larger than themselves. To repeat the obvious: One has to give the voter a reason to be happy they are voting, that is, inspire them with the legitimate belief that a high and beautiful ideal can still be realized in this nation.

So I propose that the major theme of the convention address—which will incorporate *all* sub-themes, is that Bill speak out on something that I believe is not only true to his beliefs but is indeed the reason I support him. I think he ought to consider saying that if elected, he will dedicate, he will consecrate the next four years to bringing whites and blacks, blacks and whites, together. He will mend the wound of racism or consider his administration a failure no matter what else it achieves. He will offer that as the climax to his address, and will have arrived at that point of declaration by speaking of the two fears that paralyze hope in America—the fear of joblessness and the fear of crime. He will make the argument that the two are profoundly inter-related. Joblessness came to us because the emphasis in the American economy for the last twelve years has been on marketing products instead of producing them well. We are suffering from the long economic malnutrition that results from gussying up the surface of economics (marketing) rather than the guts, which is production. The consequence has been a lack of interest in work, indeed a bitterness on the work-station that reflects resentment over welfare as well as unspoken rage at the huge profit-taking at the top. Crime is the violent expression of such profound unhappiness in working people. Good quality in production, therefore, is most likely to improve *organically* as the problems of welfare and excessive profit-skimming are reduced. The key to it all is an improvement in relations between white and black and it is for that reason I dedicate my administration, etc. If I can bring a large and happy improvement to that one problem, even if it calls for a crusade of all that is best in each of us, black and white, both I repeat, openness and charity of feeling in black and white both we can have a rebirth of the idea that two great races can live and learn from the genius and creativity of the other, then the twelve-year era of mean-mouthed and manipulative men pretending to be our leaders while they enrich themselves and augment their power will at last be over.

59

Depression, Desperation, Fascism II

(DREAMS AND NIGHTMARES: MAILER'S AMERICA, 2000)

Mailer returned again and again to the link between major economic down-turns and incipient fascism, recalling how the string of German economic crises in the early 1930s led to a ruinous fascistic regime led by Adolf Hitler.

If one's a leftist, there's really no political hope in America. To be a leftist now only offers a good opportunity to exercise one's critical opinions. If you look at the best left magazine in America, which is the *Nation*, what you find are a series of people who are complaining all the time. They complain with good style. The magazine is well written. They have a lot of sharp points to make. They will show everything that's wrong with everything that Clinton's doing, what the Republicans are doing, and they show it very nicely. It's a good, sharp magazine, but there's no program. They really don't know how to regain power. They have no idea of how to do it. My feeling, and it's a gloomy feeling, is that as long as global capitalism succeeds in being successful, economically successful, nothing will happen in politics. My guess is that global capitalism is not going to work for more than a decade or two before huge disasters overtake it. And I could be wrong. I'm often wrong. I know very little about economics. But the sad fact is that until there's a depression there's no hope for the Left, and one hardly wants a depression to come, because fascism could come to power long before the Left could even get organized. So, as far as politics go, I'm very gloomy.

60

BLACK JUSTICE/WHITE JUSTICE: O. J. SIMPSON

(*NEW YORK*, OCTOBER 16, 1995)

On October 3, 1995, after a nine-month trial, Black former pro-football star O. J. Simpson was found not guilty of the murders of his ex-wife, a white woman, Nicole Brown Simpson, and her friend, Ronald Goldman. The legal proceedings were the subject of massive reportage and heated debate in the country. In 1997, a civil lawsuit found Simpson to be responsible for their deaths and ordered him to pay compensatory and punitive damages of $33.5 million. He was later arrested for armed robbery and after serving a nine-year term was released in 2017. The following commentary on Simpson's acquittal, excerpted from an interview with Mailer conducted by his son Michael, focuses on the verdict and its painful impact on race relations.

When everyone in America was agog that the jury in the O. J. Simpson trial had come back with a decision in less than four hours, I was having dinner with a close friend, Ivan Fisher, the defense attorney. Ivan, like many another good lawyer, could not decide in that hour what the verdict would be, but he was certain of one thing: The jury had reacted in anger. Indeed, they did. The anger was vast. And I would say it came out of looking at American life from a black point of view.

Most blacks consider it vainglorious for any white to dare to speak from their point of view, but I am a novelist, and my occupation does require me to try to enter people's minds. I'd be happier in a world where women could write about men, men about women, and the Japanese could have real insights into the Irish. So I'll plunge ahead. I'll say that right now, whites are very angry. They feel that the jury paid no attention to the evidence, nor to the trappings of the law, which virtually demand that a jury argue the evidence back and forth before moving on to a decision.

Of course, these whites are not taking account of the attitude of most blacks toward American justice. Blacks see it as white justice; therefore, it's not justice. It's a game waged by players, sometimes very skillful players. When one team has considerably more money than the other, the varsity ends up playing the junior varsity. That's been the black experience going to court. Poor blacks have court-appointed defenders. So they see it as a game they usually lose.

As whites, however, we strive to hold on to the idea that justice is a chalice and our law courts are the altar. We don't care to recognize that not only in criminal cases, but even more in civil cases, a trial remains a game. Sometimes it is played for low stakes, sometimes for very high stakes, sometimes by mediocre players, occasionally by extraordinarily skillful players; but even at its best, the most we can say for the process of law in the courts is that it's a game where even justice may occasionally be served.

I think the black attitude in general—and of course I am generalizing; sometimes you can only encounter the truth by marshaling your generalizations against others—but yes, I think the general black attitude might be that white people place a huge emphasis on innocent or guilty because that way they can discard large social questions, sweep them off the court. A focus on individual innocence or guilt works to the white Establishment's advantage.

Once you say that justice must be served in every individual case, it enables you to take one hundredth of the highly imperfect social body and pretend that this is justice for all. Thereby whites can even feel a little less guilty about racism, disproportions of wealth, and the homeless. But from the black point of view, it's a shell game. The whites are holding the pea.

By now blacks are suffused with a sense of the evils that have been done to them over several centuries. From a black point of view, it almost doesn't matter whether O. J. is innocent or guilty. He is not guilty because this game has to be won. That will give a little recompense to the past. By black logic, it's neither good nor proper to allow the case to be sequestered away from all their other ills. So to hell with whether whites feel that it was a terrible injustice that O. J. went free. Let whites recognize that there were immense numbers of injustices that blacks suffered and for which they received no compensation. O. J. is their reward.

In effect, blacks are saying: "We are not interested in serving your white justice. We prefer our kind. Our justice is obtained from being able to arrive at our own sense of personal balance. And that can only come from emotional compensation. Compensation for what has been done to us in the past."

Let me give an example that is a little off to the side. When I was running for mayor of New York in 1969, several influential whites came to us and said, "If you could develop a good welfare program, people might begin to take you seriously." So Jimmy Breslin and I went up to talk with a women's welfare group in Harlem, and on the top floor of a tenement was a small apartment and two big, powerful black women sitting there at a long table. We never got a chance to open our mouths. One of them said, "Mrs. Goldplate on Fifth Avenue, she says I'm being paid welfare and I got a Cadillac. I say, 'My Cadillac is in the garage all the time and it's twelve years old and I can't afford the payments.' And she's got a Rolls-Royce and a chauffeur." The other one said, "Mrs. Silverspoon over on Park Avenue, she says I have five illegitimate children and I'm receiving welfare money for all of them. I say, Fuck her. I gave birth to my children. She didn't. She had seven abortions."

Then this woman said, "We want our share of the waste."

Where was an answer? Could we pretend that there was not prodigious waste at the top? We all know the example of Lee Iacocca asking his workers at Chrysler to settle for a little less while he's making $17 million a year.

The verdict was good for black emotion but terrible for whites. They now feel that black reactions are totally irresponsible. How can you live and work, whites will claim, with people who have no regard for the facts and don't live emotionally in our society, don't understand our feelings? Of course, blacks feel the same way about whites. My anxiety from the beginning has been that if we can't find some way for blacks and whites to come together, this country is going to head for fascism. We won't go that far unless there's a serious depression. But if we have a major economic wipeout in America, we're on the way toward barbed wire. If liberals think Republicans are getting too tough on blacks now, consider what will happen in a real depression. As soon as there are riots in the ghettos, a lot of unused army bases will become holding camps. We'll have a de facto fascism with increasing repression of the media. The only thing we can be certain of is that however the leaders will describe it, it won't be called fascism. . . . Ron Goldman's father, no matter the extent of his suffering, certainly seems determined to start a war between blacks and whites. When he said, "The prosecution didn't lose today, America lost," that's an open appeal to racial antagonism.

Start with the assassination of JFK. Then two more terrible assassinations, Martin Luther King and Bobby Kennedy. Vietnam through all of that. Then Watergate. And the years in which Ronald Reagan and George Bush tripled the national debt in order to combat the Evil Empire. Whites can see these events in many a way, but from a black point of view, one may arrive at more consensus, for blacks can see themselves as inhabitants, willy-nilly, of a powerful, vain, imperial-minded country that's shooting itself in the foot. Only they are the foot.

For 40 years, we were led to think of the Russians as godless, materialistic, and an Evil Empire. When the Cold War ended, we suddenly discovered that Russia was a poor Third World country. They had not been equipped to take over the world. In fact, they were just trying to improve a miserable standard of oppressive living, and couldn't. They had to spend too much on arms buildup. We didn't win the Cold War: we bankrupted the Russians. In effect, it was a big bank exhausting the reserves of a smaller one.

Now, people in America didn't necessarily think all that through. But they felt it. It was as if for 40 years we had all been magnetic filings, all lined up in the same direction. There we were, unified against the Evil Empire. Now it's as if a big switch has been thrown. The magnetic field no longer exists. All the filings are free to scatter. We don't have an external enemy to hate any longer. But we still have 40 years of hate and fear built up toward an Evil Empire that isn't there anymore. So everyone in America is now reckoning with random, quickly focused hate for just about everyone else in America. And that has been the background for this case. It has brought us together like nothing since the Cold War. We were in a magnetic field again.

So I say again: Let's try as whites to look at things from the black point of view, at least a little. Maybe a few blacks will even come to look at whites from more of our point of view. Until the two races begin to understand the great divide between their basic premises, we are nowhere. Take a very large generalization: Whites, for example, believe in technology. Blacks, I would say, have more of a belief in divine forces, dark and light.

The net effect of this case is to increase the potentiality for totalitarianism in America. And if you say, "What do we do about it?" because that's always the basic American question—"What do we do about it?"—sometimes you just have to stop and feel the emotional and philosophical fatigue of an unhappy matter and say, "I don't know yet." After all, it's not the only one of our problems. We have many, some of them immense, and maybe out of the sum of these problems (because democracy, one hopes, one always hopes, has resources yet untapped), we will find solutions, or at least continuations. But at this moment, all I can say is that if you're dealing with someone who's not well and he or she suddenly comes down with one more abominable illness, you can't pretend that something good has happened. I repeat: The O. J. case was a spiritual plague for America from beginning to end, no matter who won.

61

THE RAGE OF SLAVERY

(INTERVIEW WITH CHRISTOPHER HITCHENS,
NEW LEFT REVIEW, MARCH/APRIL, 1997)

Mailer's criticism of both liberalism and conservatism in this interview, as well as Blacks and whites, demonstrates the complex and destructive divisions in American life. He speaks here with the urgency of an Old Testament prophet in his call for self-examination by all sides and factions in order to preserve the commonweal.

If America goes towards fascism, which could easily happen, given the terrible state of relations between black and white, then I'm worried about the fate of the world. I'm not sure but it seems to me that the rest of the world will very quickly become fascistic too, at least the superpowers will be hard put not to get into equally authoritarian forms of government. And then, given the new info highway, my God, we're under the thumb. We could be under the thumb for a century. So I think the first line of defense is to stop fascism. It's that old 1930s cry turned around: stop the advent of fascism in America. If we avoid a depression, we'll probably be able to avoid fascism. But if we don't avoid that depression, I don't see what's going to prevent it. I think that the Left has to have a total house cleaning. We have to recognize that we're much darker and bloodier and complex and at cross purposes than the Left has ever understood. Despite the conservatism that sees human nature as ugly, and that caters to that, we've got to find a way to say human nature is both ugly and beautiful, and we have to deal with both. We have to live with the fact that every hope we have can be destroyed by the fact it is humans that are carrying out these hopes, and we bloody up everything in sight and we mess up everything. And once liberalism takes on a certain modesty and stops thinking that because one's well educated, one can dominate existence with one's brain, once liberalism loses this notion that a control freak is the highest product ever developed by humankind, then maybe the Left can regenerate itself. But for now all we can see is what's wrong with the opposition, and we never take a good look at ourselves. And we're narrow-minded and futile. And the Right have just cut us to pieces in this country. What we need are a couple of great theoreticians to come along. Oh, that a Marx would rise among us, a new one. Doesn't mean they have to be right. Just to give us blood and some enthusiasm and some juice.

I think Jimmy Baldwin was trying to tell us, tell white people, because he had many friends among white people, that it's not the way you think it is. I, Jimmy Baldwin, am not as sweet and friendly as you believe, and all those blacks that you know and love are not that friendly either. We're full of rage. Get it through your head we're full of rage. And we've been able to measure that rage over the last thirty years. It's the rage of slavery, it's the rage of being ripped out of one's country. I mean, at least other Americans came here voluntarily. Blacks were ripped out of their country. They were betrayed by their own leaders and sold into slavery. So they have that rage which they can't quite face perhaps, together with all the other vast rages at what was done to them once they came here. And that built, and that was enormous. And so what happened is that, as far as whites were concerned, when almost all liberal whites and half of even the reactionary whites in America were finally ready to accept the blacks as coming into the society and we had this beautiful idea, equal whites and equal blacks and so forth and so on, that the blacks were so full of rage that part of all the backlash now has come out of the fact that they began to express themselves. And that expression was full of murderous fury. I mean, if you want a measure of the change in these thirty years you can go from the kind of music that Miles Davis was playing, or Sonny Rollins, or Thelonious Monk, that sort of marvelous, intricate music that spoke of the complexity of human life, and the beauty of it, and the difficulty of it, and how you got your orgasm, all that wonderful stuff in jazz, and now you compare it to gangsta rap, which is as intense and hateful as the worst pages of the Old Testament. Especially when it comes to talking about women. You measure those two and you can see what's happened.

Part of the true problem is that, before there can be better white and black relations, the blacks have to come to a recognition that they are half responsible for everything bad that's happened. Because they've taunted whites. They've attacked them. They've given us to believe that there's nothing good about us. You can't do that to people. They know themselves you can't do that to people, because we've done it to them. And so, before white and black relations can improve, there's got to be a recognition that the two great armies of feeling are going to have to meet midway. And if the blacks are not willing to do it—I'm not sure they are, it may be that their deepest feeling by now is a hatred so intense and so deep that they'd rather be exterminated, dammit, than take one positive step toward whites. Because a positive step toward whites in their mind is an odious, unpleasant, repugnant step. Now, if that's true, if that's the real state of relations in the inner heart of the black kingdom, then we're nowhere. We will have fascism and the blacks will be the first victims of that fascism. Because the way it'll come about is, if we have a depression in this country, the one thing you can certainly count upon is that the ghettos will suffer first. And if there are outbreaks in the ghettos, comparable to Los Angeles, you're going to have military police, especially if you have a right-wing government running this country. And after the military police you're going to have internment camps with barbed wire. And after that you're going to have the press starting to be pinched and finally cut down and curtailed, and then you'll have a de facto totalitarianism. There won't be uniforms, they won't call it fascism, but it'll be an oppressive totalitarian state. And then slowly, probably, the uniforms and the music will come too. But it's up to the blacks as much as it is up to the whites to save this country, America, at this point. And if they don't want to, we're doomed.

62

A LONG TALK WITH REPUBLICAN PRESIDENTIAL CANDIDATE PATRICK BUCHANAN

(*ESQUIRE*, AUGUST 1996)

Patrick Buchanan (b. 1938), right-wing political commentator and two-time Republican candidate for president (1992, 1996), was a major force in the party's hard turn right in the 1990s. He borrowed the slogan "America First" from the isolationist group that opposed the entry of the United States into World War II, and this slogan was reused by Donald Trump. Buchanan, however, was sharply critical of the power of corporations, a concern shared by Mailer, who used it as a wedge in this conversation in which he suggested that Buchanan join forces with a Democratic presidential candidate, black civil rights leader Jesse Jackson (b. 1941).

Perhaps it could be said that close to fifty years of the cold war had to go by before Patrick J. Buchanan and Norman Mailer could speak to each other through a long afternoon.

Since it was Norman Mailer who sought the interview, we may as well begin with the motive. He was approaching a conservative as far to the right as Pat Buchanan. Why? The answer, clear to hand, is that during the Republican primary in New Hampshire, Buchanan had spoken not as a conservative but as a left-conservative. Since Mailer had for years been assuming that he was the only left-conservative in the land, he now had the curious pleasure of discovering that he was half of a two-man band. Of course, the novelist, by his own measure, was two-thirds left and one-third conservative, whereas Buchanan had to be, at quick estimate, three-quarters conservative. Nonetheless, some agreement might be found. Mailer had become so exercised, so infuriated, by what was happening in the country, the Congress, and the Clinton administration that he had been ready to run in the Democratic primary for president. . . . Nonetheless, he was no recognizable grade of presidential timber. Yet it gnawed at his opinion of himself that Clinton's nomination in 1996 would not be contested. Having belonged to the legion of enthusiasts for Bill and Hillary in '92, he had been hopeful that the candidate and his wife would help to bring forth a new era for a nation addicted, by the end of the Cold War, to a host of foul habits. Before long, he had been bitterly disappointed.

Clinton was too many things to too many: pro-choice, pro-feminist, pro-black, pro-gay, pro church-on-Sunday, pro-family values, pro-Hollywood, even pro-corporate business to the degree they would accept him; if it came to it, and it would, he would be pro-military, pro-combat. Wars were the first emolument of incumbency!

It certainly had to be said: Bill was, by now, bedded down with every special-interest group in the Democratic party and with a good fraction of the opposition—a species of political diddling that Mailer had come to call Boutique Politics. Clinton had not steered a navigable course. Instead, the vessel of the Democratic party was becalmed. Separate banks of oars, strained upon by separate echelons of galley slaves in the White House, pulled in opposite directions. Where were the gays to be found who would pool resources with blacks? Or vice versa? And everyone knew that the leader was not going to die for a political idea unless it was pro-choice. There, he had no choice. Female liberationists would dismember Bill Clinton if he wavered. Indeed, it may have been the only matter on which he had not compromised with the Republicans.

Of course, the inanition of Clinton's Administration was but in part his fault. With the end of the Cold War, the United States had lost an essential paranoid fiction, precisely that dramatic myth that had supported the well-being of the American system for forty-five years. We had an evil empire as our enemy, and it had been invaluable to us. What a shock to the system to discover by the end of the Cold War that this evil empire was but a poor thing—a Third World country— that needed our economic support to prevent a descent into chaos.

The abrupt disappearance of this once trustworthy fiction helped to produce a distrust of our government so profound that many a militia patriot was ready to fight the FBI down to the last man. Paranoia being a state of imbalance that lives on absolute answers, the militia, in company with some sizable number of Americans, had come to believe that the federal government was engaged in a worldwide plot to hand America over to international bankers. Indeed the International Monetary Fund was giving $10 billion to the Russians.

Our erstwhile candidate suspected, however, that the militia was mistaking the American government for another force that might be dominating our lives more closely. The feds, after all, were a gaggle of highly separated institutions, bureaucratic mills, and grassroots extensions; we all know how they aid and certainly impede the average American in a thousand if not a million ways.

Yet on reflection, it is hard to conceive of the federal government as owning so purposeful a will that it controls an alien force that is able to come creeping into our beds A more appropriate name for the source of the phenomenon—creepage!—has to be technology with its half-compatible parents, the U.S government and the U.S. corporation. And of the two, it was the corporation (if you were seeking to detect an invisible force able to control your life despite yourself) that looked to be the likelier villain. . . . Mailer could even recognize that he hated this Second Government, the Corporation, with something like the same intensity that the militias brought to their passion against the U.S. government.

Onto this stage of the author's mind enters Buchanan into the Republican primaries of '96. He wins early in Louisiana, comes in second in Iowa, and then proceeds to thrive in New Hampshire. Moreover Buchanan is acting in much the way Mailer had expected to carry himself if he had run. Pat is being himself. He is saying "Here I am with my quick wit and my caustic tongue, my offbeat laugh and my political passion and my gaffes. I haven't been prepared in advance for you, freeze-bagged and microwaved by political technologies, I'm a brilliant boy with a lot of faults, but I'm here on the hoof, and you can take an honest look at me."

Buchanan had scored in New Hampshire! There had been an energy in his campaign, an off-the-cuff virtuosity one had not seen in years. While what he said remained for the most part ultraconservative, right to life, pro-NRA, and he called for fences to keep out illegal immigrants, he also kept after the Corporation like an attack dog. Its loyalty, he told all who would listen, was no longer to America but to money.

His crowds loved him. There was a subtext to all he was saying, and it was ultrapopulist. "Wisdom," declared this subtext, "is not to be found in the think tanks of the experts but in the experience of the people."

Soon enough, Mailer began to play with the idea of doing an interview with Buchanan. It could prove costly, however, to the hard-earned equanimity of the author's days. Buchanan had reverence for icons, and the first was Ronald Reagan.

Yet Buchanan's raids on the sanctity of the Corporation might be a trumpet call to some kind of new politics. For years, Mailer, dreaming of a left-right coalition, had known it must start on the Right. People on the Right, oriented to the Sacramental, were suspicious, stingy. Most of their ideas were fixed in Perma-bond, whereas people on the Left were more flexible, more—it could be said—more desperate in their political isolation. Ergo, they were more ready to take on a new idea. At the least, one could explore the possibilities. Would Buchanan, for example, be inclined to a serious reduction in military outlay? All the other concerns of Mailer's good political day—medical support for the sick and the elderly, the restoration of the environment, workfare, some honest revision of welfare, a reduction of the deficit, even a reduction of the hatred between black and white—could be in part resolved by downsizing the Pentagon.

Of course, when it came to politics, Mailer knew that he was part of the ongoing naïveté of the majority of Americans. At the age of seventy-three, he was still looking for hope in outlandish places. To think that Buchanan, who had made this one startling move to the left, could be the harbinger, if not the protagonist, of a profound realignment in American politics was naive indeed, yet Mailer was weary into the grinding grit of his soul with the tiresome, wholly condemnatory politics of the American Left and the American Right. Neither spoke of the other except to excoriate or misrepresent, and all the while, capitalizing on their mutual animadversion, the Corporation was enjoying lavas of greed while taking in avalanches of appropriation. So, too (via TV), had flourished Roman circuses of mind-leaching entertainment for the populace.

It was time to have a dialogue between Right and Left. Might there be some potential for agreement? If Mailer went to talk to Buchanan, however, it must not be with a set of preformed media stereotypes of the man. He would not be there to scold Buchanan for being loyal to Larry Pratt of the Gun Owners of America nor to assume he was anti-Semitic; no, such routine media baggage would make their dialogue mutually fail-safe and sterile. On the contrary, if he wished to elicit a new point of view, he would have to take Buchanan on his own terms and assign as much purpose to the candidate as he gave to his own ideas.

Besides, Mailer was intrigued by the political possibilities. In the military sense—and where was any pleasure to be found in campaign analysis without a military analogy?—Buchanan had anchored his right flank on pro-life. Abortion, he had made clear, could never be acceptable. His right-wing credentials impeccable, therefore, Buchanan was free to move as far as he wished to the left, the economic left; the Corporation could now be attacked from the left *and* the right. A crucial difference. The Corporation, monarch of the center, could be deposed only if both ends attacked in combination. Left-conservatism! For forty-five years, it had been no more than an oxymoron. Now, with Buchanan, there was a gleam of possibility, call it no more than a wink, but the possibility was there. How far to the economic left was Buchanan willing to go?

Buchanan was taller than he appeared to be on television, perhaps six feet, and his weight was trim. They shook hands, and, after a moment or two of mutual recollection of Chicago in the summer of 1968 (where they had both been in the same group of shocked and startled onlookers on the nineteenth floor of the Hilton, looking down on Michigan Avenue when Mayor Daley's police proceeded to beat the demonstrators), they now sat down, tape recorder on the coffee table, not quite twenty-eight years later, and began to talk.

They had met again a few times in the intervening years, once in a Washington restaurant sometime in the eighties and again in a corridor of the Astrodome in Houston during the Republican convention of 1992. Man to man, face to face, Mailer liked Buchanan well enough. Given the fragmentary basis of these brief meetings, Buchanan looked to have humor; your heart would not sink if he turned out to be the passenger who sat next to you on a long flight. They both sat in high-backed upholstered chairs about six feet apart, and Buchanan set his body at a full 45 degree angle away from his interviewer; their eyes did not often meet.

Norman Mailer: I followed your campaign in New Hampshire and enjoyed sheer hell out of it. I thought you are certainly one of the more strong-willed and strong-opinioned conservatives in the country. Yet you uttered the most radical set of remarks that any candidate for the Democratic or Republican parties has spoken in years. You were saying that a large part of our problem is the American corporation.

Patrick Buchanan: The truth is, I used to believe Charlie Wilson [president of General Motors] when he would say, "What's good for General Motors is good for America." In the fifties, 98 percent of their employees were Americans; they were the highest-paid industrial workers in the world. But when General Motors figures it's in its best interests to move its next factory to Mexico and take it out of Michigan, then what's good for General Motors is no longer good for America. When these corporations see that the advancement of their bottom line means getting rid of these costly American workers and moving to Singapore or Mexico or China, where they can cut their labor costs by 90 or 95 percent, then what's good for corporate America is no longer good for America. This could be the death of the Republican party if it continues to carry water for these corporations.

NM: All right. This is our area of agreement. But it seems to me—and maybe you won't go along—that the Republican party is the Corporation, that is, the Republican party is the political arm of what I call the Second Government, the corporation.

PB: The Republican party is going to have to cut those ties, or it's never going to be the nation's majority party.

NM: But the Republican party, I will say again, is the political arm of the Corporation. By this logic, you can no longer be a Republican.

PB: It's the old question: Do we stay inside the country club and try to open up its admissions policy, or do we leave in protest and start our own club? That's the decision before us.

NM: I have an ax to grind. My feeling is that your future is in the Democratic party. I do see it as the other political arm of the Corporation, the minor political arm, but all the same, the party is closer to that huge mass of Americans who don't like greed.

PB: Let me tell you this, Norman. In Louisiana, I spoke at the library in a tiny town about fifty miles outside of Lake Charles, over near Texas. The mayor introduced me and gave me the key to the city, and they cut loose, they were cheering, yelling. And as I was leaving, because I had come there as a presidential candidate, the mayor said, "Why did you come here? There's only two Republicans in the whole town." They were all Democrats, but they loved what we were saying about the corporations.

So our problem is this: A significant slice of our coalition is in the Democratic party. Where Democrats could vote in Republican primaries, we did best. A significant slice is Ross Perot [third-party candidate for president in 1992 and 1996] supporters; a significant slice is Republican. The best way to get that all together, we believe, was to capture the Republican nomination and then reach out to those Perot voters and those grassroots Democrats and say, "We are populist, conservative, traditionalist; we are against big government, big corporations. America first, and we're running against the establishment." Our problem is, Republicans tend to be loyalists. When we ran against George Bush in 1992 in the New Hampshire primary, 80 percent of New Hampshire Republicans said they agreed with me, not with George Bush.... The party is strong. The problem is the establishment in Washington. Can you overcome and displace the establishment? Or is it just too strong, too determined?

NM: You are running into the stonewall of all time if you're trying to separate the Republican party from the Corporation.

PB: Well, we could have if we had gotten the nomination. Let that part of the party go; let it walk away. Where is it going? Let *them* ride in the back of the bus. You can get the grassroots of the party, the Perot people, these grassroots Democrats. Of course, it would be tough. The entire establishment—the media, the corporate establishment, and all the others—will try to stop you from the nomination. But once you could get the grassroots, I think it would be one of the great, glorious contests of all time.

NM: But the key problem—and you stated it clearly—is, if you leave the Republican party, many of those loyalists will not vote for you, no matter how sympathetic they are.

PB: Yep. And you have to take a look at the possibility that you're not a third party but a fourth or fifth or sixth party. You've got the Libertarians there and Ralph Nader and Ross Perot.

NM: Becoming a Democrat opens up something extraordinary, however. One of the ironies besetting the Democratic party now is that this country is a Christian country—not a Judeo-Christian country but a Christian country, first and foremost.

PB (laughing): That puts you in trouble, Norman!

NM (laughing): Being Jewish, I probably can afford to say it's a Christian country. One small advantage to being Jewish! But here's my point: The average Democratic congressman who dares to invoke the name of Jesus Christ is doomed!

PB (laughing): Go on.

NM: The president can be a practicing Christian—he can go to church and invoke the name of God—but the average urban white Democratic congressman certainly cannot. The result is that the Republicans have picked up a great many Democratic voters whose religious faith is more important to them, finally, than their politics. You have more or less said the same thing. The power that you would set loose in the Democratic party by saying, "We are for more economic justice and, at the same time, reinvigorating some sense of the spirit" would be enormous. What you're up against, and I will say this over and over, is, I can't conceive of the Corporation ever letting go of the power they have in the Republican party.

PB: You're exactly right. The corporations are not going to let go. But we had almost taken over. Almost. Six points more in Arizona. If we had broken through there, it might have carried us over the top in Georgia. One week after Georgia came Florida, Mississippi, Tennessee, Oregon, Texas, Oklahoma. That's Super Tuesday.

NM: You would have had a chance at Super Tuesday?

PB: Georgia was the key southern state. If we'd beaten [Republican presidential candidate Robert] Dole there, the whole South would have been up for grabs. All you needed after New Hampshire was to go over the top in Arizona and then in Georgia . . . but it didn't happen.

NM: I don't mind if some people make twenty or thirty times as much as others, but I don't think the ratio should be five hundred to one. That breeds all social disease.

PB: If the middle-class and working-class folks were seeing a steady increase in their standard of living, as they did in the fifties and early sixties, I don't think people would pay much attention to someone making a lot of money. But they do if they're slipping themselves. You look at some of these corporate executives. When their companies do badly, their incomes remain astronomical. There's a sense that an enormous amount of rip-off is going on. The return is in no way justified.

NM: And the products are not getting better.

PB: Right. The products are not getting better. I think it increases the national—almost contempt—of the capitalists. Eventually, this will translate into contempt of the system. We're getting to the point where the big corporations are being seen as increasingly unpatriotic. It is a new era, but most of the Republican party at the national level is still very much a Cold War party. It can't let go. It misses the Soviet empire, all the Cold War paraphernalia.

NM: Would you agree that the war gave a free ride? We had an enemy. That enemy was godless materialism.

PB: It made everything easy. It provided clarity.

NM: But at a huge cost. Because it was a drug. Absolutely a drug, that Cold War. Here, you may disagree profoundly, but I think the Cold War was over twenty years before it ended.

PB: People watched Jimmy Carter talk about, We've gotten over our "inordinate fear of communism," and all of a sudden Iran is gone, they're holding Americans hostage; the Red army's in Afghanistan, Ethiopia, Angola; they're in Grenada; they even have a beachhead in Nicaragua. I was in Ronald Reagan's White House. We were doing our best to expel the Soviet beachhead in Nicaragua. It all collapsed— you're right; I think it was hollow by then, and you anticipated that . . .

NM: Hollow! The Soviet Union was endlessly hollow, and I think there were certain people who knew it. But you guys bought it, that this was an expanding empire.

PB: Here's the thing, here's the thing: Why was everyone saying, "We have to watch Reagan; he will get into a war with this mighty empire"? Reagan did not directly confront the Soviets. He challenged their empire around the periphery, the Soviet empire would not feel its *vital* interests were threatened. He moved the Stingers into Afghanistan. Moved aid to the Angolan resistance and aid to the Nicaraguan resistance. Moved even into Mozambique. He bled the empire dry. It was a gradual and consistent pressure, and I think he built up America's defense establishment until he finally broke them. And it collapsed.

NM: Well, I could put it another way entirely. The Soviets were a worn-out palooka by 1970.

PB: You know, the one thing I think the American people do believe is that we did win. People ask me: Can you name one good thing that government has done? Yes. We won the Cold War.

NM: Well, I try to take that away.

PB: Look, Norman, look, it seems to me—I was there with Nixon, remember, in 1972, '73, '74. The United States lost the Vietnam War, or at least, the West lost the Vietnam War. The demoralization of the United States in the seventies was incredible. I believed, generally, at the end of the 1970s that we were in danger of losing the Cold War.

NM: There we disagree. The Soviets didn't have it anymore. Under Stalin, it was a great threat. He, no question, was insane. An evil empire, if you will, back in the fifties. But I think Khrushchev alleviated the worst Soviet strictures to a considerable degree. If America had gone through several revolutions and several overthrows of government, and had had a hideous system for over fifty years and an incredible war in which twenty million people were killed and another twenty million expired over several decades in prisons and camps, how much will to fight would be left? I've never been in a country where so many people were depressed as in Russia in 1984. You were there earlier than I was, and you saw the same thing: this prodigious depression. When you have a country where everyone is down that low, it is not about to wage a major war. They knew by then that they certainly didn't have the stuff to conquer the world.

PB: Eurocommunism was a very big thing in the late 1970s. I think Ronald Reagan really provided the leadership, the philosophical offensive, the economic offensive, the Reagan Doctrine. The Soviet Union collapsed without firing a shot, and it was a phenomenal victory for the West. Now, it could have been we overestimated, although I don't think we overestimated how strong they were militarily.

NM: Well, that's arguable. They couldn't even win Afghanistan.

PB: One of the reasons is we provided Spanish mortars and Stinger missiles. I think Reagan made the Soviet Union pay a hellish price for its empire.

NM: Would you agree that we, too, paid a great price for the Cold War?

PB: Oh, we paid an enormous price.

NM: Not only economically. Spiritually. For four decades. We assumed that we had an enemy who was dangerous, lethal, godless, and evil. All our hatred—and a lot of hatred exists in this country—was focused on those Soviets. I've used this image before, and I'll use it again. We were all like iron filings in the same magnetic field. With rare exceptions, we all pointed in the same direction. And when the war ended, when the Cold War ended, it was like you threw a switch. The magnetic field no longer existed. The filings began to scatter. But the hatred was still there. America has been more divided in the last four or five years than at any time I can recall. Everybody is hating everybody. Hating your enemy is no longer as comfortable as it used to be. For politicians, the Soviet Union had been invaluable. It was like having a dependable mother-in-law, the one you can blame for everything.

PB: I think there was a genuine feeling in this country, and it was valid, that we had a mortal enemy outside the gates, and it took a measure of unity and solidarity to face that enemy. Suddenly, the enemy is gone. So we go back into the house, and all the old disputes that existed before the threat have now come to the surface. I think what happened in the conservative movement is that a lot of us have gone home to where we came from—the idea that America ought not to be an empire. That we ought to tend to our own business and stop meddling in other countries' affairs. We see that the war is over. We ought to come home, retrench, repair, reorganize, and rebuild our own country, our own nation. All right. Some communists have been reelected in Eastern Europe. But I think this second-generation communism is not what the earlier one was. It doesn't have the spiritual hold on any one. It's no longer, quite frankly, a threat to the United States of America. The United States ought to take a look at the world as it is. The potential threats and menaces to American security are very, very few, and they're very far away. I think we ought to be a normal country in a normal time. Look, if Russia rises again, it's not going to look around for an enemy halfway around the world. It's mainly going to be a threat to its neighbors. I don't think the United States ought to counter threaten them with military force or hot war or blockade or all-out war. I would say to the Russians this: We know you can invade the Baltic republics and Poland. There's nothing we can do about it militarily. You can overrun them in two days. But if you do, here's what's going to happen: You'll be diplomatically isolated; you'll be politically isolated; you're probably going to force massive rearmament in Western Europe, which we will assist. You're going to be alone in the world. You're going to have problems with the Muslim countries, which we're not going to help you with. You'll have the hostility of Western Europe, which we're not going to help you with. You're probably going to have the hostility of China and Japan. You will be friendless on the earth. Why are you going to do it? Why are you going to reestablish an empire that you people had to give up because it was bankrupt and the people hated you? Do you want to remain friends with the United States? There is no natural conflict between Russia and America or between the Russian people and the American people. Why create one?

NM: You'd be willing to reduce the size of the Pentagon?

PB: Surely. I think that's right. I believe the United States should remain superior, on the seas, in the air, in technology, and we have to have the finest fighting men in the world, but you don't need a hundred miles of American troops sitting in the middle of Germany, guarding a border that doesn't exist against an enemy who went home six years ago. Eventually, the South Koreans, who are twice as populous and have six times the economy of North Korea, have to take full responsibility for their own defense. I think the United States should confine its treaty commitments to air and naval power. We're not going to put another army on the ground in Southeast Asia.

NM: So you are saying that we don't need a military organization which attempts to control the affairs of countries all over the world?

PB: Now that the Cold War is over, Europe is as prosperous as we are. It has more people than we do. It is as technologically advanced. There is no reason why Europeans cannot handle the defense of Europe themselves. We aren't the Romans protecting an empire ...

NM: I think Americans felt subtly betrayed by how the Soviet Union came to an end. Do you agree that part of the huge distrust of government is that people felt lied to? Systematically. Where were those terrible, terrible Russians? We're suddenly taking care of them.

PB: I think there's a lot of sense of what in heaven's name are we doing now, giving them foreign aid and loans?

NM: If they're not evil now, why weren't they not evil then?

PB: Well, speaking for the folks for whom I speak—we think we won the war—

NM: And I keep saying you bankrupted them.

PB [laughing]: Okay! We bankrupted them. Better we bankrupt them than we exchange weapons with them.

NM: Come on, you know and I know that if you beat a man in a poker game because you have more money you can't take the same kind of pride in it.

PB: All right, right, there's something of a letdown, there's no doubt about it. It didn't end with a bang. It did end with a whimper.

But I was glad that all those Eastern European countries broke free, virtually without firing a shot. Look, the Cold War is what brought me into active politics; it's what activated my journalism in St. Louis; it's the reason I supported Goldwater; it's one reason I was with Nixon all the way, even though Nixon had his own vision. It's why I was in Reagan's White House. It was "Get the communists out of Nicaragua"—it was our whole life. And I feel now we've got a second life. The war's over.

NM: Well, with all due respect—

PB: You don't think the war *existed*.

NM: It never existed to the extent . . . you guys exaggerated.

PB: You're saying we exaggerated . . .

NM: My basic argument is that you fellows exaggerated the danger of the Soviet Union by at least one order of magnitude. You were calling 10 percent 100 percent. Nineteen hundred marines went into Grenada, and I don't know if they knew it in advance or discovered it to their huge embarrassment, but they were up against a thousand construction workers. They kept it secret for three days, the embarrassment was so immense. But it was used, it was used. The country celebrated.

PB: The country loved it.

NM: Let's talk about what it would take for you to become president.

PB: Sure.

NM: One of the fundamental problems in America now is the gulf between blacks and whites. It seems to me that an economic sufficiency for the working people of America is tied into an economic sufficiency for blacks. Clinton does have a little showpiece here for black people and another little showpiece there, but nothing's happened. He's really changed nothing. There's a huge dialogue still waiting to be held between blacks and whites. Half of the trouble in the Democratic party is their reliance these days on what I call Boutique Politics. Five or six unrelated political causes. For example, the problems women have in America, or gays, are minor compared to the gulf between blacks and whites. Unless we learn to live with each other, we may not survive as a country. Not in the form we know

now. We could break down into race riots and ghettos with barbed wire around them. I mean, this country will hold so long as we don't get into a depression. . . .

PB: You're talking about the major social problem of our time. We've got to start the income of working men and women rising again, especially those who work with their hands, tools, and machines, many of whom are black and Hispanic and rural white. Three ways to do this: One, stop forcing Americans to compete with folks who can work very hard and very well for a lot less—stop illegal immigration into this country cold. Two, I believe you should have a temporary halt to legal immigration. There are twenty million such people here, many of whom work very hard and undercut the wages of working men and women. Three, you have to get rid of these trade deals that force American working men and women into competition with Mexican folks who work for a buck an hour, a buck-fifty an hour, or Chinese who work cents an hour. In other words, you have to return to the idea that the American market is for the American worker first and foremost. People deride this as protectionism, but it is economic nationalism, which has as its goal a plenitude of jobs where the wages of working men and women rise every year, as they used to do in the 1940s and 1950s and early '60s . . .

NM: You were saying this in New Hampshire and other places—I kept listening. And I kept waiting for you to say a little more. I believe the only way your ideas will work here is to create more interest in production itself. I think some very bad habits formed in the American working class over the last thirty or forty years, a cynicism about the job that comes out of the very monotony of the work in manufacturing jobs. In addition, there's not enough real self-interest for working well. It seems to me that a good part of profit that goes to the top of the corporation has to be plowed back in the form of bonuses for workers.

PB: A stake in the profit margins.

NM: A large stake. A team with pride. This country certainly thrives on the idea of competitive teams. . . . I think you can't begin until the emphasis moves from marketing to production. What we have now is a huge amount of needless advertising.

PB: You sound like my old friend Earl Butz when he was sec-retary of agriculture. He'd show you a loaf of bread, take out all the pieces, and say. "How much of this goes to the farmer?" He would take one slice of bread and a half slice and say: "This is what goes to the farmer who produces everything that's in here. And the people who put the package together and sit it in the supermarket, that's where all the rest of this is going." It was a very powerful message. But how do you restructure the whole?

NM: What we're really talking about is the mind of America. My argument is that you're paying for it whether you know it or not. The prices on products are higher because of excessive advertising. If five products are about equal, like any five automobiles out there, then don't spend 10 or 15 percent of your budget on promotion in order to try to get some phony advantage over the others. . . . Go back to the father of capitalism, Adam Smith. His idea was that if there is a free play of workers doing their jobs, the best products will win. And a healthy society will come out of that. We've gone far away from such a concept. By now, in marketing, the real pleasure is to sell something that's crappy. Anyone can sell something that's good. But to market a mediocre product successfully, that shows skill.

PB: Aren't you sort of just complaining? Television is here. We're not going back.

NM: There are ways it could be changed.

PB: How?

NM: Let the American worker begin to take a little pride in what he or she is making.

PB: I think it's crucial. Let me tell you, this is what I've talked about. There's tens of millions of Americans who don't get any sat-isfaction at all from what they do. The number of people who do good work with their hands and with tools is being reduced to a smaller and smaller share of the American labor force. I agree with you 100 percent that you don't want to have just the assembly-line job where people do the same thing hour after hour after hour. Now, your thought of advertising is something I haven't given a great deal of thought to, but there's no doubt about it, there's an enormous amount of the wealth, of the business budget, that is spent not on producing the finest product but producing the most effective ad to outsell the competition. Sure.

NM: I've been suggesting that unless you make some major move to double your constituency, there's no Buchanan presidency on the horizon. Suppose you had won the Republican nomination; could you have made such a move to Jesse Jackson?

PB: There was no doubt we were looking at some people outside the Republican Party. We looked outside. You mentioned Jackson—if someone could bring you 20 percent of the black vote without losing you something, you'd win the election. But I think if you went outside the Republican Party, you probably would have exacerbated your basic problem, which is to put the party together.

NM: I vow on my nine children, I'm not here as an emissary—but what, for instance, if you and Jesse Jackson could do something together within the Democratic party?

PB: That would be exciting within the Republican party, too, Norman.

NM: Certainly would.

PB: No, I'm saying that the differences between me and Jesse are so great on so many other issues that if you move into an alliance like that, you forfeit a significant part of our constituency.

NM: *He'd* forfeit a significant part of his constituency.

PB [laughing]: Let me say this: Jesse, I think, is on the right side of NAFTA for the right reasons. He sees these deals as putting working-class black folks in America into direct competition with people who have considerable skills and work for 10 percent of the wages that a black American gets paid in a factory. Now, we could come together as we did on NAFTA and GATT—a non-interventionist foreign policy. But a considerable part of my base is with social and cultural conservatives and traditionalists. And Jesse has gone south on right to life.

NM: I confess I'm a little bewildered by some of the NRA arguments.

PB [laughing]: I know what you mean. I'm not going to get into an argument with you about it.

NM: I can understand people who want to keep their firearms. I can accept that they are sincere. But this idea that militiamen need assault arms to defend themselves against the government is not a real argument. We all know that the Army won't care whether you've got a rifle or an assault gun when they go in with their tanks. To me, that's where the National Rifle Association goes off the rails. It violates the notion that a citizen is entitled to small arms for personal defense.

PB: I think many of the people in the Second Amendment movement believe that the ultimate objective of the gun-control movement is to disarm the American people incrementally. Take what seem to be reasonable positions against unpopular weapons. Then use incidents to get the camel's nose into the tent. The goal is the registration of all firearms.

NM: All right. That's what the goal is. That doesn't mean the goal can be achieved. I think the worst thing one can ever get into politically is to start defending a notion in which one does not really believe. I think the NRA lost their high ground by defending assault weapons. . . .

At Yale that winter, Mailer had given the Chubb Lecture, and he now proceeded to quote from it: "Will the time come," he had written, "when we can cease concerning ourselves with the fiction that the rich need large profit incentives in order to keep our economy going? Just as a poor man does all he can to survive under the most wretched circumstances, so will the rich continue to be rich (although less so) if their profits are reduced by the recognition that a modern society cannot take an honest breath until it manages to provide for all its citizens . . . "

PB: On first reading, I don't disagree with that. You don't need a salary that's 140 times the average worker's when the boss used to have one that was 20 times. I don't think you need those enormous profits or rewards to give people adequate incentive. But let me tell you, I don't believe in policies to end that. People have to be able to reach for the stars. It doesn't bother me that Bill Gates has his $12 billion or that Ted Turner has his $2 billion—as long as the person being rewarded is treating his people fairly and well and generously. So I don't have a problem making sure there's no roof over any man's head as long as the floor of decency is under every man's feet.

NM: How about the idea that a modern society cannot take an honest breath until it provides for all its citizens?

PB: An affluent society like the United States has a moral obligation to take care of the less fortunate among us now. There are differences over how that should be done. The welfare state has become a total monstrosity. It's loaded with so many traps. I think the American people are generous and good-hearted people. I don't think the government approach works. There's no doubt of our obligation to charity to those less fortunate.

NM: But then you end up with another kind of welfare. See, my point here is that welfare may be god-awful, but then look at all the rich who do not work a damned bit, who never produce anything. They consume and they're filled with envy for those richer than themselves. Who are they to judge the poor? Yet they're the ones always saying, "Those welfare people don't do a damned thing, and they're living off the fat of the land."

PB: Well in that sense, they don't have a moral standing to judge the poor, but a fundamental difference is that a lot of people think, Whatever the wealthy are doing or not doing, they're doing it with their own money or their daddy's money. They're not doing it with *mine*. The objection of the middle class and their hostility to welfare is that while I am earning my own way, they are not. They're living off *me*.

NM: You mean they don't disapprove of those who were lucky enough to inherit money: they're just disapproving of the bad luck of the poor?

PB: How you're going to deal with that problem is you get into an inheritance tax on the superrich. A hundred percent over a million dollars, zero underneath.

It was frustrating. So near, so far away. Yet a few of Buchanan's sentiments had actually traveled further to the left than anticipated. Mailer was finally beginning to comprehend the cost of real politics. In order to gain one's desired end, you had to surrender a good many feelings in which you had long invested. And often they were your most generous feelings. To live the life of a congressman—or, even more excruciating, a statesman!—would, for a man with conscience, be equal to suffering the ardors of a wrestling match through every hour of one's working existence. "I will sacrifice my shoulder socket in order to keep a hold on your neck."

Yet if some inner peace did not come to America in the next few years, fascism would be pressing at the gates. The irony was that Buchanan, who had been named and feared by the media elite as a demagogue, a potential leader of fascists, was, more likely, an antidote, harsh to the taste, but, ultimately, a man of reason. It was only the Corporation that commanded enough to metamorphize us, step by step, into a totalitarian state.

Contemplating the specter of drugs, AIDS, crack, welfare mothers, and the homeless, Mailer took it for granted that there were power centers in the Corporation that had come to the conclusion (and the freshman Republicans were certainly there to abet them) that the effective solution to their endangered interests was to keep applying heat to the downtrodden toes of the problem. With a little luck, riots would, in fact, commence. If white neighborhoods were invaded by the rioters, there would be martial law to ring every ghetto. If matters escalated, then free speech would be curtailed in a few newspapers, then in a great many. It would be totalitarianism without a name, and corporate capitalism would live happily in a new concept of democracy. A somewhat curtailed democracy. They would not call it fascism.

Given such a perspective, Mailer could even contemplate the temporary closure of immigration for which Buchanan had been calling. The American internal situation might be bad enough to require such an action as a palliative. It was an idea that would in other years have seemed outrageous to him, but there was almost a palpable need to stabilize the raw, outraged, bewildered, and furious nerves of the nation. For a time! All sedatives become poison if used for too long, and a protracted closure of immigration would certainly be destructive to all that was most noble about America. Could he really give assent, however, to a limited period without immigration?

A MYSTERIOUS COUNTRY

Was this another pill he must prepare himself to swallow for a left-right coalition?

Buchanan kept coming back to how he could win the Republican nomination. Mailer was obliged to recognize that his hope that Buchanan would move to the Democrats had certainly contracted by late afternoon. Nonetheless, he kept telling Buchanan that he could not win as a Republican.

NM: You present the Corporation with a huge problem. In effect, you have said that you are their enemy. You are never going to get the Republican nomination. They'll change the rules before they'll let you have it!

PB [laughing]: But we came close.

NM: You did and you didn't. It's true that you came so near it was like watching a boxer who's fighting beautifully for four rounds, and suddenly he's counted out in the fifth round. And one never saw the punch. After it was over, I said to myself, "Why did he ever think he could win?" Because I knew if you did—I have a hundred disagreements with you, but I knew if you won, everything was going to be open again in American politics, all the questions that have been buried for decades under a blanket. The blanket of the Cold War.

PB: It would have been a very exciting time right about now. (Laughs.)

In the four years that remained before the millennium, startling dislocations in the body politic were bound to occur. It was not impossible he had planted one small seed in Buchanan's presidential ambitions. Not likely, but not impossible. Indeed, if Buchanan ever came over to the Democrats, a fruitful chaos might result in party ranks. For the party was in need of a vast housecleaning.

63

HILLARY, BILL, AND MONICA

(*LONDON OBSERVER*, AUGUST 29, 1998)

Mailer's essay on President Clinton's problems stemming from his sexual liaison with Monica Lewinsky, a White House intern, moves from the scandal to a critique of Clinton's "boutique politics," a poor substitute, in Mailer's view, for engaging head-on the racial disharmonies of American life. He also makes it clear that he believes Hillary Clinton would be a better leader.

In the late thirties, there used to be any number of dirty jokes circulating about Franklin D. Roosevelt and Eleanor, but they worked their way out of the side of one's mouth. It was the time, after all, of eight-page cartoon books featuring Popeye and his King Kong prong, or Olive Oyl having one on the house (or the horse). Now, in the years of Bill Clinton, the jokes are on the Internet or come to you by e-mail: "How is Clinton different from the Titanic?" "Why, only 240 women went down on the Titanic." Monica Lewinsky told a friend: "You could say I earned my presidential knee-pads."

In America, the mood is almost gay. A trifle nauseated, but gay, like a rough trip on an amusement ride. Once again, the American spirit is investing in a matter about which few knew anything, yet the ignorant were certain they would keep being rewarded. If Clinton had to resign, then we'd have a new media era. The old one, after all, was getting dull.

On Cape Cod, a land much exposed to wind and tide, there is a local expression: If you don't like the weather, wait ten minutes. The Clinton years have been like that. Two weeks ago, Clinton was on the way out. Last week, he was back. Quite likely, he'll stay. Two weeks ago, Clinton was a broken pustule on the American flag. Last week, the independent prosecutor Kenneth Starr had become the glop. If you don't like your weather, wait ten minutes.

Of course, the Clintons must receive due credit for turning it around. They know that they are the biggest soap opera in town. Hillary's defense of her husband on the *Today Show* (where else?) was monumental. Indeed, for that mob of voting citizens out in the big middle of our land who get up to take TV with their first coffee, there was reason to be impressed. Here was a woman who had been accused of every crime from murder to illegal manhandling of official files, and she was undented, she was undaunted, indeed, she was better-looking now, at least in the soft-focus of newspaper photographs, than when Hill and Bill took office five years ago.

Humiliated over the years by a hundred sexual encounters large and small, real or suggested, that her husband had had or was supposed to have had, legendary for her temper concerning such infidelities (and where in the world is the wife who can forgive any kind of association with a girl who looks like Paula Jones?)—what iron in the lady! And there is Bill with his trousers now famous for being shucked down to his ankles. Yes, Hillary has suffered humiliations on a scale few women in history can match. Yet, there it is. She comes out early on the morning of Bill's State of the Union speech and defends her man with fury, conviction, and purpose. He is—like O. J. Simpson—"100 percent not guilty." Her man is not guilty. Hillary is on the way to becoming a legend. How many millions of wives in America are now obliged to say to themselves: Could I ever defend my guy like that? Hillary is wonderful.

Hillary *is* wonderful. She not only defends, she attacks. She speaks of a right-wing conspiracy to destroy her husband. It satisfies our deep need in America to find a new conspiracy every year. What powerful instincts are in Hillary. The first lady's features, when studied, are remarkable. On the brow and mouth of very few women is written so vast and huge a desire for power. Of course, she is loyal to her Bill, loyal certainly by her good side, but even more loyal out of darker and more powerful urges. For if she remains loyal to him she will yet become a legend in America, and that is necessary to satisfy what may be her true aim—to become the first woman elected president of the United States.

If [Democratic presidential candidate] Al Gore should win and have two terms, then the year is 2008. Should Gore not win in the year 2000, then 2004 is her moment. The price is to be loyal to a man she might prefer to brain with a brick. She must know the old Italian saying: "Revenge is a dish that people of taste eat cold." How much better to wait and put him in a position of being First Man. Bill will not feel comfortable to find himself in Denis Thatcher's old slot.

On Tuesday evening, January 27, after Hillary's performance on *Today*, Bill gave his State of the Union speech to a vast audience of Americans, and it was not different from all his big speeches over the years. It was more than an hour long, and it touched upon something like fifty national and international problems. For each, he had a specific social solution. To improve education, he would reduce the average number of children in public school classes from twenty-two to eighteen. He would put all of our future surplus from a reduced budget into Social Security. Never argue that such savings would never be enough to take care of Social Security for more than a few years, or that eighteen children might be no happier in a classroom than twenty-two if they were going to study under the same wan fluorescent lights that are ubiquitous now in our classrooms. Just keep the speech going. So it went. And it went, and a solution came up to meet each problem, conducting you to a pew as deftly as an usher.

There were no deep projects proposed, there were no serious suggestions of undertakings that might unhorse your status quo or mine, no, it was all tints and hues, a small program for a modest social wrinkle here, a little spot remover to put on there. It was, when all was said, a cosmetician's catalogue, but it had been developed by a consummate pitchman who could project a sweetness of mien, a steadfastness of purpose, and the healthy, earnest suggestion that no citizen of America who was in want could possibly be alien to him.

Like all the other major speeches he had given, very few of the proposed programs would be obtainable once they entered the jaws of the Republican Congress. And whatever did get done would not change much. It was reminiscent of the products you buy when it is late at night, the critical powers are weak, and the TV infomercial becomes convincing. Yet, how good he is at it! This Tuesday night, he gave the greatest of all the hour-long empty itemized speeches he has delivered year after year.

But on this night, Bill Clinton was the real substance. It was a wow. He never faltered once, he never gave a hint there was a girl named Monica Lewinsky and she had a tale or two or three or four to tell. He showed why he was president. Millions of American men also out there watching had been caught once or twice in infidelities by their wives. So they knew what it takes. When it had happened to them, they could barely function. For weeks, they had had to run on empty, but here was a guy who could put all his troubles in a box and act like he had not a care in the world but to be good and effective and aware of all the things to be done. No wonder he was the president. Yes, he had finally convinced the American people. Maybe he had dodged getting into a soldier's uniform, but he was still a man. Because now he had shown that he could stand up in public and exhibit grace under pressure. In America, we care only for heroes. Grace under pressure suggests that you are one of the boys who deserve to be invited into the club.

Clinton had hitherto been—to use the nicest word—a house pet for the Republicans. They would never admit it, but he had been wonderful for them. His proposed medical program had sunk of its own dolorous complexity, and that was because he had attempted to keep everyone happy. Of course, he never bit the bullet long enough to say: Let's just pay for it. Let's go to bed at night knowing the poor and the old and the sick can also sleep. If we are a Judeo-Christian nation, let us put our money where our mouth is. No, he kept his medical program complicated and he lost. But then, he had lost before he began. To guarantee future defeat, he had tried earlier to get the gays accepted in the military. So, the Republicans could love what he did for them. Clinton had managed to mess up his first two years sufficiently to bring in a yahoo Republican Congress in 1994. Afterward he never tried to fight them. It was easier to leach what remained of the bedraggled spirit of the Democratic Party by moving himself into the middle of the Republican Party.

Clinton then ended welfare as we know it, which was just what the Republicans wanted. However, he did not end corporate welfare. He did not assume the rich were no more entitled to a free ride than the poor. Instead, he used his mouth. He spoke of beautiful social programs. Little social programs on low budgets. But by his acts, he completed the scenario of Reaganism. He took apart what was left of the safety net for the poor in order that the maximization of profit for the rich might be maximized more. Under Clinton, the rich got vastly richer. All the while, on his spiritual saxophone, Clinton played tender resonant ballads for blacks and women. Some of them even got high-end jobs. It was gilt-edged tokenism. Measured as a Democrat, however, who might retain some real social purpose, he was a dork and a nerd.

On the other hand, but for the possible exception of Hillary, he was the most powerful Clintonite in the country; he was, indeed, a mighty lion of a Clintonite—he was his own most important and powerful project. That is true of more than a few of us. The crucial difference here is that Clinton is most mighty as a lion when his favorite project, himself, is threatened. He is at his best when wounded. How many can say that? Yes, he certainly comes through when it is a matter of projecting for one dramatic night what a wonderful all-seeing, all-doing American president he is.

What he does not deliver, of course, is any vision of the world larger than himself. How can he? His deepest relations are not with the world but with himself. So, his political charm is beyond measure when the occasion presents an appropriate contest for him. That field of contest is to go out and save himself. This he succeeds in doing by standing up superbly in public when everyone else would be supine with panic before the media onslaught.

He, however, knows better. He knows that the media is like Madame de Stael, who threw her friends into the pool for the pleasure of fishing them out again. He knows that if he shows up, if he speaks and never misses a beat, it will, under the circumstances, come over to the audience as an impressive work of oratory.

64

TO SAL CETRANO

(MARCH 28, 1999; *SELECTED LETTERS OF NORMAN MAILER*, 2014)

A New York City teacher and poet, Cetrano (b. 1948) was one of Mailer's many Republican friends. Like many others, Mailer was dismayed by the major cutbacks in welfare payments to the poor made by the Clinton administration, which he saw as a betrayal of both the principles of a compassionate government and Judeo-Christian ethical standards.

Dear Sal,

We've never talked about your Republicanism since the few times we were lucky enough to share a meal together, why would one want to bring that up? I'll only say—and I've not really written about this yet—that while the Democrats, and Clinton first, disgust me with what I call their "boutique politics"—a little bit here, a little bit there, and served with loads of bullshit slathered over it—the Republicans are a psychotic monstrosity. On the one hand, they're God, flag, and family—although few of them would know Jesus Christ if he were standing at the next urinal pissing along with them—and an astonishing number never served in the armed forces nor heard a bullet, and being politicians, they cheat like jackrabbits on their wives and families. But all right, what's the use of being a politician if you can't make a living at being a hypocrite? The point is, the Republican Party is schizophrenic: on the one hand, they are, as I say, for God, flag and family, but on the other they are for the unbridled expansion of capitalism, and thereby leave out something that might still be important to you which is that Jesus, like Karl Marx, thought that money leaches out all other values. Indeed, it does. If the whole country is going to pot, and it certainly is, I think you could graph the decline not only in morals, but in a sense of social éclat and social standards—I think you could plot the decline right next to the rise of the Dow Jones—the higher the Dow, the lower the standards. Money destroys all other values. I can even respect the right wing Republicans for holding to a few standards, as they do, but they never take on capitalism, which, unbridled, is the worst scourge of human value that we have right now. There may have been a time when Communism was a worse scourge, but now we're the leaders, and I suggest you consider living with the notion that the party of your choice is paralyzed in its moral centers. . . .

As for Clinton, leave him to heaven. His crime is not that he messed around in the White House—you become, after all, a successful politician by pressing the flesh, and after a while it is like a meal for a hungry man, and I don't see Hillary ladling food anywhere but at a soup kitchen—but his real crime was to end Welfare "as we know it" without ending Welfare as we don't know it—that is, corporate Welfare. It's a monstrosity in my mind, to save money by lecturing the poor and kissing the ass of the wealthy. As the old song goes, "that ain't healthy."

65

LARGER THAN THE ATOM BOMB

(*BBC NEWSNIGHT*, APRIL 2, 2002)

Mailer made the following statement about the 9/11 attack to a BBC inter-viewer about seven months after the attacks. He was in Provincetown, Mas-sachusetts, when the planes crashed into the Twin Towers but got a firsthand account of the event from his daughter Maggie, who watched it happen from his apartment in Brooklyn Heights where she had a clear view of southern Manhattan.

I think 9/11 was even larger, this is a huge remark to make, but larger than the atom bomb that fell at the end of the Second World War. 9/11 has had an enormous impact. I was living in Massachusetts, on the tip of Cape Cod, so I was 300 miles away from New York when it happened. My children, who live in New York, were furious at me, because they felt that my reaction was not huge enough. Everybody in New York was walking around stunned, apparently. They still haven't gotten over it.

I think it was a matter of emotional scale, if you will. In America, people get mad at each other, but despite all of the stories about mur-der and killing and violence in America, the fact is most Americans are peaceful, essentially. They just can't conceive of anyone hating them that much. "How can anyone hate us? We're a sweet nation. We're a good nation. We want good for everyone." Most Americans are pretty innocent. The worst thing that can be said about my coun-try in one sentence is that they don't like any question that takes longer than ten seconds to answer.

I think that Allah is a concept that's absolutely foreign to Americans. It's as if a great divide is coming upon the world. On the one hand, no matter what lip service one pays to religion, no matter how often one invokes the name of Jesus Christ, the majority of people are living their lives with the idea that they're not going to worry about death. They're just going to do as much as they can to hold off death as long as possible. You see, it's become a money culture. "I live for my life," they say, everyone says. And in effect, they are very practical, so far as life goes, and have absolutely no concept that's at all enriching about death. On the other hand, you have Islam, which says this world is a total bloody mess, most of us are poor. Those who are rich at the top are awful and corrupt. We have this abominable life, but we have heaven if we live, and die, especially, for Allah. What you've got is a huge war shaping, in which what you've got, let me speak like a Jamaican for a moment, we've got "Allah versus the Almighty Dollah."

66

AMERICA'S CRUMBLING SPIRITUAL ARCHITECTURE

(WHY ARE WE AT WAR?, 2003)

The following excerpts are taken from Why Are We at War? *(a compilation of interviews with and essays by Mailer from 2002 and early 2003), which was published in April 2003, a month after the beginning of the Iraq war. Mailer's warning about the disastrous repercussions of the war have proven remarkably prescient. As of this writing, October 2022, Iraq still does not have a functioning parliament, and its factional political groups are deeply divided. It appears to be settled wisdom now that the Middle East is far less stable as a result of President George W. Bush's impetuous and unjustified invasion. In 2004 and 2005, Mailer did several interviews with John Buffalo Mailer about the war's deleterious effect on the US, collected in* The Big Empty *(2006). In mid-2005 he had open heart surgery. His last two books, a novel,* The Castle in the Forest, *which depicts the early life of Hitler, and* On God: An Uncommon Conversation, *conversations with J. Michael Lennon on his theological and spiritual beliefs, both appeared in 2007. He died on November 10, 2007.* Why Are We at War? *is arguably Mailer's most comprehensive, incisive, and impassioned analysis of the imperiled state of American democracy and stands as a cogent summation of many of the key themes and ideas of this collection.*

9/11 is one of those events that will never fade out of our history, for it was not only a cataclysmic disaster but a symbol, gargantuan and mysterious, of we know not what, an obsession that will return through decades to come.... What in God's name was happening? It is one thing to hear a mighty explosion. It is another to recognize sometime after the event that one has been deafened by it. The United States was going through an identity crisis. Questions about our nature as a country were being asked that most good American men and women had never posed to themselves before. Questions such as, Why are we so hated? How could anyone resent us that much? We do no evil. We believe in goodness and freedom. Who are we, then? Are we not who we think we are? More pressing, who are "they"? What does it all mean? . . .

A mass identity crisis for all of America descended upon us after 9/11. . . . Our response was wholly comprehensible. We were plunged into a fever of patriotism. If our long-term comfortable and complacent sense that America was just the greatest country ever had been brought into doubt, the instinctive reflex was to reaffirm ourselves. We had to overcome the identity crisis—hell, overpower it, wave a flag. We had had a faith. The ship of the United States was impregnable and had been on a great course. We were steering ourselves into a great future. All of a sudden, not to be able to feel like that was equal to seeing oneself as a traitor to the grand design. So we gathered around George W. Bush. That he had not been elected by a majority even became a species of new strength for him. . . .

The transient, still-forming, fresh national identity could not for a moment contemplate the fact that maybe Bush should not even be in the White House. Why? Because now the country had to be saved. A horror had come upon us. There were people on earth so eager to destroy us that they were ready to immolate themselves. That went right to the biblical root. Samson had pulled down the pillars of the Temple. Now there were all these Muslim Samsons. A ripple went through the country, a determining wind. In its wake, flags rippled everywhere. Nearly everyone in America was waving a flag. For a few of us, this great indiscriminate wave of patriotism was not a joy to behold. . . .

We had a parade in Provincetown on the Fourth of July, 2002. A rather nice looking, pleasant fellow—he looked to me like a young liberal lawyer—came up and smiled and handed me a small American flag. And I looked at him and just shook my head. And he walked on. It wasn't an episode in any way. He came over with a half-smile and walked away with a half-smile. But I was furious at myself afterward for not saying, "You don't have to wave a flag to be a patriot." . . .

Free-floating patriotism seemed like a direct measure of our free-floating anxiety. Take the British for contrast. The British have a love of their country that is profound. They can revile it, tell dirty stories about it, give you dish on all the imperfects who are leading the country. But their patriotism is deep. In America it's as if we're playing musical chairs, and you shouldn't get caught without a flag or you're out of the game. Why do we need all this reaffirmation? It's as if we're a three-hundred-pound man who's seven feet tall, superbly shaped, absolutely powerful, and yet every three minutes he's got to reaffirm the fact that his armpits have a wonderful odor. We don't need compulsive, self-serving patriotism. It's odious. When you have a great country, it's your duty to be critical of it so it can become even greater. But culturally, emotionally, we are growing more arrogant, more vain. We're losing a sense of the beauty not only of democracy but also of its peril.

Democracy is built upon a notion that is exquisite and dangerous. It virtually states that if the will of the populace is freely expressed, more good than bad will result. When America began, it was the first time in the history of civilization that a nation dared to make an enormous bet founded on this daring notion—that there is more good than bad in people. Until then, the prevailing assumption had been that the powers at the top knew best; people were no good and had to be controlled. Now we have to keep reminding ourselves that just because we've been a great democracy, it doesn't guarantee we're going to continue to be one. Democracy is existential. It changes. It changes all the time. That's one reason why I detest promiscuous patriotism. You don't take democracy for granted. It is always in peril. We all know that any man or woman can go from being a relatively good person to a bad one. We can all become corrupted, or embittered. We can be swallowed by our miseries in life, become weary, give up. The fact that we've been a great democracy doesn't mean we will automatically keep being one if we keep waving the flag. It's ugly. You take a monarchy for granted, or a fascist state. You have to. That's the given. But a democracy changes all the time. . . .

A quick review of the two years since George W. Bush took office may offer some light on why we are where we are. He came into office with the possibility of a recession, plus all the unhappy odor of his investiture through an election that could best be described as legitimate/illegitimate. America had learned all over again that Republicans had fine skills for dirty legal fighting. They were able to call, after all, on a powerful gene stream. The Republicans who led the campaign to seize Florida in the year 2000 are descended from 125 years of lawyers and bankers with the cold nerve and fired-up greed to foreclose on many a widow's home or farm. Nor did these law-yers and bankers walk about suffused with guilt. They had the moral equivalent of Teflon on their souls. Church on Sunday, foreclose on Monday. Of course their descendants won in Florida. The Democrats still believed there were cherished rules to the game. They did not understand that rules no longer apply when the stakes are immense.

If Bush's legitimacy was in question then from the start, his per-formance as President was arousing scorn. When he spoke extem-pore, he sounded simple. When more articulate subordinates wrote his speeches, he had trouble fitting himself to the words.

Then September 11 altered everything. It was as if our TV sets had come alive. For years we had been watching maelstrom extrav-aganzas on the tube, and enjoying them. We were insulated. A hun-dredth part of ourselves could step into the box and live with the fear. Now, an invasion from the Beyond! An Appearance! Gods and demons were invading the United States, coming in right off the TV screen. This may account in part for the odd, unaccountable guilt so many felt after September 11. It was as if untold divine forces were erupting in fury.

And, of course, we were not in shape to feel free of guilt about September 11. The manic money-grab excitement of the nineties had never been altogether separated from our pervasive American guilt. We were happy to be prosperous, but we still felt guilty. We are a Christian nation. The *Judeo* in *Judeo-Christian* is a grace note. We are a Christian nation. The supposition of a great many good Christians in America is that you were not meant to be all that rich. God didn't necessarily want it. For certain, Jesus did not. You weren't supposed to pile up a mountain of moolah. You were obligated to spend your life in altruistic acts. That was still one half of the good Christian psyche.

The other half, pure American, was, as always: Beat everybody. One can offer a cruel but conceivably accurate remark: To be a mainstream American is to live as an oxymoron. You are a good Christian, but you strain to remain dynamically competitive. Of course, Jesus and Evel Knievel don't consort too well in one psyche. Human rage and guilt do take on their uniquely American forms.

Even before September 11, many matters grew worse. America's spiritual architecture had been buttressed since World War II by our near-mythical institutions of security, of which the FBI and the Catholic Church were most prominent, equal in special if intangible stature to the Constitution and the Supreme Court. Now, all that was taking its terrible whack. . . . Then after September 11 came the pedophile lawsuits against the Catholic Church, and that opened a grieving abyss of a wound in many a good Catholic home. It certainly wounded the priesthood grievously. How could a young or middle-aged man wearing the collar walk down the street now without suffering from the averted eyes and false greetings of the parishioners he met along the way? . . .

America had been putting up with the ongoing expansion of the corporation into American life since the end of World War II. It had been the money cow to the United States. But it had also been a filthy cow that gave off foul gases of mendacity and manipulation by an extreme emphasis on advertising. Put less into the product but kowtow to its marketing. Marketing was a beast and a force that succeeded in taking America away from most of us. It succeeded in making the world an uglier place to live in since the Second World War. One has only to cite fifty-story high-rise architecture as inspired in form as a Kleenex box with balconies, shopping malls encircled by low-level condominiums, superhighways with their vistas into the void, and, beneath it all, the pall of plastic, ubiquitous plastic, there to numb an infant's tactile senses, plastic, front-runner in the competition to see which new substance could make the world more disagreeable. To the degree that we have distributed this crud all over the globe, we were already wielding a species of world hegemony. We were exporting the all-pervasive aesthetic emptiness of the most powerful American corporations. There were no new cathedrals being built for the poor—only sixteen-story urban-renewal housing projects that sat on the soul like jail.

Then came a more complete exposure of the economic chicanery and pollution of the corporations. Economic gluttony was thriving at the top. Criminal behavior was being revealed on the front page of every business section. Without September 11, George W. Bush would have been living in the nonstop malaise of uglier and uglier media. It could even be said that America was taking a series of hits that were not wholly out of proportion to what happened to the Germans after World War I, when inflation wiped out the fundamental German notion of self, which was that if you worked hard and saved your money, you ended up having a decent old age. It is likely that Hitler would never have come to power ten years later without that runaway inflation. By the same measure, September 11 had done something comparable to the American sense of security.

For that matter, conservatism was heading toward a divide. Old-line conservatives like Pat Buchanan believed that America should keep to itself and look to solve those of its problems that we were equipped to solve. Buchanan was the leader of what might be called old-value conservatives, who believe in family, country, faith, tradition, home, hard and honest labor, duty, allegiance, and a balanced budget. The ideas, notions, and predilections of George W. Bush had to be, for the most part, not compatible with Buchanan's conservatism.

Bush was different. The gap between his school of thought and that of old-value conservatives could yet produce a dichotomy on the right as clear-cut as the differences between communists and socialists after World War I. Flag conservatives like Bush paid lip service to some conservative values, but at bottom they didn't give a damn. If they still used some of the terms, it was in order to avoid narrowing their political base. They used the flag. They loved words like *evil*. One of Bush's worst faults in rhetoric (to dip into that cornucopia) was to use the word as if it were a button he could push to increase his power. When people have an IV tube put in them to feed a narcotic painkiller on demand, a few keep pressing that button. Bush uses *evil* as a narcotic for that part of the American public which feels most distressed. Of course, as he sees it, he is doing it because he believes

America is good. He certainly does. He believes this country is the only hope of the world. He also fears that the country is rapidly growing more dissolute, and the only solution may be—fell, mighty, and near-holy words—the only solution may be to strive for world empire. Behind the whole push to go to war with Iraq is the desire to have a huge military presence in the Middle East as a stepping-stone to taking over the rest of the world.

That is not a small statement, but this much can be offered directly: At the root of flag conservatism is not madness but an undisclosed logic. If you accept its premises, it is logical. From a militant Christian point of view, America is close to rotten. The entertainment media are loose. Bare belly-buttons pop onto every TV screen, as open in their statement as wild animals' eyes. The kids are getting to the point where they can't read, but they sure can screw. One perk for the White House, therefore, should America become an international military machine huge enough to conquer all adversaries, is that American sexual freedom, all that gay, feminist, lesbian, transvestite hullabaloo, will be seen as too much of a luxury and will be put back into the closet again. Commitment, patriotism, and dedication will become all-pervasive national values again (with all the hypocrisy attendant). Once we become a twenty-first-century embodiment of the old Roman Empire, moral reform can stride right back into the picture. The military is, obviously, more puritanical than the entertainment media. Soldiers are, of course, crazier than any average man when in and out of combat, but the overhead command is a major everyday pressure on soldiers and could become a species of most powerful censor over civilian life. To flag conservatives, war now looks to be the best possible solution. Jesus and Evel Knievel might be able to bond together, after all. Fight evil, fight it to the death! Use the word fifteen times in every speech.

There is just this kind of mad-eyed mystique to Americans: the idea that we Americans can do anything. Yes, say flag conservatives, we will be able to handle what comes. We have our know-how, our can-do. We will dominate the obstacles. Flag conservatives truly believe America is not only fit to run the world but that it must. Without a commitment to Empire, the country will go down the drain. This, I would opine, is the unstated, ever-denied subtext beneath the Iraqi project, and the flag conservatives may not even be wholly aware of the scope of it, not all of them. Not yet.

Besides, Bush could count on a few other reliable sentiments that will buttress the notion. To begin with, a good part of American pride sits today on the tripod of big money, sports, and the Stars and Stripes. Something like a third of our major athletic stadiums and arenas are named after corporations—Gillette and FedEx are two of twenty examples. The Super Bowl could only commence this year after an American flag the size of a football field was removed from the turf. The U.S. Air Force gave the groin-throb of a big vee overhead. Probably half of America has an unspoken desire to go to war. It satisfies our mythology. America, goes our logic, is the only force for good that can rectify the bad. George W. Bush is shrewd enough to work that equation out all by himself. He may even sense better than anyone how a war with Iraq will satisfy our addiction to living with adventure on TV. If this is facetious, so be it—the country is becoming more loutish every year. So, yes, war is also mighty TV entertainment....

Flag conservatives may yet be hoping to send some such message as this to China: "Hear ye! You Chinese are obviously bright. We can tell. We know! Your Asian students were born for technology. People who have led submerged lives love technology. They don't get much pleasure anyway, so they like the notion of cybernetic power right at their fingertips. Technology is ideal for them. We can go along with that. You fellows can have your technology; may it be great! But, China, you had better understand: We still have the military power. Your best bet, therefore, is to become Greek slaves to us Romans. We will treat you well. You will be most important to us, eminently important. But don't look to rise above your future station in life. The best you can ever hope for, China, is to be our Greeks."

In the 1930s, you could be respected if you earned a living. In the nineties, you had to demonstrate that you were a promising figure in the ranks of greed. It may be that Empire depends on an obscenely wealthy upper upper class who, given the in-built, never-ending threat to their wealth, is bound to feel no great allegiance in the pit of its heart for democracy. If this insight is true, then it can also be said that the disproportionate wealth which collected through the nineties may have created an all but irresistible pressure at the top to move from democracy to Empire. That would safeguard those great and quickly acquired gains. Can it be that George W. Bush knows what he's doing for the future of Empire by awarding these huge tax credits to the rich?

Of course, terrorism and instability are the reverse face of Empire. If the Saudi rulers have been afraid of their mullahs for fear of their power to incite terrorists, what will the Muslim world be like once we, the Great Satan, are there to dominate the Middle East in person? Since the administration can hardly be unaware of the dangers, the answer comes down to the unhappy likelihood that Bush and Company are ready to be hit by a major terrorist attack. As well as any number of smaller ones. Either way, it will strengthen his hand. America will gather about him again. We can hear his words in advance: "Good Americans died today. Innocent victims of evil had to shed their blood. But we will prevail. We are one with God." Given such language, every loss is a win.

Yet so long as terrorism continues, so will its subtext, and there lies the horror to its nth power. What made deterrence possible in the Cold War was not only that there was everything to lose for both sides, but there was also the built-in inability on either side to be certain it could count on any particular human being to flip the apocalyptic switch over to world domination. In that sense, no final plan could be counted on. How could either of the superpowers be certain that the up-to-now wholly reliable human selected to push the button would actually prove reliable enough to obliterate the other half of the world? A dark cloud might come over him at the last moment. He could fall to the ground before he could do the deed.

This human unreliability does not apply, however, to a terrorist. If he is ready to kill himself, he can also be ready to destroy the world. The wars we have known until this era, no matter how horrible, could offer at least the knowledge that they would come to an end. Terrorism, however, is not attracted to negotiation. Rather, it would insist on no termination short of victory. Since the terrorist cannot triumph, he cannot cease being a terrorist. They are a true enemy, far more basic, indeed, than Third World countries with nuclear capability that invariably appear on the scene prepared to live with deterrence and its in-built outcome-agreements after years or decades of passive confrontation and hard bargaining.

If much of what has been argued so far has been restricted to neocon mentality, there is a wing of the flag conservatives' campaign to invade Iraq that does have liberal support. Part of the liberal media, columnists at *The New Yorker* and the *Washington Post* and some at the *New York Times*, is joined with Senators Hillary Clinton and Dianne Feinstein, Joe Lieberman and John Kerry, in acceptance of the idea that perhaps we can bring democracy to Iraq by invasion. . . .

It is as if these liberal voices have decided that Bush cannot be stopped and so he must be joined. To commit to a stand against fighting the war would guarantee the relative absence of Democrats at the administration tables that will work on the future of Iraq. It is an argument that can be sustained up to a point, but the point depends on many eventualities, the first of which is that the war is quick and not horrendous.

The old Bill Clinton version of overseas presumption is present. The argument that we succeeded in building democracy in Japan and Germany and therefore can build it anywhere does not necessarily hold, Japan and Germany were countries with a homogeneous population and a long existence as nations. They each were steeped in guilt at the depredations of their soldiers in other lands. They were near to totally destroyed but had the people and the skills to rebuild their cities. The Americans who worked to create their democracy were veterans of Roosevelt's New Deal and, mark of the period, were effective idealists.

Iraq, in contrast, was never a true nation. Put together by the British, it was a post–World War I patchwork of Sunnis, Shiites, Kurds, and Turkomans, who at best distrusted one another intensely. A situation analogous to Afghanistan's divisions among its warlords could be the more likely outcome. No one will certainly declare with authority that democracy can be built there, yet the arrogance persists. There does not seem much comprehension that, except for special circumstances, democracy is never there in us to create in another country by the force of our will. Real democracy comes out of many subtle individual human battles that are fought over decades and finally over centuries, battles that succeed in building traditions. The only defenses of democracy, finally, are the traditions of democracy. When you start ignoring those values, you are playing with a noble and delicate structure. There's nothing more beautiful than democracy. But you can't play with it. You can't assume we're going to go over to show them what a great system we have. This is monstrous arrogance.

Because democracy is noble, it is always endangered. Nobility, indeed, is always in danger. Democracy is perishable. I think the natural government for most people, given the uglier depths of human nature, is fascism. Fascism is more of a natural state than democracy. To assume blithely that we can export democracy into any country we choose can serve paradoxically to encourage more fascism at home and abroad. Democracy is a state of grace attained only by those countries that have a host of individuals not only ready to enjoy freedom but to undergo the heavy labor of maintaining it.

The need for powerful theory can fall into many an abyss of error. One could, for example, be wrong about the unspoken motives of the administration. Perhaps they are not interested in Empire so much as trying in good faith to save the world. We can be certain at least that Bush and his Bushites believe this. By the time they are in church each Sunday, they believe it so powerfully, tears come to their eyes. Of course, it is the actions of men and not their sentiments that make history. Our sentiments can be flooded with love within, but our actions can produce the opposite. Perversity is always looking to consort with the best motives in human nature. . . .

For those of the rest of us who are not ready to depend on the power of prayer, we will do well to find the rampart we can defend over what may be dire years to come. Democracy, I would repeat, is the noblest form of government we have yet evolved, and we may as well begin to ask ourselves whether we are ready to suffer, even perish, for it rather than preparing ourselves to live in the lower existence of a monumental banana republic with a government always eager to cater to mega-corporations as they do their best to appropriate our thwarted dreams with their elephantiastical conceits. . . .

What scared the hell out of me was a recent poll that indicated half the people in America are willing to accept a certain curtailment of their liberties in return for more security. If, already at this point, 50 percent of the people are ready to give up some of their liberties in return for that dubious security, then what's going to happen if something truly bad ensues? Our belief that Americans are free individuals has suffered erosion in the last ten years from too much stock market and the greed it inspired. You know, Marx and Jesus Christ do come together on one fundamental notion, which is that money leaches out all other values. . . .

I must say it again: In a country where values are collapsing, patriotism becomes the handmaiden to totalitarianism. The country becomes the religion. We are asked to live in a state of religious fervor: Love America! Love it because America has become a substitute for religion. But to love your country indiscriminately means that critical distinctions begin to go. And democracy depends upon these distinctions.

A good Englishman has a certain sense of his national life. . . . The British have memory in a way we don't. That is the scariest single thing about American democracy to me: We don't have roots the way other countries do. Relatively, we are without deep traditions. So the transition from democracy to totalitarianism could happen quickly. There could be fewer impediments here, those brakes and barriers that true conservatives usually count upon. Without the stops and locks, a nation can swing from one extreme to the other. . . .

Freedom. The freedom that I've had in my life. Who has ever had the opportunities I've had, the extraordinary freedom to be able to think the way I think, for better or worse? No, the best thing in America is that freedom. I had the great good luck that very few people have, to be a writer and earn a relatively independent income by the age of twenty-five. It didn't continue to be always that simple, but generally speaking, I've had more time to think than most people. I've had that advantage, that luxury. I can hardly hate the country. I don't want to make this a sentimental journey, but I have been treated very well. . . . I have had great freedoms here in America, and I don't want to see them lost to the people who come after me. But I repeat: Freedom is as delicate as democracy. It has to be kept alive every day of our existence. So, yes, I do love this country. [But] if our democracy is the noblest experiment in the history of civilization, it may also be the most singularly vulnerable one.

67

HERMANN GÖRING SPEAKS

(*THE BIG EMPTY*, 2006)

Mailer did extensive research for his final novel about Hitler and World War II and was familiar with the trial transcripts and interviews with Nazi war criminals, including one with Hitler's vice chancellor, Hermann Göring. Göring was sentenced to death by hanging for war crimes, but on October 15, 1946, the night before his scheduled execution, he committed suicide with a secreted potassium cyanide tablet.

I quote from a man who arrived at objectivity a little too late in life:

> Naturally, the common people don't want war, but after all, it is the leaders of a country who determine the policy, and it is always a simple matter to drag people along whether it is a democracy, or a fascist government, or a parliament, or a communist dictatorship. Voice or no voice, the people can always be brought to the bidding of the leaders. This is easy. All you have to do is tell them they are being attacked, and denounce the pacifists for lack of patriotism and exposing the country to danger. It works the same in every country.

That was Hermann Göring speaking at the Nuremberg trials after World War II. It is one thing to be forewarned. Will we ever be forearmed?

68

HOPE FOR THE FUTURE

(WILKES UNIVERSITY COMMENCEMENT ADDRESS, MAY 27, 1995)

Speaking at a Wilkes University commencement ceremony, Mailer enunci-
ated his metaphor of how the changes caused by major geopolitical upheavals
resemble the way magnetized filings scatter in chaos when power to the mag-
net goes off. The simile captures Mailer's abiding notion that large historical
changes—wars, depressions, natural disasters, assassinations, etc.—often lead
to the repression of free speech, livid patriotism, populist leaders, and authori-
tarian regimes. And yet, he also points out the potential for a positive outcome
for this young generation as they plow through the existential circumstances
they have been dealt, forging the events that will come in the twenty-first
century and beyond.

Well, I graduated from college in 1943, so it has taken me fifty-two
years to become a Doctor. I thank you.

It is most agreeable to talk to you today because I feel, oddly
enough, an identity with many of you, since I came from a family
where almost no one had gone to college before me, and I owe an
enormous amount to my parents to go to school, to go to college, and
I understand the special intensity of such an education.

What adds to my pleasure is that I have been to many graduations.
In fact, I could say to all you good friends and family who are in the
bleachers on either side that since I have nine children, and all but
one have finished their education, I have been to so many graduations
that if some of you fall asleep while I am speaking, I will be the last
to judge. . . .

We had the dubious benefit from 1946 on ... of a Cold War which established all the signs. It was very easy, looking back on it now, for us to function as a nation. We had an enemy and they were Godless and materialistic, which God knows we are not, and they were determined to destroy us. And so it was very simple for ninety-five, ninety-eight percent of Americans to find their way in a social structure.

Looking back on it, we were like magnetic filings in the power of a huge electromagnet, the Cold War, and almost all of us pointed in the same direction. When the Cold War ended, it was as if the great switch on this huge electromagnet was released and now all the fragments went in all directions. Filings were scattered, and being so scattered we discovered that the anger and the rage that we have been able to channel toward the Soviet Union was now being directed toward ourselves in every way. And we had become a nation—we were always famous for being contumacious with each other as Americans—but now we have become a nation in which there is more acrimony and more dislike between groups and enclaves than any time I can recall. And that is the depressing side of the situation into which you go.

But, the promising side is that you will not have to face what fifty years of students graduating from college had to go into, which is that they were going into a structured world in which their rise was going to be slow because everything was understood. The world had a shape, and we had an enemy, and so it was as if you were all going off into a vast social army and starting at the bottom.

Now, that no longer exists. The people of my generation and the people who came after me for the next forty years who built their understanding of the world, society, and even of the hereafter on the firm foundation of the Cold War are now superannuated; myself, among the others. We no longer know how things are going to turn out. We don't have a clear sense of the future. And you will go forth on the rare position of being—in the spiritual sense—of being pioneers because you are going into a new and undiscovered frontier. It is the frontier of the last of this century, and the twenty-first century to come where all the guide rules of the nineteenth and twentieth century have been used up.

And so for those of you who are bold and intelligent, which I suspect is the majority of this class, you have a great and exciting world to go into if you do not despair. If you like the idea that the world is free again, then perhaps we can regain that dream on which this country was founded.

The idea—and it was unique in world history when it arrived on the scale with which America was created—the idea that if you take the mass of human beings and if you believe that there is more good than evil in the sum of humanity, then democracy can prevail. For if that's not true, we must live in an oppressive system and live under authority. But, if it is true, as a totality, as a sum we have more good in us than evil, then we can begin again to create and amplify that extraordinary dream of democracy.

And so I salute you as a class and wish, and I don't even have to wish it for you, you are going to have it, I beg you to anticipate the glorious, and exciting, and fearful, and incredible days and years that await you.

ACKNOWLEDGMENTS

Magazines

Esquire, December 1963: "March on Washington for Jobs and Freedom"; *The New Yorker,* May 20, 1974: "Nixon's Fall"; *New York Times Magazine,* September, 26, 1976: "A Visit with Jimmy Carter"; *Parade,* October 23, 1983: "A Talk with Clint Eastwood"; *New York Times,* April 18, 1988: "Jesse Jackson for President"; *Vanity Fair,* November 1991: "Warren Beatty: One on One"; Hitchens interview, *New Left Review,* March/April 1997: "The Rage of Slavery"; *Esquire,* August 1996: "Patrick Buchanan"; *New York,* October 16, 1995: "O. J. Simpson"; *London Observer,* August 29, 1998: "Hillary, Bill, and Monica"; *BBC Newsnight,* April 2, 2002: "Larger than the Atom Bomb"; *Provincetown Arts,* 2008: *"*Hitler on My Mind*"*; *Vanity Fair,* May 1991: "Black Power."

Interview Transcript

Dreams and Nightmares: Mailer's America, copyright © 2000. Used by permission of Films d'Ici. All rights reserved.

Books

Excerpt from *The Naked and the Dead: 50th Anniversary Edition* by Norman Mailer. Copyright © 1948, renewed 1976 by Norman Mailer. Reprinted by permission of Henry Holt and Company. All Rights Reserved.

The Presidential Papers by Norman Mailer, copyright © 1976. Used by permission of Penguin Random House LLC. All rights reserved.

Selected Letters of Norman Mailer, copyright © 2014. Used by permission of Penguin Random House LLC. All rights reserved.

The Deer Park by Norman Mailer, copyright © 1964. Used by permission of Penguin Random House LLC. All rights reserved.

Barbary Shore by Norman Mailer, copyright © 1963. Used by permis-

Source Notes

The place of first publication for all of the collected excerpts in this volume is given in the notes below, followed by the books where Mailer reprinted them. (Some of these reprints were changed in various ways by Mailer.) In all instances, the final book version has been our source, excepting only those excerpts that have not been previously published or collected. Additional detail can be found in the standard bibliography, Norman Mailer: Works and Days *(2018), published by the Mailer Society and edited by J. Michael Lennon, Donna Pedro Lennon, and Gerald L. Lucas. Most of Mailer's work has been reissued by his longtime publisher, Random House. Mailer's papers were purchased by the University of Texas–Austin in 2005 and now reside in the university's Harry Ransom Center. A finding aid for the holdings is available online. A second Mailer archive containing the bulk of Mailer's five-thousand-book library and some of his manuscripts has recently been established at Wilkes University, where Mailer's Provincetown writing study has been re-created.*

Opening Remarks: *The Big Empty*, Nation Books, 2006 (hereafter BE); *The Presidential Papers*, Putnam's, 1963 (hereafter PP); *Dreams and Nightmares: Mailer's America*, Films d'Ici, Paris, 2000 (hereafter MA).

1. The General's Lecture: *The Naked and the Dead*, Rinehart, 1948.
2. Letter to Beatrice Mailer, August 8, 1945: *Selected Letters of Norman Mailer*, ed. J. Michael Lennon, Random House, 2014 (hereafter SLNM).
3. Hitler on My Mind: Interview with J. Michael Lennon, *Provincetown Arts*, 2008.
4. Frontiers of Violence: *MA*.
5. Russia, the Progressive Party, and Henry Luce: *MA*.
6. Roots and Paranoia: *MA*.
7. Depression, Desperation, Fascism I: *MA*.
8. McLeod Tells All: *Barbary Shore*, Rinehart, 1951.
9. Letter to Arthur Miller, early September, 1950: *SLNM*.

10. The Depths of Democratic Strength: *MA*.

11. Eitel Tells All: *The Deer Park*, Putnam's, 1955.

12. Eisenhower and Corporate Power: *MA*.

13. Jackie Robinson and Black Rage: *MA*.

14. Jazz and the White Negro: *MA*.

15. "The White Negro": *Dissent*, summer 1957; reprinted in *Advertisements for Myself*, Putnam's, 1959.

16. J. Edgar Hoover and Stalin, *MA*.

17. "Superman Comes to the Supermarket": *Esquire*, November 1960; reprinted in *PP*.

18. Living Like Cockroaches: *MA*.

19. "The Existential Heroine: Jackie Kennedy": *Esquire*, July 1962; reprinted in *PP*.

20. Letter to *Playboy*: December 21, 1962: *SLNM*.

21. A Long Season of Dread: *Esquire*, April 1963; reprinted in *PP*.

22. March on Washington for Jobs and Freedom: *Esquire*, December 1963.

23. "The Leading Man": Review of *J.F.K.: The Man and the Myth* by Victor Lasky: *New York Herald Tribune*, September 29, 1963; reprinted in *Cannibals and Christians*, Dial, 1966 (hereafter *CC*).

24. Letter to Mickey Knox, December 17, 1963: *SLNM*.

25. Ike's GOP Convention Speech, 1964: "In the Red Light: A History of the Republican Convention in 1964," *Esquire*, November 1964; reprinted in *CC*.

26. Goldwater: Sincere Demagogue: "In the Red Light," reprinted in *CC*.

27. Letter to Eiichi Yamanishi, April 17, 1964: *SLNM*.

28. Review of *My Hope for America* by Lyndon B. Johnson: *New York Herald Tribune*, November 1, 1964; reprinted in *CC*.

29. "A Speech at Berkeley on Vietnam Day": *The Realist*, June 1965; reprinted in *CC*.

30. Letter to William F. Buckley, Jr., April 20, 1965: *SLNM*.

31. A Second Letter to William F. Buckley, Jr., October 18, 1965: *SLNM*.

32. A Sharp Searing Love for His Country: *Harper's*, March 1968; reprinted in *The Armies of the Night*, New American Library, 1968 (hereafter *AON*).

33. The Marshal and the Nazi: *Harper's*, March 1968; reprinted in *AON*.

34. A Love Affair with America: Interview with Eric James Schroeder in his collection, *Vietnam, We've All Been There: Interviews with American Writers*, Praeger, 1992.

35. Robert Kennedy's Magic: unpublished.

36. The Reporter Observes the Wasps: *Miami and the Siege of Chicago: An Informal History of the Republican and Democratic Conventions of 1968*, New American Library, 1968 (hereafter *MSC*).

37. Richard M. Nixon, GOP Convention, 1968: *MSC*.

38. Ronald Reagan, GOP Convention, 1968: *MSC*.

39. Eugene McCarthy I: *MSC*.

40. Eugene McCarthy II: *MSC*.

41. Mayor Daley, Clansman: *MSC*.

42. Hippies, Yippies, and Schizophrenia: *MSC*.

43. Good Cops, Bad Cops: *MSC*.

44. A National Disorder: *MSC*.

45. Bobby Kennedy Remembered: *MSC*.

46. Pat Nixon: Portrait of a First Lady: *St. George and the Godfather* (hereafter *SGG*).

47. Lunch with Kissinger: *SGG*.

48. Nixon's Fall: *The New Yorker*, May 20, 1974.

49. A Visit with Jimmy Carter in Plains, Georgia: *New York Times Magazine*, September 26, 1976.

50. Letter to Mary Bancroft, October 18, 1976: *SLNM*.

51. Letter to President Jimmy Carter, March 2, 1977: unpublished.

52. Nixon's Curtain Call: "Of a Small and Modest Malignancy, Wicked and Bristling with Dots," *Esquire*, November 1977; reprinted in *Pieces and Pontifications*, ed. J. Michael Lennon, Little, Brown, 1982.

53. A Talk with Clint Eastwood: *Parade*, October 23, 1983.

54. Married to America: *MA*.

55. Jesse Jackson for President: *New York Times*, April 18, 1988.

56. Black Power, Political Parties, and Prison Camps: "How the Wimp Won the War," *Vanity Fair*, May 1991; reprinted in *How the Wimp Won the War*, Lord John Press, 1992.

57. Warren Beatty: One on One: *Vanity Fair*, November 1991.

58. Letter to Hillary Clinton, June 26, 1992: *SLNM*.

59. Depression, Desperation, Fascism II: *MA*.

60. Black Justice/White Justice: O. J. Simpson: *New York*, October 16, 1995.

61. The Rage of Slavery: Interview with Christopher Hitchens, *New Left Review*, March/April 1997.

62. A Long Talk with Republican Presidential Candidate Patrick Buchanan: *Esquire*, August 1996.

63. Hillary, Bill, and Monica: *London Observer*, August 29, 1998.

64. Letter to Sal Cetrano, March 28, 1999: *SLNM*.

65. Larger than the Atom Bomb: *BBC Newsnight*, April 2, 2002.

66. America's Crumbling Spiritual Architecture: *Sunday Times Magazine* (London), September 19, 2002; *American Conservative*, December 2, 2002; reprinted in *Why Are We at War?* Random House, 2003.

67. Herman Göring Speaks: *BE*.

68. Hope for the Future, Wilkes University commencement address, May 27, 1995: unpublished.